Tourism and National Identities

By understanding tourist destinations through the lens of national identity, the tourist may develop a deeper appreciation of the destination. Further, tourism marketers and planners may be better equipped to promote and manage the destination, particularly with regard to expectations of the potential visitor.

Tourism and National Identities is the first volume to explore fully the relationship between tourism and national identities and the multiple ways in which cultural tourism, events and celebrations contribute to national identity. It examines core topics critical to understanding this relationship, including: tourism branding, stereotyping and national identity; tourism-related representation and experience of national identity; tourism visitation/site/event management; and the relationship to cultural tourism.

The book looks at a range of international tourist sites and events and combines multidisciplinary perspectives and international cases to provide a thorough academic analysis. The interconnecting area of cultural tourism and national identity has been largely overlooked in academic literature to date; this volume gives considerable analysis to the complex relationship between the two domains and, indeed, the multifaceted strategies used to define that relationship.

Written by an international team of leading academics, *Tourism and National Identities* will be of interest to students, researchers and academics in tourism and related disciplines such as events, cultural studies and geography.

Elspeth Frew is a Senior Lecturer at La Trobe University, Melbourne, Australia.

Leanne White is a Lecturer in the School of Hospitality, Tourism and Marketing, and a research associate in the Centre for Tourism and Services Research at Victoria University, Melbourne, Australia.

Contemporary geographies of leisure, tourism and mobility

Edited by C. Michael Hall

Professor at the Department of Management, College of Business and Economics, University of Canterbury, Christchurch, New Zealand

The aim of this series is to explore and communicate the intersections and relationships between leisure, tourism and human mobility within the social sciences.

It will incorporate both traditional and new perspectives on leisure and tourism from contemporary geography – for example, notions of identity, representation and culture – while also providing for perspectives from cognate areas, such as anthropology, cultural studies, gastronomy and food studies, marketing, policy studies and political economy, regional and urban planning, and sociology, within the development of an integrated field of leisure and tourism studies.

Also, increasingly, tourism and leisure are regarded as steps in a continuum of human mobility. Inclusion of mobility in the series offers the prospect of examining the relationship between tourism and migration, the sojourner, educational travel, and second home and retirement travel phenomena.

The series comprises two strands:

Contemporary geographies of leisure, tourism and mobility aims to address the needs of students and academics, and the titles will be published in hardback and paperback. Titles already published:

The Moralisation of Tourism
Sun, sand . . . and saving the world?
Jim Butcher

The Ethics of Tourism Development
Mick Smith and Rosaleen Duffy

Tourism in the Caribbean
Trends, development, prospects
Edited by David Timothy Duval

Qualitative Research in Tourism
Ontologies, epistemologies and methodologies
Edited by Jenny Phillimore and Lisa Goodson

The Media and the Tourist Imagination
Converging cultures
Edited by David Crouch, Rhona Jackson and Felix Thompson

Tourism and Global Environmental Change
Ecological, social, economic and political interrelationships
Edited by Stefan Gössling and C. Michael Hall

Cultural Heritage of Tourism in the Developing World
Edited by Dallen J. Timothy and Gyan Nyaupane

Understanding and Managing Tourism Impacts
C. Michael Hall and Alan Lew

Forthcoming:

An Introduction to Visual Research Methods in Tourism
Edited by Tijana Rakic and Donna Chambers

Routledge studies in contemporary geographies of leisure, tourism and mobility is a forum for innovative new research intended for research students and academics, and the titles will be available in hardback only. Titles already published:

1 **Living with Tourism**
Negotiating identities in a Turkish village
Hazel Tucker

2 **Tourism, Diasporas and Space**
Edited by Tim Coles and Dallen J. Timothy

3 **Tourism and Postcolonialism**
Contested discourses, identities and representations
Edited by C. Michael Hall and Hazel Tucker

4 **Tourism, Religion and Spiritual Journeys**
Edited by Dallen J. Timothy and Daniel H. Olsen

5 **China's Outbound Tourism**
Wolfgang Georg Arlt

6 **Tourism, Power and Space**
Edited by Andrew Church and Tim Coles

7 **Tourism, Ethnic Diversity and the City**
Edited by Jan Rath

8 **Ecotourism, NGOs and Development**
A critical analysis
Jim Butcher

9 **Tourism and the Consumption of Wildlife**
Hunting, shooting and sport fishing
Edited by Brent Lovelock

10 **Tourism, Creativity and Development**
Edited by Greg Richards and Julie Wilson

11 **Tourism at the Grassroots**
Edited by John Connell and Barbara Rugendyke

12 **Tourism and Innovation**
C. Michael Hall and Allan Williams

Tourism and National Identities

An international perspective

**Edited by
Elspeth Frew and Leanne White**

Routledge
Taylor & Francis Group

LONDON AND NEW YORK

First published 2011
by Routledge
2 Park Square, Milton Park, Abingdon, Oxon OX14 4RN

Simultaneously published in the USA and Canada
by Routledge
270 Madison Avenue, New York, NY 10016

Routledge is an imprint of the Taylor & Francis Group, an informa business

© 2011 Selection and editorial matter, Elspeth Frew and Leanne White; individual chapters, the contributors.

The right of Elspeth Frew and Leanne White to be identified as editors of this work has been asserted by them in accordance with the Copyright, Designs and Patents Act 1988.

Typeset in Times New Roman by
Book Now Ltd, London

Printed and bound in Great Britain by
CPI Antony Rowe, Chippenham, Wiltshire

British Library Cataloguing in Publication Data
A catalogue record for this book is available from the British Library

Library of Congress Cataloguing in Publication Data
A catalog record for this book has been requested

ISBN: 978–0–415–57277–4 (hbk)
ISBN: 978–0–203–85596–6 (ebk)

Contents

Illustrations

Boxes

Contributors

Dr Robert Aitken is a Senior Lecturer in the Department of Marketing at the University of Otago in New Zealand. His academic and research interests include advertising, branding, consumer behaviour, teaching and learning, communications and the media. He is a constructivist who is interested in how people make sense of the world and an idealist in wanting to know how they propose to make it a better place.

Dr Nazia Ali was awarded her doctorate in 2008. She has published in areas relating to tourism, migration and reflexivity. Theoretically, her work takes on board postcolonial perspectives to interpret the relationship between tourism and ethnicity, and her research agenda is largely ethnographic, operating within an interpretive framework to investigate tourism's relationship with such characteristics of identity as religion, culture, race and diaspora. She is currently lecturing in tourism and events management at the University of Bedfordshire in the United Kingdom.

Dr Anne Buchmann lectures at the University of Newcastle in Australia. She is a multilingual scholar with extensive experience as a public speaker as well as an active researcher. She has been specialising in researching the film tourism phenomenon in Aotearoa New Zealand since 2000, and has also gained industry knowledge through her work as a specialist tour guide. Nowadays her knowledge is disseminated via presentations and publications, including peer-reviewed journal articles, book chapters, industry publications, newspaper articles and documentaries.

Huong Thanh Bui is a doctoral student at Griffith University, Australia. Her research interests are in Asian culture, identity and backpacking. She has participated in a number of tourism development projects in Vietnam. Formerly she was a lecturer in the Faculty of Management and Tourism at Hanoi University.

Adriana Campelo is a doctoral candidate in the Department of Marketing at the University of Otago, New Zealand. Among her academic and research interests are destination marketing, consumer behaviour, place branding and advertising.

In her doctoral studies she developed expertise in qualitative research methods using video and photography, along with the more conventional techniques such as interviewing and focus group discussions.

Rob Ferguson is a faculty member in the Department of Recreation and Tourism Management at Vancouver Island University, Canada. His teaching and research interests include adventure tourism, cultural tourism and event studies. He is currently completing his doctorate at the University of Gloucestershire, examining issues associated with aboriginal tourism within protected areas.

Dr Elspeth Frew is a Senior Lecturer in Tourism Management in the School of Management at La Trobe University, Australia. Her research interest is in cultural tourism, with a particular focus on festival and event management and arts and entertainment.

Dr Lionel Frost is an Associate Professor in the Department of Economics at Monash University. He is an applied economist with research interests in the economic history of the Pacific region, social capital and social inclusion, urban and regional history and sports history.

Dr Warwick Frost teaches tourism at La Trobe University. His research focuses on the interplay between heritage, tourist attractions, popular culture and identity. He was co-editor of *Tourism and National Parks: International Perspectives on Development, Histories and Change*, editor of *Zoos and Tourism: Conservation, Education, Entertainment?*, and one of the organisers of the biennial International Tourism and Media conference series.

Dr Andrew Holden is a Professor and Director of the Institute for Research in Tourism at the University of Bedfordshire. He is a graduate in environmental sciences from the University of East Anglia, he was awarded his doctorate from the University of Reading and he is a Fellow of the Royal Geographical Society in London. He is the author of three textbooks and is on the editorial board of *Annals of Tourism*. Among his specialist research interests are sustainable tourism development, poverty reduction, and the role of tourism in identity formation. He has worked on several international research and consultancy projects.

Wei-Jue Huang is a doctoral student in the Department of Parks, Recreation and Tourism Management at Clemson University, South Carolina. She received her Master of Science in recreation, sports and tourism from the University of Illinois. Her research interests include destination image, heritage tourism and globalisation.

Dr Lee Jolliffe holds the Almond Chair in Tourism and Hospitality at the University of the West Indies, Barbados and is a Professor at the University of New Brunswick, Canada. Her research focuses on the cultural aspects of tourism, as reflected in her books *Tea and Tourism: Tourists, Traditions and Transformations* and *Coffee Culture, Destinations and Tourism*.

Dr Jennifer Laing is a Lecturer in the Tourism Research Unit at Monash University, Melbourne. She has a background in law and marketing and completed her doctorate on motivations behind frontier travel experiences. She teaches in the areas of tourist behaviour and festivals/events. Her research interests are tourist narratives, the role of myth in tourism and the use of heritage in developing tourist experiences.

Chantal Laws is a Senior Lecturer in Events Management at the University of Gloucestershire. Her interests are in cultural tourism, identity tourism, hedonic consumption and research methodology, areas in which she has contributed to books and to the journals *Managing Leisure* and *Events Management*. She regularly makes presentations at conferences of the Leisure Studies Association and the International Festival and Events Association and at the Global Events Congress. She has professional experience in the heritage and arts sectors, notably managing a multi-stage London music venue, and currently teaches events, music and festival management.

Dr Xiang (Robert) Li is an Assistant Professor at the School of Hotel, Restaurant and Tourism Management at the University of South Carolina. His research focuses mainly on destination marketing and tourist behaviour, with special emphasis on international destination branding, customer loyalty and tourism in Asia. He has worked extensively with international destination marketing organizations and companies. He is the author of nearly sixty scientific publications and currently serves on the editorial boards of the *Journal of Leisure Research* and *Tourism Analysis*. He is a frequent speaker at numerous international and industry conferences.

Agata Maccarrone-Eaglen lectures at the Centre for Research in Marketing and Strategy at the University of Salford in the UK. Her main research interests are consumer decision making, compulsive buying, cross-cultural behaviour in tourism and the role of culture in tourism marketing.

Dr Fang Meng is an Assistant Professor in the School of Hotel, Restaurant and Tourism Management at the University of South Carolina. Among her research interests are destination management and marketing, tourist behaviour, and international tourism. She has published articles in various journals, including the *Journal of Travel Research* and *Tourism Analysis*, is a member of the editorial board of the *Journal of Vacation Marketing*, and serves as an *ad hoc* reviewer for several academic journals. She is a member of professional associations in tourism and hospitality.

Anh Minh Nguyen lectures in the Faculty of Management and Tourism at Hanoi University. Her research interests are tourism information and tourist behaviour.

Dr Anthony Patterson is a Senior Lecturer in the Management School at the University of Liverpool, having previously taught at the University of Sheffield and the University of Ulster. He holds a doctorate in consumer behavior from the latter institution. His research focuses on providing a snapshot into current communications practices, such as social networking and text messaging, with a view to exploring how these phenomena impact on consumers. Other research interests are city branding, tourism and book marketing.

Dr László Puczkó is managing director and head of the tourism section at Xellum management consulting company. He is a board member of the European chapter of the Travel and Tourism Research Association, a research associate of Corvinus University in Budapest, and president of the Hungarian Association of Tourism Consultants. His main areas of expertise are in tourism research, strategy preparation, planning and management. Based on his works, several market analyses have been prepared focusing on the characteristics of theme parks, health tourism, thematic routes, heritage tourism, attraction and visitor management, destination marketing and impact analysis.

Dr Keir Reeves is a Monash Research Fellow in the Tourism Research Unit and the National Centre for Australian Studies at Monash University, Melbourne, and is a member of both the Heritage Council and the History Council of Victoria. His research is connected to Australian and Asian history, world heritage studies, mining heritage tourism and development tourism in Asia. He is currently working on Australian Research Council projects exploring international perspectives on heritage, memory and pilgrimages in the Second World War, and the promotion of harmony, multiculturalism and reconciliation through Australian rules football.

Dr Carla A. Santos is an Associate Professor in the Department of Recreation, Sport and Tourism and co-director of the Tourism Laboratory for Economic and Social Behavior Research at the University of Illinois. Her research programme focuses on the examination of communicative practices as a means of addressing the socio-political and cultural impact of tourism on the world's people and cultures.

Dr Peter Schofield is a Senior Lecturer in the Centre for Research in Marketing and Strategy at the University of Salford in the United Kingdom. His main research interests are tourism destination and events marketing, cultural heritage tourism, consumer decision-making and behavior and service quality management with particular reference to service failure and recovery strategies.

Dr Melanie Smith is a Senior Lecturer at Corvinus University, Budapest, where she is developing a Masters programme in tourism management. She has been a tourism academic for almost fifteen years, having served as director of tourism and management courses at the University of Greenwich in London. She is chair of the Association for Tourism and Leisure Education. She is also the author of several books and journal articles with research interests in cultural tourism, urban regeneration and wellness tourism.

Dr Fiona Wheeler is a post-doctoral researcher and tutor in the Tourism Research Unit at Monash University, Melbourne. Her doctoral thesis explored the process of marketing and branding rural tourism regions through a case study of north-east Victoria. She has degrees in commerce and tourism management, and has a strong strategic marketing background with experience in product and market development, customer experience management, branding and marketing research. Among her research interests are destination marketing and branding, tourism in rural communities, tourism partnerships and networks and heritage tourism.

Dr Leanne White is a Lecturer in the School of Hospitality, Tourism and Marketing and a research associate in the Centre for Tourism and Services Research at Victoria University, Melbourne. Her doctoral thesis examined manifestations of official and commercial nationalism at the Sydney 2000 Olympic Games. Among her research interests are national identity, advertising, commercial nationalism, Australian popular culture and cultural tourism. She is the author of eighteen book chapters, along with numerous refereed journal articles and conference proceedings, a reviewer for several academic journals and a member of professional associations in marketing, tourism and sport.

Dr Jacqueline Z. Wilson is a Lecturer in the School of Education at the University of Ballarat, Victoria. She gained a degree in sociology from La Trobe University, where she was awarded the David Myer University Medal, and has a doctorate in history from Monash University. She is the author of *Prison: Cultural Memory and Dark Tourism*. Her current research focuses on the role of dark tourism sites as teaching resources in the Australian history school curriculum, with a particular focus on national memory, war memorials and historical prison sites.

Dr Caroline Winter is a Senior Lecturer in tourism and teaches at the University of Ballarat, Victoria. She is passionate about the First World War. As a result, her study and research in this field takes up much of her time.

Acknowledgements

Our earlier research and feedback from colleagues suggested that the intersecting domains of tourism and national identities had to date been largely overlooked in the academic literature. This became all the more apparent when our call for chapter contributions brought about an overwhelming response from researchers around the world. As such, we acknowledge the growing number of researchers in the field of tourism and national identities and recognise that a closer examination of the relationships between these two domains is indeed a subject worthy of more detailed scrutiny.

We would like to thank the twenty-six authors who contributed to this edited volume. They have been fantastic to work with, highly responsive to our many emails and always incredibly cooperative.

On a personal level, we are grateful for the immeasurable support of our families. Elspeth would like to thank Pat, Zoe, Callum and Millie Figgis. Leanne would like to thank Clarke Stevenson and her parents – Avis and Ron White.

This book would not have been possible without a period of research leave from our respective universities – La Trobe University and Victoria University. We are especially thankful to our employers for these sabbaticals, as they provided us with the opportunity to focus on this book and a range of other publications.

We would like to thank our publisher Routledge and their affiliated organisations. In particular, we thank Emma Travis, Faye Leerink, Elisabet Sinkie, Caroline Richmond and James Cooke.

Finally, we hope that this edited volume will add to and further energise this emerging and critical area of research.

Elspeth Frew   Leanne White
La Trobe University, Australia   Victoria University, Australia

1 Tourism and national identities

Connections and conceptualisations

Leanne White and Elspeth Frew

Intersecting tourism and national identities

This edited volume explores the multiple ways in which aspects of tourism and national identity intersect, overlap and traverse. Tourism has broad appeal on account of the opportunity it gives individuals to travel to a range of destinations and become involved in a variety of new experiences reflecting aspects of their national identity. The area where cultural tourism and national identity interconnect has been largely overlooked in the academic literature to date. This complex relationship between the two domains (and, indeed, the multifaceted strategies used to define that relationship) is a subject worthy of considerable analysis. The overlapping area in need of further research attention is shown in the middle of the Venn diagram in Figure 1.1. The tourist may develop a deeper appreciation of a destination by understanding it through the lens of national identity, and in the same way tourism marketers and planners might be better equipped to promote and manage it – particularly with regard to the expectations of the potential visitor.

This introduction examines the conceptual framework, offers a brief theoretical background to the area, and then provides an overview of the rest of the book.

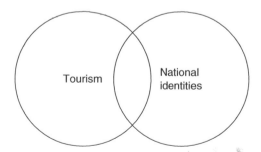

Tourism

National
identities

Figure 1.1 The important overlapping area between the domains of tourism and national identities.

The various chapters investigate case studies from around the world, exploring diverse tourism and identity issues in the United States, Ireland, Hungary, New Zealand, Australia, England, China, the Kyrgyz Republic, Canada and Vietnam. The conclusion highlights and interconnects many of the significant issues and themes explored in the volume and illuminates the path for further possible research in the area.

Nation, nationalism and national identities

The term "nation" encompasses more than simply the body of people within the borders of a particular country. Theorists of nationalism have acknowledged that the term can incorporate political, social, cultural, historical, economic, linguistic and religious factors. When an individual is said to belong to a nation, it is generally understood that that person has their foundations in that country. The word "nation" originated from the Latin term *natio*, or community of birth. Nation is therefore associated with words such as native, nature, innate, natal and renascent. While the focus of this book is on forms of national identity (within the context of tourism), connected terms include nation-state, nationality, national consciousness, national sentiment, nation-building and, to some extent, patriotism and citizenship.

While one acknowledges arguments that enter into the debate about the nation and the nation-state, such as the existence of states without nations and nations without states, the nation-state remains the effective political entity in terms of the way in which the world is organised. In a world which is operating increasingly at a global level, and where political and trade associations often emphasise regional alliances, some may argue that the nation-state may be becoming redundant. However, in the highly competitive tourism industry, where destinations and nations compete for a finite tourist dollar, the significance of national identity seems to strengthen rather than diminish with the passing of time.

There is general agreement that the historical moment when nationalism was first given full expression was in the late eighteenth century in Europe, and that the phenomenon intensified with the French Revolution of 1789. Groth suggests that the revolution suddenly brought the "ideas, slogans and institutional expressions of nationalism" to the attention of Europe and the world (Groth 1971: 86). Anderson (1983, 1991), however, traces the origin of the nation-state to an event two years before the French Revolution, the formation of the Constitution of the United States in 1787.

Smith defines nation as a "named human population", with shared territory, myths, history, culture, economy, and rights and responsibilities by all members of that community (Smith 1991: 14). While his notion is useful, it has been Anderson's (1983) theories on the subject that have made a significant contribution to the discourse of the nation in recent years. Anderson claims that the nation is an "imagined political community". Unlike previous theorists, he breaks away from the interpretation that the nation is intrinsically bound up with factors such as religion or kinship by emphasising the imagined status of the community by the people: "It is imagined because members of even the smallest nation will never know most of their fellow members, meet them, or even hear of them, yet in the minds of each lives the image of their communion" (Anderson 1983: 15). Anderson asserts that the imagined community is limited because even large communities have restricted boundaries beyond which other countries exist. His concept of the community stems from the myth of fraternity – the perceived rather than the actual comradeship (ibid.: 16). His definition of the nation presupposes a close connection both among citizens and between citizens and their country. He contends that official nationalism is the "willed merger of nation and dynastic empire" and argues that the concept came about in response to popular nationalism that emerged in Europe from the 1820s (1991: 86). He explains that official nationalism emanates "from the state" and has as its primary feature a focus on "serving the interests of the state first and foremost" (ibid.: 159).

Of the books produced on theories of nationalism over the past twenty years, Anderson's is among the most frequently cited (Culler and Cheah 2003: vii). Ozkirimli argues that his work "constitutes one of the most original accounts of nationalism to date" (Ozkirimli 2000: 151), while James claims that Anderson's key text "remains the most insightful book written in the area" (James 1996: ix). However, James departs from Anderson in characterising the nation as something more than a representation – a "distinctive kind of abstract community" (ibid.: xi).

Building on Anderson's theory of imagined community, Appadurai puts forward the term "imagined worlds" to describe "the multiple worlds that are constituted by the historically situated imaginations of persons and groups spread around the globe" (Appadurai 1996: 33). Appadurai's five dimensions of global cultural flows consist of ethnoscapes – the movement of people; technoscapes – the shifting of technologies; finanscapes – the moving of money; mediascapes – the transfer of images; and ideoscapes – the progress of ideologies. The two "scapes" which are of most relevance to the issues examined in this book are mediascapes and ideoscapes, with mediascapes providing complex repertoires of images and narratives. Bennett also states that, in as much as they are "imagined communities", nations exist and represent themselves in the form of "long continuous narratives" or "never-ending stories" (Bennett 1993: 74).

The development of the printing press, and in particular the mass production of novels and newspapers towards the end of the eighteenth century, provided the vehicle through which members of the imagined nation could share their perceived alliance. Print media "provided the technical means for 're-presenting' the *kind* of imagined community that is the nation" (Anderson 1991: 25). Commentators understand the imagined community of the nation as being maintained by cultural artefacts and institutions such as literature, art, media and the education system, and argue that a sense of nation is established and sustained "by the quotidian rhythms of print and electronic media output, along with periodic national ceremonies" (O'Sullivan *et al.* 1994: 196–7).

While the nation-state is an important concept for this book, the enormous cultural, social and economic impact of globalisation deserves some further attention. Smith contends that global culture is comprised of a number of discrete elements, including efficiently promoted mass commodities, ideological discourses concerned with human rights and values, and a constantly changing cosmopolitanism. It is a culture which is universal and timeless, fluid and fundamentally artificial (Smith 1991: 157–8). Smith's conception of a global culture is inherently postmodern in its shapelessness and lack of structure.

If global influences on culture are part of the lifestyle of the twenty-first century, one might then wonder if the ideology of the nation will continue to play a significant role in the future. Smith maintains that the nation displays little indication of being transcended and that nationalism does not seem to be failing in its power and meaning (Smith 1991: 170). He predicts that the nation will continue to produce for the people its "central cultural and political identities" fully into the next century (ibid.: 177). There appear to be two main reasons for suggesting that nationalism will remain an important ideology. Its attraction has much to do with two key elements – the issue of immortality and the flexible nature of the ideology. Participating in the national arena, even in a seemingly insignificant way, is perceived by many to transcend the personal and mortal and to enter into the more honoured realm of the immortal. Also, the different interpretations that can be placed on nationalism provide the ideology with its popular appeal.

Nationalism can be considered as either a positive or a negative force. On the positive side, it is regarded as a source of distinction, while those in the negative camp claim it to be a source of aggression. Hobsbawm raises its negative aspect when he states that nationalism by definition excludes "all who do not belong to its own nation, that is, the vast majority of the human race" (Hobsbawm 1990: 169). However, Seton-Watson explains that nationalism is intrinsically neither good nor bad. He claims national identity is at least "passively treasured by nearly all citizens of modern societies, even if they don't know it" (Seton-Watson 1982: 13). After the 11 September 2001 attacks in the United States, American citizens showed their patriotism and stance against "the enemy" by proudly flying the flag. Some might perceive this as a proud gesture, while others might argue that it may either deliberately or inadvertently promote aggression. Across the United States, around New York City and what became known as "Ground Zero" in particular, the stars and stripes were prominently displayed in an almost defiant stance.

The intensity of an individual's feelings about their national identity seems to be directly related to their level of national sentiment. Sentiment for the nation involves a sense of personal identification and empathy with something larger and greater than oneself. As a particular level of emotion is involved, national sentiment is highly subjective and can vary enormously in different circumstances. To illustrate the point, while it is possible that possessing citizenship of a country might not register any emotional involvement, it is often the case that being a member of the nation-state does carry some meaning, even if it is regarded as one of the more abstract identities enjoyed by the individual. Additionally, national sentiment might be more concentrated when the citizen is younger, and possibly more impressionable, than when they become older and increasingly aware of manipulative forces. This phenomenon might best be demonstrated by the propensity of young Australians, particularly in more recent times, to wear the Australian flag at sporting events as something of a potentially divisive jingoistic cloak (Frew and White 2007).

When confronted with the task of articulating precise definitions for concepts such as the nation, the nation-state, national identity, national sentiment, nationality and citizenship – to name a few terms that arise when examining this subject – one soon arrives at an understanding that the concepts clearly do not have fixed definitions but take on different meanings depending on the use to which they are put. Much time and energy has been spent in exploring the boundaries of definition on this topic. Hobsbawm alludes to this with his observation that a "considerable proportion of all serious analytical writing on the national question was inevitably concerned with problems of definition" (Hobsbawm 1972: 385).

Many theorists agree about the elusive nature of nationalism. When comparisons are made, one particular member of the animal kingdom is identified as providing a metaphor for nationalism. Minogue claims that nationalism is a "set of ideas" which are "chameleons that take on the colour of the locality around them" (Minogue 1967: 153), while Smith explains that "Chameleon-like, nationalism takes its colour from its context". He adds that nationalism is capable of infinite manipulation, is an "eminently malleable nexus of beliefs, sentiments and symbols" and is understood in the context of each different use (Smith 1991: 79).

Although debate about the concept of the nation has been "serious and intensive" since the 1880s (Hobsbawm 1990: 43), there remains much to learn about the phenomenon of nationalism. The lack of substantial discussion on the subject was observed by Emerson, who claimed that what is not known about it amounts to "an impressive body of ignorance and uncertainty" (Emerson 1960: 89). Nearly thirty years after Emerson made this comment, and despite a significant resurgence of interest in the subject since the late 1960s, the insufficient amount of serious research on nationalism is also noted by James, who discussed the paradoxical situation that, "While the nation continues to be, even if in a changing form, an ontological category of central importance, it has long been associated with a poverty of theorising" (James 1989: 273).

In expanding on Emerson's assessment that there is an "impressive body of ignorance", James emphasises the severity of the problem by suggesting that the word "impressive" should be substituted by "overwhelming" (James 1989: 275). The inadequacy of the debate surrounding nationalism was also made by Hobsbawm, who stated that, while nationalism is "probably the most powerful political phenomenon of our century", it is remarkably difficult to analyse, as the literature about it is generally "unsatisfactory and frustrating". He also made the comment that "virtually everything that has been written . . . is question-begging and therefore negligible" (Hobsbawm 1972: 385). The level of debate about nationalism is indeed cause for considerable concern. However, there remains much to say about the nation, and this book examines how the eminently flexible phenomenon is appropriated by the tourism industry to sell products and services.

Tourism, identity, culture and heritage

Recent studies in tourism have considered the role of heritage attractions in helping create a national identity (see, for example, Palmer 2005; Pretes 2003). Pretes notes that tourists receive messages sent to them by the creators of the sites they visit, and these sites, presented as aspects of a national heritage, help to shape a common national identity, or "imagined community", among a diverse population. He also argues that a shared identity is often an official goal of countries comprised of many different cultures where there exists a common urge to create a national identity to overcome diversity and difference. He adds that monuments in particular represent something shared by all citizens, helping to "popularize a hegemonic nationalist message of inclusion" (Pretes 2003: 127). Another perspective on diversity is offered by Spillman (1997), who maintains that, in a diverse country, diversity itself can become an aspect of national identity.

Identity tourism is a comprehensive term where "collective identities are represented, interpreted and potentially constructed through the use of history and culture" (Pitchford 2008: 3). The term encompasses the notion that tourism and finding out more about one's identity is something that has broad appeal. It also alludes to the facts that the once clear boundaries between these domains have been largely eliminated and that one's identity (particularly, and in this case, their national identity) can be combined with tourism to create a new experience and, consequently, a new genre within the broader discipline of tourism. However, identity tourism can best be contrasted with the common perception of tourism as involving "the gaze" (Urry 1990), whereby there is no interaction of the person with the destination. Rather, identity tourism frequently involves the generation of significant personal meaning for the visitor. For example, Nash (2002) considered Americans who visited Ireland, where they shared a "desire for connection, to match something in themselves to another place and to other people". She noted that, for these people, the expectations of intimacy, affinity, family likeness and finally being in the place that matters were sometimes translated into bodily registers, as "shivers down the spine" and "goose bumps", that confirmed the significance of matching up genealogy and geography (ibid.: 37).

About this book

When we announced the call for chapter abstracts in 2009, we welcomed a broad range of topics from contributors around the world, including (but not limited to) national authenticity and tourism; tourism and representation; heritage tourism and aspects of nation; media, tourism and national identity; nation and tourism images; indigenous nations and tourism; nation branding and tourism; destination marketing and the nation; representative national events; and autoethnography, national identity and tourism. As the editors of this collaborative international

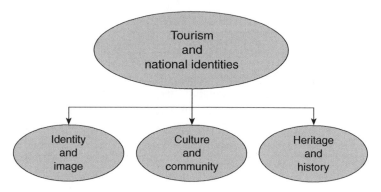

Figure 1.2 The three themed sections.

body of work, we are pleased to be able to announce that, with the help of scholars around the globe, we have produced a volume that covers all of the above topics and more.

This volume explores in detail the multiple ways in which cultural tourism, events and celebrations contribute to national identity. It contends that, by understanding tourist sites and events associated with aspects of culture and national identity, planners and destination managers can better manage such attractions and events. We are also able to understand more about the discipline of tourism by examining it in the context of discussions about nationalism and national identity. This book combines an applied practitioner's approach with solid academic analysis and critical input and is unique in that it incorporates the broader issues of identity tourism and opens the areas of nationalism and cultural tourism to both a multidisciplinary and an international approach. It is divided into three themed sections: "Identity and image", "Culture and community", and "Heritage and history" (see Figure 1.2).

Part I begins by looking at tourism and national identity in the United States. In Chapter 2, Huang and Santos explore how national identity can be incorporated into tourism discourse by examining travel-related websites for Washington, DC. The case clearly illustrates that representations of a nation's capital can be used to strengthen national identity by instilling a sense of national pride, reflecting the unique spirit and characteristics of a nation, and creating an emotional bond between tourists and the destination. In Chapter 3, Patterson illustrates how "Brand Ireland" gained its iconic status among tourists. He charts the connections between Brand Ireland and the social and cultural realm of its creation, and concludes by asking whether the success of the country as a tourist destination is sustainable over the longer term. In Chapter 4, Smith and Puczkó examine the construction of national identity and tourism in Hungary, arguing that most post-socialist countries share similar dilemmas regarding how far to promote their socialist or pre-socialist heritage while at the same time creating a European and global identity. They suggest that multi-level identity creation is desirable if a country's history, traditions, contemporary culture and lifestyle is to be properly reflected. In Chapter 5, Buchmann and Frost investigate how the *Lord of the Rings* films affected tourism and national identity in New Zealand. They explore how the blockbuster trilogy both initiated a growing film tourism sector and came to present a "national product" that reinforced the existing identity of a green and clean country with spectacular scenery. Finally, in Chapter 6, White explains how the horse and the notion of horsemanship have played a central role in Australian national identity and focuses on the ways in which certain tourism and leisure industries in particular work to manufacture and sustain the powerful myth.

The middle section of the book – "Culture and community" – begins with Ali and Holden's evaluation of the influence of travel to the homeland on identity formation among the Pakistanis of Luton, England. Based upon interpretive ethnographic fieldwork, the theoretical framework for this chapter is developed from the "myth of return" and Benedict Anderson's concept of "imagined communities". The results demonstrate that tourism to the homeland is an important component of identity formation. Chapter 8 examines the 2008 Beijing Olympic Games and China's national identity from the perspective of the host community in Beijing. Meng and Li provide insights into tourism development and the building of national identity and discuss the impact of China's tourism development on the country's biggest nation-building exercise. Tourism and national identity in the Kyrgyz Republic is explored by Schofield and Maccarrone-Eaglen in Chapter 9, which focuses on the socio-cultural, economic and political transformation of the country, examining Kyrgyz identity and its connection to tourism. The authors look at cultural heritage tourism, particularly those aspects relating to the country's nomadic tradition. In Chapter 10, Laws and Ferguson analyse the annual Canada Day celebration in a small community. They argue that this national celebration carries multiple narratives of identity and that participants play an active role in deriving meaning from the relatively modest event. In the final chapter of the section, Frew undertakes a study of novelty world championship events and explores how these relate to national identity. Having examined a sample of such events, she determines that those that are location-specific often reflect the culture and identity of the region in which they are staged.

Part III presents chapters under the theme of heritage and history and begins, in Chapter 12, with a discussion by Wheeler, Laing, Frost, Reeves and Frost as to how specific outlaws such as Jesse James, Billy the Kid, James MacKenzie and Ned Kelly have become icons of frontier destinations. In these instances, national identity is projected to tourists in terms of frontier anti-heroes. In Chapter 13, Thanh Bui, Jolliffe and Nguyen examine the central role of Vietnam's Ho Chi Minh Museum in highlighting aspects of nation for both domestic and international visitors. Visitor statistics and comments show that this museum effectively conveys the nation-state dialogue of contemporary Vietnam. Battlefield tourism and Australia's national identity is examined in Chapter 14. Winter argues that, while the Gallipoli campaign helped to form a new identity for Australia and distinguish it from Britain, the achievements on the Western Front were largely forgotten. It is suggested that tourism will play a significant role in connecting contemporary Australians with these lesser-known European battlefields. In Chapter 15, Campelo and Aitken consider narratives and place in the Chatham Islands, off the coast of New Zealand, providing an insight into the distinctive destination where narratives of history and the influence of genealogy intertwine with the dramatic natural environment to create a strong sense of place identity. In Chapter 16, Wilson explores dark tourism and national identity in the Australian history curriculum. It is argued that excursions to sites identified as having key significance in the historical process of nation-building form a central component of the curriculum at both primary and secondary level, with prisons a popular choice for teachers. While such sites often have iconic status in the national memory, their historical meaning can be ambiguous.

This book – a reference text aimed principally at the academic market – is designed to address the significant void that currently exists in tourism and national identity discourse. This stimulating volume could become a prescribed text for postgraduate coursework units and/or recommended reading for advanced undergraduate and postgraduate students in a number of discipline areas. It is also of interest to the many academics around the globe and other interested stake-holders, including those in the tourism industry, government bodies and community groups. We trust that you will be inspired and energised by the diverse international cases of tourism and national identity that are explored here.

References

Anderson, B. (1983) *Imagined Communities: Reflections on the Origins and Spread of Nationalism*. London: Verso.

Anderson, B. (1991) *Imagined Communities: Reflections on the Origins and Spread of Nationalism*. 2nd edn, London: Verso.

Appadurai, A. (1996) *Modernity at Large: Cultural Dimensions of Globalization*. Minneapolis: University of Minnesota Press.

Bennett, T. (1993) "The shape of the past", in G. Turner (ed.) *Nation, Culture, Text: Australian Cultural and Media Studies* (pp. 72–90). London: Routledge.

Culler, J., and Cheah, P. (eds) (2003) *Grounds of Comparison: Around the Work of Benedict Anderson*. New York: Routledge.

Emerson, R. (1960) *From Empire to Nation*. Cambridge, MA: Harvard University Press.

Frew, E., and White, L. (2007) "Australia Day alternative events: an exploration of national identity and nationalism", in B. O'Mahony, R. Harris and J. Mair (eds) *Proceedings of the Fourth International Event Research Conference*. Melbourne: Victoria University.

Groth, A. (1971) *Major Ideologies: An Interpretative Survey of Democracy, Socialism and Nationalism*. New York: Wiley-Interscience.

Hobsbawm, E. (1972) "Some reflections on nationalism", in T. Nossiter *et al.* (eds) *Imagination and Precision in the Social Sciences*. London: Faber & Faber.

Hobsbawm, E. (1990) *Nations and Nationalism since 1780: Programme, Myth, Reality*. New York: Cambridge University Press.

James, P. (1989) "National formation and the 'rise of the cultural': a critique of orthodoxy", *Philosophy of the Social Sciences*, 19(3): 273–90.

James, P. (1996) *Nation Formation: Towards a Theory of Abstract Community*. London: Sage.

Minogue, K. (1967) *Nationalism*. London: Batsford.

Nash, C. (2002) "Genealogical identities", *Environment and Planning D: Society and Space*, 20(1): 27–52.

O'Sullivan, T., Hartley, J., Saunders, D., Montgomery, M., and Fiske, J. (1994) *Key Concepts in Communication and Cultural Studies*. 2nd edn, London: Routledge.

Ozkirimli, U. (2000) *Theories of Nationalism: A Critical Introduction*. Basingstoke: Macmillan.

Palmer, C. (2005) "An ethnography of Englishness: experiencing identity through tourism", *Annals of Tourism Research*, 32(1): 7–27.

Pitchford, S. (2008) *Identity Tourism: Imaging and Imagining the Nation*. Bingley: Emerald.

Pretes, M. (2003) "Tourism and nationalism", *Annals of Tourism Research*, 30(1): 125–42.

Seton-Watson, H. (1982) "The history of nations", *Times Literary Supplement*, 27 August.

Smith, A. (1991) *National Identity*. London: Penguin.

Spillman, L. (1997) *Nation and Commemoration: Creating National Identities in the United States and Australia*. New York: Cambridge University Press.

Urry, J. (1990) *The Tourist Gaze: Leisure and Travel in Contemporary Societies*. London: Sage.

Part I
Identity and image

2 Tourism and national identity in the United States

The case of Washington, DC

Wei-Jue Huang and Carla A. Santos

Introduction

Identity is one's understanding of the question "Who am I?" It is generally divided into two categories: individual and collective. National identity, as a type of collective identity, is a cultural identification based on either territory or ancestry (Smith 1993). As one's self-identity indicates how "self" is different from "other," national identity also encompasses unique psychological characteristics that differentiate one nationality from another (Renshon 2005). In this respect, national identity is related to tourism because of the shared need for uniqueness and difference, a central element in tourism marketing. An important goal of tourism marketing is to create a unique image which sets a particular destination apart from other places. Therefore, national identity can be incorporated into tourism branding as a way of showcasing how each country is exceptional and worthy of a visit.

The relationship between tourism and national identity is evident in capital city tourism. National capital cities require a unique hosting environment to perform their political, economic and symbolic functions (Gottmann 1983). For pragmatic purposes, the capital demands more office buildings and facilities and better infrastructure (Gordon 2006; Ritchie and Maitland 2007). To represent national identity, image and prestige, the capital is usually kept clean and well maintained and beautified with parks, memorials and monuments (Hall 2002; Campbell 2003). Political capitals are those cities created to be the seat of government but lacking other urban functions – for example, Ottawa, Canberra, Brasilia and Washington, DC (Hall 2000). Their environment is distinctively planned and developed to serve their national capital function and thus is different from those of other types of capitals and metropolitan centers.

Capital cities are popular travel destinations. The planned nature of the environment makes for a distinctive tourism setting. Clusters of memorials and monuments provide not only famous attractions but easily accessible tourist zones (Gordon 2006). Furthermore, the infrastructure and transportation systems in capitals facilitate domestic and international travel (Ritchie and Maitland 2007). But, apart from the practical advantages of their status, the symbolic function of political capitals also impacts their tourism development (Gottmann 1983;

Dube and Gordon 2000). The national capital has buildings, memorials and monuments that represent the nation and its national identity (Daum 2005), the meanings and messages of which are often used in tourism marketing and promotional materials.

This chapter explores the uniqueness of the capital city environment and how it is appropriated in tourism discourse. The language of tourism has the power to construct and control the "toured" people, cultures and environments (Dann 1996). Promotional materials seek to create a perfect image of the destination in order to appeal to potential visitors. Such representations are usually constituted by stereotypical images and the toured environment is depicted in certain ways to create a "sense of place" (Urry 1995; Stokowski 2002). This chapter therefore aims to unravel the representational dynamics of the environment within the discourse of tourism. Travel-related websites for Washington DC, such as the DC Chamber of Commerce, the DC Visitor Information Center and Cultural Tourism DC, are examined to reveal the underlying themes and structures in the representation of its environment. It demonstrates how the language of tourism can be used to showcase national pride and identity to international tourists while constructing and reinforcing the national identity of domestic visitors.

Capital city tourism

The significance of tourism in capital cities was first acknowledged outside the field of tourism. Research in urban planning has identified the unique features of capitals, many of which are beneficial for tourism development. Gottmann was the first to specify the attributes of capital cities, including "a special hosting environment," a variety of ancillary activities, and "good accessibility" (1983: 88). Specifically, capital cities are different in that they are "larger, more subsidized, or more bombastic" (Campbell 2003: 4) and marked by monuments, government buildings, universities, theatres and concert halls (Hall 2000). These facilities are usually grouped together, allowing tourists to visit all the sites with ease (Gordon 2006).

Hall was the first in tourism studies to call attention to capital cities and their implications, arguing that, while the capital acts as "showpiece" for a nation, this role also has "positive spin-offs for tourism" (2002: 246). The distinctive features of capital city tourism were summarized as national focus, clusters of cultural resources, and connectivity (Ritchie and Maitland 2007). Capitals may have positive impacts on destination marketing (Haven-Tang *et al.* 2007; Smith 2007) as well as negative implications (Mules *et al.* 2007; Peirce and Ritchie 2007). They therefore often face dilemmas in market positioning (Byrne and Skinner 2007; Puczkó *et al.* 2007).

In order to explore the relationship between tourism and national capitals, it is necessary to understand the original purpose of the planning and designing of such cities. Gottmann indicated that "the position of the capital reflects many practical and also symbolical, actually *iconographic*, elements in the selection of its chosen place" (1983: 89). A capital may be located in the geographical center of a nation for the practical reason of easier accessibility to and from other parts of the country. Symbolically, the central location also represents the heart of a nation. For example, Washington, DC, is situated centrally on the eastern coast of the United States, Tokyo between the east and west regions of Japan, Canberra between the major cities of Sydney and Melbourne, and Brasilia in the central part of Brazil.

The city itself is designed for both practical and symbolic purposes. According to Dube and Gordon, "planning for cities that include a seat of government often involves political and symbolic concerns that are different from those of other urban areas" (2000: 6). The practical functions of a political capital include "serving as the formal seat of the head(s) of state and the government" and "hosting parliamentary sessions, publishing laws, and receiving the envoys and ambassadors of other states" (Daum 2005: 13). Its symbolic function is to "convey meanings through the spatial signifiers it contains: the form of the urban plan, the architecture used by government and parliament, and the presence of national memorials" (ibid.: 16–17). The environment is constructed to represent the nation and its national identity.

Washington, DC

Founded in 1790, Washington, DC, is located centrally along the eastern seaboard of the United States, just south of Maryland and north of Virginia. It was the first political capital of the "New World" and has become a role model for other planned capital cities. According to Gottmann, "the United States has set the fashion of capital cities of moderate size, away from the main metropolis" (1983: 91). For example, the Australian Capital Territory was carved out of a state as a separate district following the model of the District of Columbia (Gordon 2000), and Ottawa's improvement plan in 1893 was to become the "Washington of the North" (Gordon 2002: 183). The location of DC was deliberately chosen to act as a hinge between the north and south of the eastern United States and as a commercial connector between the Atlantic Ocean and the inner continent (Abbott 2005). Named after the first president of the United States, George Washington, the city was planned and developed to serve as America's permanent capital. In 2008, its population was approximately 5,358,000, ranking as the ninth largest metropolitan city in the country (US Census Bureau 2009).

According to the Washington DC Convention and Tourism Corporation, tourism is the city's primary industry after the federal government. Tourism generates over $10 billion in direct spending every year and sustains 260,000 jobs (WCTC 2007). Another source indicated that, in 2007, domestic travel expenditures to the area amounted to $5.7 billion (US Travel Association 2007). Washington is usually ranked in the top ten visited cities in the United States. For example, it was eighth in the "Top cities visited by overseas travelers," with 1,481,000 international visitors in 2000 and 1,470,000 in 2008 (US Department of Commerce 2009). With

36.9 million visitors and 22.8 million hotel rooms sold in 2006, it was ranked sixth in Forbes Traveler's list of "America's 30 most visited cities" (*USA Today* 2007). Washington is home to many national treasures, with such popular attractions as the White House, the Washington Monument, the Lincoln and Jefferson memorials, the US Capitol, the Library of Congress and the Smithsonian Institution.

DC tourism and national identity

Thirteen public and government-related websites on tourism in Washington, DC, were selected for this study through purposive and snowball sampling. A total of 329 webpages were collected, and the contents, both text and images, were scrutinized through qualitative content analysis, focusing on the themes and meanings behind the representation of the city. Overall, the environment of DC is depicted on travel-related websites such as the Official Tourism Site of Washington DC and Cultural Tourism DC through three main themes: glorifying the nation and its capital, reflecting the American ideal, and arousing patriotic emotions. The environment is used in the first theme to represent the grandeur and prominence of the nation, through the display of history, wealth, power and superiority, and in the second to symbolize American ideals and values, such as democracy, liberty/freedom, justice, equality and diversity; in the third it is portrayed in such a way as to arouse feelings of patriotism through the use of national symbols and references to wars. The third theme may seem contradictory at first because, in order to arouse patriotic emotions, the websites demonstrate not the strength of the nation and the victory of war, but rather the painful history and the casualties, the sacrifices and the "price" of war.

Such touristic yet nationalistic images of Washington, DC, suggest that political ideology is incorporated into the language of tourism. Through the exhibition of its planned, political environment on tourism websites, the city is not only promoting itself as the national capital but also constructing the nationhood of the United States of America. The three focal themes signify the underlying structure in the representation of national identity. Each of these themes is further divided into sub-categories, explored in detail below.

Glorifying the nation and its capital

Needless to say, tourism websites generally portray a positive image of the destination they seek to market. Travel-related websites for Washington, DC, also paint a pleasant picture of city while incorporating certain political elements to create a sense of a great capital within a great nation. Four key elements are most commonly used to glorify the nation and its capital: history, wealth, power and pride.

Washington's environment reflects its place in American history, and tourism websites emphasize its historic significance. According to the DC Chamber of Commerce website (2008), history is what makes the city a unique destination: "Washington, DC – our nation's capital – is unlike any other travel destination in the world. Its storied history extends back to the founding of our country, and virtually every neighborhood offers a glimpse into the past." History resounds in every neighborhood, through "the city's inspiring sacred structures, historic black churches, landscaped cemeteries, and presidential houses of worship" (Cultural Tourism DC 2007). The ExploreDC.org website (2001) provided detailed accounts of the history and heritage reflected in the city's sites, buildings and neighborhoods. Altogether, it was depicted as a tribute to American history:

> Our nation's history and heritage is embodied in Washington, DC . . . Washington is an archive of Civil War, African American, and literary history and as well as striking public and domestic architecture and artistic treasures. Its neighborhoods, houses of worship, hidden monuments, museums, cemeteries and military sites tell the story of our culture, governance, politics, and the development of our democratic institutions.
>
> (Ibid.)

Such representation emphasizes Washington's role in American history and reinforces its status as the national capital. The USA is generally considered a modern and advanced country, with a relatively short history in comparison to that of many Asian and European countries. Nevertheless, history defines who we are, and likewise it plays an essential role in shaping a nation's identity. Even for New World countries, there is a need to commemorate the tales of the nation and its founding heroes in the construction of its national ideology. The USA therefore highlights and celebrates its historic importance in order to compensate for what may be perceived as a shorter global history. The physical environment of DC is commonly portrayed on tourism websites as the setting of historic incidents and associated with American national heroes in order to bring a sense of historic pride and glory to the nation.

The wealth of a nation can be demonstrated through the physical environment of its capital city. In their portrayal of Washington, websites frequently mention the materials that make up the buildings and monuments. For example, the exterior of the Russell Senate Office Building is "lined with a colonnade of Doric columns and faced with white marble and limestone" (US Senate 2007). Moreover, some websites tend to emphasize the precious value of the construction materials. For example, the Washington Monument is "topped off with a nine-foot pyramid made of aluminum, which was then considered a precious metal" (District of Columbia n.d.). And, in the construction of the Supreme Court Building, "marble was chosen as the principal material to be used and $3 million worth was gathered from foreign and domestic quarries" (Supreme Court 2007).

Another way to exemplify the wealth of the nation is to provide figures associated with the construction cost. For example, the Vietnam Veterans' Memorial recently paid for a $1 million renovation just for the lighting system (DC Visitor Information Center 2007). The Union Station underwent a $160 million renovation between 1978 and 1988, which was "the largest, most complex public/private restoration project ever attempted in the US" (US Senate 2007), and, "at a cost of over $830 million, the Washington Convention Center is the city's largest building" (District of Columbia n.d.). The frequent use of numbers on these tourism websites appears to be a means of impressing and inspiring a sense of awe in potential visitors to the capital by parading its wealth.

A great nation must be powerful, with the ability to protect its land and citizens. Power is associated with many places in Washington, DC, particularly the Pentagon, the White House and the Capitol Building. As the headquarters of the US Department of Defense, the Pentagon is recognized as "the world's largest office building and the command center for our nation's defense" (US Senate 2007). The enormous size of the building is emphasized to signify the country's strength. The White House is the office and residence of US presidents – "the men who have held one of the most powerful offices in the world" (ExploreDC. org 2001). Therefore, it has also come to be "identified with the power of the presidency" (District of Columbia n.d.) and to signify "the important decisions made within its walls over the years" (DC Chamber of Commerce 2008).

The monuments and buildings in Washington also symbolize the strength of the nation. For example, the World War II Memorial portrays "two American eagles hold[ing] the victory laurel aloft with an impressive bronze-sculpted ribbon" and a wreath which "symbolizes the combination of strength and bounty imperative to America's mighty war effort" (District of Columbia n.d.). As home to the Constitution, the Declaration of Independence and the Bill of Rights, National Archives building is not only fireproof but designed with high-tech security devices:

> This "holy trinity" of American political documents is displayed in an altar like setting in the rotunda of the Archives. Enclosed in airtight, helium-filled cases, the documents are perhaps the most well protected parchments on earth. Each evening the display cases are lowered into a crypt 20 feet below the rotunda, safe from deterioration, theft or even nuclear attack.
> (ExploreDC.org 2001)

In short, through the expression of its military strength and national security in Washington, DC, the United States can claim its national power and reinforce its global authority.

It is necessary for a nation to develop a sense of pride and, as the national capital, Washington also wishes to assert its leading position. A sense of pride can be created through the use of superlatives. Numerous buildings and monuments in DC are depicted as the first, the best, the oldest or the largest nationwide or worldwide. The Library of Congress is described as "the nation's oldest federal cultural institution and serves as the research arm of Congress. It is also the largest library in the world" (DC Chamber of Commerce 2008). The National Museum of Women in the Arts is hailed as "the world's first museum dedicated to the artistic achievements of women" (US Senate 2007).

Washington, DC, exemplifies its prominence by emphasizing its international fame and leading status in the world. For example, the National Mall area is "known worldwide and depicted on everything from currency to the nightly news" (NAMA 2008). Furthermore, the city is often associated with political leaders. For example, the Franklin Delano Roosevelt Memorial is a tribute to "a world-wide leader who brought America through the Great Depression and World War II and changed the course of the nation and the world" (US Senate 2007). The portrayal of US presidents as international leaders is used to signify the city and the nation's leading position.

Reflecting the American ideal

While history, wealth, power and pride are of universal value, it is equally necessary for a nation to establish its unique identity. The identity of a nation is formulated upon its founding values and beliefs, which can often be reflected through the symbolic function of its capital city. For example, the National Mall and Memorial Parks area of DC is "a testament to America's past and present where the values of our nation . . . are presented" (NAMA 2008). In other words, Washington reflects the unique American ideals and values, particularly those of democracy, freedom, justice, equality and diversity.

The United States takes great pride in its status as being the first liberal democratic nation in the world. Its capital city is said to "truly embody the American Experience" and is described as "a powerful symbol not only of our nation but also of democracy and freedom" (WCTC 2007). Located at the center of the city, the National Mall is "the heart of the Nation's Capital and of the entire United States of America. Here, the nation celebrates, honors, and demonstrates its commitment to democracy" (NAMA 2008). The value of democracy is promoted not only to American citizens but also to international tourists. Visitors are encouraged to "explore the symbolism behind the city and the buildings that are the homes of American democracy" (ExploreDC.org 2001). Among all the buildings and monuments, the US Capitol is most closely associated with democracy and is commonly described as "the most recognized symbol of democratic government in the world" (US Senate 2007). Other places also emphasize democracy. For example, the Smithsonian Institution reflects "the Enlightenment ideals of democracy and universal education" (Smithsonian Institution 2008).

Democracy, equality and freedom are the founding values of the United States. The thirteen original colonies fought for their freedom from Britain and the American Civil War sought to end the conflict between freedom and slavery. Washington, DC, is recognized as a powerful symbol of freedom, and the National Mall "celebrate[s] the United States' commitment to freedom and equality" (NAMA 2008). The memorial to Thomas Jefferson, the man who shaped American ideals, "stands as a symbol of liberty and endures as a site for reflection and inspiration for all citizens of the United States and the world" (NAMA 2008). Atop the US Capitol's east dome sits "the Statue of Freedom" (District of Columbia n.d.; US Senate 2007); located in the National Archives are "the Charters of Freedom" – the Declaration of Independence, the Constitution and the Bill of Rights (ExploreDC.org 2001); and the African American Civil War Memorial "features Ed Hamilton's 'Spirit of Freedom' sculpture" (ibid.).

Equality and justice form another vital component of the American ideal. As stated in the US Declaration of Independence: "We hold these truths to be self-evident, that all men are created equal, that they are endowed by their Creator with certain unalienable Rights, that among these are Life, Liberty and the pursuit of Happiness" (Library of Congress 2008). In the 1863 Gettysburg Address, Lincoln stressed the importance of equality: "Four score and seven years ago our fathers brought forth, upon this continent, a new nation, conceived in Liberty, and dedicated to the proposition that all men are created equal" (ibid.). In this city the value of justice and equality is exemplified by the US Supreme Court. Etched in white marble on the building's west pediment is the phrase "Equal Justice under Law," which expresses the court's constitutional role (ExploreDC.org 2001). And above the east entrance is the phrase "Justice the Guardian of Liberty," as the court stands as "the final arbiter of the law and guardian of constitutional liberties" (Supreme Court 2007).

The United States is a nation composed of immigrants, from early European settlers to the more recent Africans, Asians and Latinos. This has resulted in the ethnic multiplicity of the nation, and the concept of diversity has become deeply rooted in American ideology. Travel-related websites often promote the diverse ethnic neighborhoods of the capital. For example, "Washington, DC is a city of colorful and diverse neighborhoods, filled with hip boutiques and galleries, historic homes and small museums, urban parks and spectacular gardens" (WCTC 2007). Nowadays, it is recognized as a global, international and cosmopolitan center. Its rapid expansion in the last century created "a rich and diverse culture, represented by people from across the globe" (DC Chamber of Commerce 2008). Its neighborhoods attract tourists for their cultural diversity. For example, the suburb of Adams Morgan, an immigrant community with diverse cultures, has long been a "multicultural hub" and, today, "its restaurant scene is a veritable global village ranging from Ethiopian and Thai to Mexican and Indian" (WCTC 2007). The downtown area is where "thousands of newcomers to Washington – Jews, Germans, Chinese, Greeks, Italians – and many others got their start . . . Their religious structures remain as monuments to their historic presence and offer a fascinating social history" (Cultural Tourism DC 2007).

The values of democracy, freedom, justice, equality and diversity are intertwined to form the ideal American consciousness. Equality is the foundation of justice, justice is the guardian of freedom and democracy, and it is because of the beliefs of freedom, justice and equality that the nation can embrace its cultural and ethnic diversity. As the national capital, Washington embodies the American ideal and reflects these values through its tourism representations.

The beliefs and values of a nation constitute its national identity. For Americans, the United States is different from other nations because of its emphasis on democracy, freedom, equality and diversity. Being a relatively new nation, there was neither feudalism nor an aristocracy in the country (Hodgson 2009). In fact, as stated in the Declaration of Independence, the nation was founded based on the concept that "all men are created equal." Although it has been argued that such equality was not achieved until much later in the nation's history, the values of democracy and freedom remain central to the American identity (ibid.). In addition to their shared belief in democratic government and the principles of equality and freedom, Americans take pride in the nation's cultural diversity and its ability to accommodate people of different origins and ethnicities. And, since these national ideals are embedded in tourism websites, tourism discourse also plays a role in constructing and reaffirming national identity.

Arousing patriotic emotions

The third focal theme in the websites' representation of Washington, DC, is patriotism. The environment is designed and depicted in certain ways so as to arouse patriotic emotions and reinforce national identity. This underlying purpose can be achieved through the use of American national symbols and reference to wars and casualties.

Images of national symbols and references to their meanings can arouse patriotic emotions. The main symbols of America are the national flag, stars and the bald eagle. The most popular pictorial element used on the websites is the American flag. Flags are shown atop or in front of almost every building and monument. In particular, the Washington Monument is surrounded by a circle of "50 flags . . . representing the 50 states" (District of Columbia n.d.). The Statue of Freedom at the top of the US Capitol wears an eagle-shaped helmet surrounded by stars, and the World War II Memorial features four American eagles holding the victory laurel and 4,000 sculpted gold stars, honoring the 400,000 who sacrificed their lives.

The national anthem of the United States also symbolizes the American spirit. A national anthem is usually a patriotic song which describes the history of the nation, the virtue of its people, and the struggles and progress of the nation's development. The Fort McHenry National Monument is the home of "The Star-Spangled Banner," the American national anthem:

> Fort McHenry is best known for its role during the War of 1812. As the linchpin of Baltimore's defenses, Fort McHenry withstood a grueling 25 hour bombardment by the British fleet. In spite of the rockets and bombs, Francis Scott Key saw the fort's 30ft x 42ft flag waving after the battle. Full of emotion, he penned a poem that would later become the National Anthem for the United States of America.
>
> (US Senate 2007)

The above passage serves to arouse patriotic emotions by describing the hardship of war and inducing negative feelings towards the British.

Wars and casualties are frequently mentioned in the websites' description of the tourist sites in the city. Making reference to wars may provoke feelings of patriotism and generate emotional connection to the environment. Patriotic emotions can be aroused by emphasizing the human cost of war in the defense of the nation and its founding values. In Washington, DC, "national monuments dominate the skyline, recognizing the sacrifice of those American heroes – from our founding fathers to the brave men and women in the armed forces – whose resolve and sacrifice helped to shape our country into the great nation it is today" (DC Chamber of Commerce 2008). The image thus created is that this capital city is not a place for fun, but rather a place where people come to contemplate, commemorate and be inspired. Tourists are encouraged to question: "How can memorials to the dead become inspiration to the living? Why is it important to 'never forget' the human loss required to keep our land free?" (ExploreDC.org 2001).

Of all the wars that took place on American soil, the most prominent is the Civil War, which led to the temporary division of the nation. The historic sites associated with the Civil War usually inform the visitors of the great number of casualties. For example, the Gettysburg National Memorial Park was the site of the bloodiest battle in American history: "on July 1, 2, and 3, 1863, more men fought and more men died than in any other battle before or since on North American soil . . . with 51,000 casualties" (US Senate 2007). Similarly, other war or veterans' memorials make a point of specifying the number of people who sacrificed their lives. The World War II Memorial "honors the 16 million who served during WWII and those who supported the war effort from home" (DC Chamber of Commerce 2008). The Vietnam Veterans Memorial "bears the names of more than 58,000 servicemen killed or missing in the Southeast Asia conflict between 1959 and 1975" (District of Columbia n.d.). By emphasizing the enormity of the loss, these monuments remind tourists of the courage and sacrifice of their forefathers who fought to protect the nation and inspire feelings of patriotism and appreciation.

Another important war in American history is that between Britain and the United States in 1812, when British troops burned several buildings in DC. This violent action is mentioned repeatedly on travel-related websites – for example: "This was how the Capitol appeared in August 1814 . . . when British troops burned the Capitol and other public buildings in Washington" (US Senate 2007); "3,000 volumes [of books] fell to the flames when the British burned the Capitol in 1814" (ExploreDC.org 2001). Similar passages can be found in the depiction of the White House: "The Octagon House . . . served as James Madison's White House following the destruction of the real White House by the British in 1814" (US House of Representatives 2008). The frequent reference to the War of 1812 and the burning of the Capitol and the White House perhaps arouses patriotic emotions and even antagonism towards the British. It is necessary for the nation to distinguish itself from Britain to strengthen its national identity.

Conclusion

National capital cities require a unique environment to perform their political functions. In particular, political capitals are designed and constructed with that specific purpose in mind, including the pragmatic function of hosting government offices and organizations and the symbolic function of representing the image and identity of the nation. Political capital cities are also tourist destinations, with many reporting the highest visitation rates for their particular nations. Their distinctive environment is favorable for tourism development in terms of attractions and accessibility, and their political capital status impacts their destination marketing strategies. In other words, the representation of the city in promotional materials is influenced by the political agenda of the city as well as the nation. The purpose of this chapter was to identify and discuss the focal themes in the representation of the capital city environment by examining some travel-related websites for Washington, DC. The analysis focused on the political messages embedded in the language of tourism to reveal the underlying structure and ideology of tourism discourse and representation in the context of political capitals.

It is worth noting that the three themes outlined above are not mutually exclusive. For example, historic reference to Fort McHenry can create a sense of historic importance and also provoke patriotic emotions. Moreover, while the first and the third themes may appear to be contradictory with regard to war, they are akin to the two sides of a coin, portraying the city and the nation from two different angles. The meaning of war can be interpreted in at least two ways. The first theme focuses on the victory in war and the power of the nation, while the third stresses the painful memory of war and the price of maintaining a unified nation. In fact, the three themes are inextricably linked together. A nation's history involves both pain and glory. Through remembrance of past wars and sacrifices, people can learn to cherish the present and appreciate the glory and ideals protected by the nation. The three themes therefore come together to create a complete image of the national capital and construct the identity of the nation.

One current concern is the impact of national capital status on tourism development. Previous research has identified the beneficial features of this, such as activities, facilities, attractions and infrastructure (Hall 2002; Pearce 2007; Ritchie and Maitland 2007). Seeking to depart from a discussion of these pragmatic features, this chapter explored the symbolic functions of a national capital and its connection to tourism promotion and representation. The environment of this city is designed to represent the image and prestige of the nation. Making use of its national capital status, Washington, DC, markets national history, culture, ideals, values and historic figures to tourists. The city is portrayed not only as a destination but also as a symbol of the nation and the American experience.

Touristic representations of Washington demonstrate the relationship between tourism and national identity. The city represents both the materialistic achievements and the spiritual ideals of the United States. It is an exhibit of the history, pride and glory of the nation as well as a symbol of the American creed.

Moreover, when tourists visit the city itself or its travel-related websites, they can not only learn what America stands for but also grow to identify with the nation's founding values of democracy, freedom and cultural diversity. For capital city tourism, promoting patriotism and destination loyalty is relevant because both involve a sense of place attachment and shared experience between tourists and the destination. The case of Washington, DC, clearly illustrates how the language of tourism can be used to strengthen national identity by instilling a sense of national pride, reflecting the unique spirit and characteristics of a nation, and creating an emotional bond between the nation and its citizens.

References

Abbott, C. (2005) "Washington and Berlin: national capitals in a networked world", in A. W. Daum and C. Mauch (eds) *Berlin – Washington, 1800–2000: Capital Cities, Cultural Representation, and National identities*. Cambridge: Cambridge University Press.

Byrne, P., and Skinner, H. (2007) "International business tourism: destination Dublin or destination Ireland?", *Journal of Travel and Tourism Marketing*, 22(3/4): 55–66.

Campbell, S. (2003) *The Enduring Importance of National Capital Cities in the Global Era*, URRC Working Paper, University of Michigan.

Cultural Tourism DC (2007) www.culturaltourismdc.org/ (accessed 20 January 2008).

Dann, G. (1996) *The Language of Tourism: A Sociolinguistic Perspective*. Wallingford, Oxon: CAB International.

Daum, A. W. (2005) "Capitals in modern history: inventing urban spaces for the nation", in A. W. Daum and C. Mauch (eds) *Berlin – Washington, 1800–2000: Capital Cities, Cultural Representation, and National Identities*. Cambridge: Cambridge University Press.

DC Chamber of Commerce (2008) http://dcchamber.org/ (accessed 17 January 2008).

DC Visitor Information Center (2007) www.dcvisit.com (accessed 17 January 2008).

District of Columbia (n.d.) www.vrc.dc.gov/vrc/site/default.asp (accessed 10 January 2008).

Dube, P., and Gordon, D. (2000) "Capital cities: perspectives and convergence", *Plan Canada*, 40(3): 6–7.

ExploreDC.org. (2001) http://exploredc.org [no longer active].

Gordon, D. (2000) "Planning Canberra and Ottawa: more differences than similarities", *Plan Canada*, 40(3): 20–21.

Gordon, D. (2002) "Ottawa-Hull and Canberra: implementation of capital city plans", *Canadian Journal of Urban Research*, 11(2): 179–211.

Gordon, D. (2006) "Capital cities and culture: evolution of twentieth-century capital city planning", in J. Monclus and M. Guardia (eds) *Culture, Urbanism and Planning*. Burlington, VT: Ashgate.

Gottmann, J. (1983) "Capital cities", *Ekistics*, 299: 88–93.

Hall, C. M. (2002) "Tourism in capital cities", *Tourism*, 50(3): 235–48.

Hall, P. (2000) "The changing role of capital cities", *Plan Canada*, 40(3): 8–12.

Haven-Tang, C., Jones, E., and Webb, C. (2007) "Critical success factors for business tourism destinations: exploiting Cardiff's national capital city status and shaping its business tourism offer", *Journal of Travel and Tourism Marketing*, 22(3/4): 109–20.

Hodgson, G. (2009) *The Myth of American Exceptionalism*. New Haven, CT: Yale University Press.

Library of Congress (2008) www.loc.gov/visit (accessed 25 January 2008).

Mules, T., Pforr, C., and Ritchie, B. W. (2007) "The impact of domestic tourism on perceptions of Australia's national capital", *Journal of Travel and Tourism Marketing*, 22(3/4): 35–54.

NAMA (National Mall and Memorial Parks) (2008) *National Mall & Memorial Parks*. Online. Available: www.nps.gov/nama (accessed 25 January 2008).

Pearce, D. (2007) "Capital city tourism: perspectives from Wellington", *Journal of Travel and Tourism Marketing*, 22(3/4): 7–20.

Peirce, S., and Ritchie, B. W. (2007) "National capital branding: a comparative case study of Canberra, Australia and Wellington, New Zealand", *Journal of Travel and Tourism Marketing*, 22(3/4): 67–78.

Puczkó, L., Ratz, T., and Smith, M. (2007) "Perception, positioning and promotion of Budapest", *Journal of Travel and Tourism Marketing*, 22(3/4): 21–34.

Renshon, S. A. (2005) *The 50% American: Immigration and National Identity in an Age of Terror*. Washington, DC: Georgetown University Press.

Ritchie, B. W., and Maitland, R. (2007) "Marketing national capital cities", *Journal of Travel and Tourism Marketing*, 22(3/4): 1–5.

Smith, A. (2007) "Monumentality in 'capital' cities and its implications for tourism marketing: the case of Barcelona", *Journal of Travel and Tourism Marketing*, 22(3/4): 79–94.

Smith, A. D. (1993) *National Identity*. Reno: University of Nevada Press.

Smithsonian Institution (2008) www.si.edu (accessed 23 January 2008).

Stokowski, P. (2002) "Languages of place and discourses of power: constructing new senses of place", *Journal of Leisure Research*, 34(4): 368–82.

Supreme Court of the United States (2007) www.supremecourtus.gov (accessed 26 January 2008).

Urry, J. (1995) *Consuming Places*. London: Routledge.

USA Today (2007) "The 30 most visited US cities", www.usatoday.com/travel/destinations/2007-07-27-most-visited-US-cities-forbes_N.htm?POE=click-refer (accessed 6 December 2007).

US Census Bureau (2009) "50 largest metropolitan statistical areas in 2008 – components of population change: 2000 to 2008", www.census.gov/compendia/statab/2010/tables/10s0021.xls (accessed 20 October 2010).

US Department of Commerce, International Trade Administration, Office of Travel and Tourism Industries and Bureau of Economic Analysis (2009) *Overseas Visitation Estimates for U.S. States, Cities, and Census Regions: 2008*, www.tinet.ita.doc.gov/outreachpages/download_data_table/2008_States_and_Cities.pdf (accessed 1 November 2010).

US House of Representatives (2008) www.house.gov/house/Visitor.shtml (accessed 25 January 2008).

US Senate (2007) "Capitol Visitor Center", www.senate.gov/pagelayout/visiting/a_three_sections_with_teasers/visitors_home.htm (accessed 26 January 2008).

US Travel Association (2007) "Domestic travel expenditures by state: 2007", www.census.gov/compendia/statab/2010/tables/10s1227.pdf (accessed 10 April 2010).

WCTC (Washington, DC, Convention and Tourism Corporation) (2007) www.washington.org (accessed 15 January 2008).

3 Brand Ireland

Tourism and national identity

Anthony Patterson

Introduction

Despite Ireland's heavy reliance on tourism to bolster its general economic health, tourism in the country remains understudied (Deegan and Dineen 2003). With this in mind, the purpose of this chapter is to explore tourism in Ireland, focusing specifically on what tourists find so appealing about its unique brand of national identity. The chapter is unusual in that it does not, as other studies in tourism tend to do, consider a place or country merely via its surface manifestations and immediate imagery (see Curtis-Wilson *et al.* 2006). Instead a cultural perspective is adopted, similar to that currently advocated by some branding theorists (Holt 2004; Schroeder and Salzer-Mörling 2006). The aim of the chapter is to chart the connections between tourism in Ireland and the social and cultural realm of its creation. To this end, it will begin by considering the country's popularity and by revisiting the dramatic historical changes in Irish history that inadvertently caused contemporary tourism to undergo rapid growth. This will provide a springboard for defining and detailing the three incarnations of Brand Ireland suggested here as the main features that attract tourists: Generic-Ireland, Regional-Ireland and Ireland-Plus. The chapter will conclude by asking whether the success of Ireland as a tourist destination is sustainable over the longer term, especially at a time when its credibility in the marketplace is increasingly under scrutiny (Bielenberg 2006; Courtney 2007).

Ireland's popularity

Tourists began visiting Ireland centuries before the Irish government became both a leading exponent of tourism marketing and, in the 1990s, a pioneer of "nation branding". According to Hooper (2001), throughout history tourists have found Ireland a compelling place to visit. He compiles a fascinating collection of travelogue extracts that detail the universal fascination that has brought tourists to the island. Interestingly, it is the strangeness of the country that Hooper notes functions as a chief draw. Often tourists experience "an incredulity at how a country so geographically proximate to other European cultures and civilizing influences could remain so alien" (ibid.: xvi). Yet, in earlier times at least, the country was frequently perceived as a frightening nation of unruly barbarians living bleak, brief lives on desolate bog land. This is a world apart from the Ireland of today, which is said to offer a "postcolonial aura of privileged victimhood" (Witoszek *et al.* 1998: 1) and "idealized ethnicity" that together create an inimitable cult of Celtic chic that sells everywhere (Foster 2002; Negra 2006).

What is it then that has led to Ireland's popularity as a tourist destination? Looking beyond the annual worldwide and public espousal of all things Irish on St Patrick's Day, the creation of which is in no small measure down to clever promotion on the part of the Irish government, it is clear that a main source of competitive advantage that draws tourists to Ireland is its outstanding cultural imagination (Smyth 2001). Ireland's well-honed trait of inventiveness is perhaps the result of over a century of practice, acquired at the culture-promoting feise-anna and Oireachtas festivals that have been organized since the 1890s (Koch 2006). Or perhaps it is simply the enactment of the Celtic stereotype, discussed at length elsewhere (Aherne 2000; O'Loughlin and Szmigin 2007; Patterson and Brown 2007). Whatever the reason, the Irish indisputably excel at generating tourist-friendly goods whose principal ingredients are creativity, quick-wittedness and imagination.

In music, passing swiftly over Bono, Daniel O'Donnell and Ireland's seven winning Eurovision entries, Westlife's cloying brand of identikit pop is probably not particularly representative of the nation's ideals, but it is a good example, if not of musical talent, then certainly of skilful marketing (Ferriter 2005). In dance, the thunderous stepdance that marks the climax of *Riverdance* might, by now, be a cliché too far, but the show remains on permanent world tour. Solid exemplars of Ireland's tourism assets, though, exist in the literary market, where writers such as Roddy Doyle, John Banville, Seamus Deane, Seamus Heaney, William Trevor, Edna Longley and Edna O'Brien have achieved widespread critical acclaim by writing stories about Ireland's intemperate society that, Holt (2004) might argue, resolve cultural contradictions embedded in Irish nationality. It is even alleged that the Irish write better English than the English (Lesinska 2005). Unsurprisingly, Irish creatives of a different genus are frequently the star draw on the interna- tional comedy circuit. The loquacious wiles of Dara Ó Briain, Dylan Moran and Jason Byrne spring most readily to mind.

In film, too, Ireland has a proud tradition with which tourists the world over are familiar. It seems to subscribe to what is named here as the 4Ps of Celtic tour- ism marketing – poets, priests, pubs and poverty. This tradition began with the controversial documentary of island life *Man of Aran* (1934), which, while a remarkable anthropological movie, was fiercely criticized for pretending that the Aran islanders still engaged in the then long-dead tradition of capturing basking sharks (Ellis 2000). Later the romantic comedy *The Quiet Man* (1956) heightened the fictionalization of Ireland by portraying Irish life in a fashion which, depend- ing on an individual's perspective, can either be castigated as excessively senti- mental (see McLoone 2002) or celebrated as a exemplar of marketing abundance, excess and overload that all Irish products should emulate (see Brown and

Patterson 2000). *The Quiet Man*, according to Gibbons *et al*. (2002: 3), came to represent the "blueprint for subsequent travelogue films promoting Ireland as a tourist destination". Today, similar sweeping scenes of rural Ireland are the stock in trade of the Irish tourist board, Bord Fáilte.

The story of Irish national identity understood as a tourist asset, on the one hand, is comprised of the manifold and protean journalistic, fictional and literary representations that depict the Irish as ethnically distinct. On the other, it is equally true that fixed stereotypes and stock imagery are associated with Ireland. As consumers we immediately understand that tartan, bagpipes and shortbread belong to Scotland and, in a similar vein, that shamrocks, *craic* and leprechauns are integral to Ireland. Nonetheless, it is impossible to fix upon what Ireland means to everyone, since its meaning is different for each person. Any material distinctiveness, signification or meaning depends entirely upon how it is perceived by individual consumers. As Batey (2008: xiii) eloquently acknowledges, "Meaning can be elusive: It flows and drifts and is often hard to pin down. No matter – the search for meaning in all its forms is hardwired into our psyches. The millennia may have passed, but we are still hunters and gatherers – of meaning." This chapter will try, therefore, neither to indulge in essentialist thinking nor to impose a reductive definition of what constitutes "this thing that Ireland is". Ireland will always remain what O'Toole (1994: 53) calls "a bizarre accumulation of heterodox imaginings". Nor is this ambiguity of national identity a feature restricted only to Ireland, for, as Giddens (1990) asserts, the character of every nation-state is extraordinarily difficult, if not impossible, to conceptualize.

The birth of contemporary Irish tourism

To appreciate fully the social construction of Irish popular history that has created the contemporary tourist influx, it should be understood that it was born out of Ireland's struggle to escape from, and be nationally unlike, its all-pervasive neighbour England. The English in Elizabethan times feared cultural pollution from the "inferior" cultures that surrounded them, and they expected the Celtic nations – particularly Ireland – to assimilate to their "superior" culture (Catey 2008). Even the great Charles Darwin argued in the nineteenth century that the Irish posed a serious threat to England, saying that "The careless, squalid, unaspiring Irishman multiplies like rabbits", and would, unless something was done, eventually outnumber and overrun the English (Paul 2008). To justify a policy of assimilation, England's philosophical position was, according to Steingart (2008), that the absorption of the entire world under English rule would bring the end of all wars, and, since the Irish were regarded as savages, drunkards and troublemakers, their fate was of no concern. Destroying their culture was for the greater good. One practice, for instance, used by the British against the Irish in order further to justify their racist policies involved the use of craniometry. Irish skulls, like those of black Africans, were said to be shaped like those of apes or Cro-Magnon men (Carroll 2003). With such policies in evidence, unsurprisingly a colony was established to civilize the "lazy" natives and garner resources for the Crown. Colonial administrators such as the poet Edmund Spenser were ceaseless in propagating the notion of Irish inferiority and savagery, as well as introducing institutions of civilization to Ireland. The favoured instruments of control used by the British against the Irish were warfare, slaughter, terror and the confiscation of land (Catey 2008).

The Great Famine marks another milestone in the development of Brand Ireland and the emergence of the postcolonial sensibility that helped forge Ireland's fierce nationalism. Many thousands of Irish peasants fled the country as a consequence of the poverty which was –rightly or wrongly – perceived to have been caused by both British oppression and the ravages of the devastating potato blight that struck Ireland between 1845 and 1852. Over the course of the disaster and the following decades, well over a million people left. Starving, sickly and wretched, they travelled by whatever means they could to the cities of Britain, Canada, Australia and the United States, creating a mass migration. Neither transportation nor cities could cope with the tide of human misery. Liverpool – the first step for many on the journey to America – presented scenes of turmoil and tragedy. Lodging house owners, ships' captains, American employers' agents, loan sharks and charlatans all touted for trade among the dispossessed, who were desperate to escape from famine (Kissane 1995).

The peculiar and powerful reverence in which Ireland is held can be attributed partly to the wistful and nostalgic yearnings of its many immigrant descendants scattered across the United States, Britain, Australia and other corners of the world. Their conception of Ireland is almost entirely unencumbered by actual experience, but instead finds potent expression in the realm of the imagination. As a onetime Irish immigrant explains, "What I could not discover I invented. Ironically, freedom to do so was greater than if I had remained in my own country, bound by the actuality and truth of its place, its people, its food, its place-names" (Boland 1996: 14). O'Toole (1997) sees this imagined Ireland as a creation not only of immigrant nostalgia but also of the emptiness felt by those who were left behind. Thus a shared victimhood was cultivated that was jointly sanctioned by the 70 million abroad who claim Irish ancestry and the Irish still living in Ireland. Nor, until quite recently, did centuries of British rule (which culminated in the separation of the island in 1922 into two political entities: the Republic of Ireland (the Irish Free State from 1922 to 1949) and the Province of Northern Ireland) do anything to ease tensions. In fact, it spurred the IRA (Irish Republican Army) into existence and gave it cause to attempt the reunification of one nation (a 32-county Ireland) and freedom from another (Britain).

Ireland was naturally, then, full of loathing for the many injustices perpetrated against it by Britain. One response to continued British rule and the anti-Irish racism that accompanied it saw the Irish intelligentsia, at the end of the nineteenth century, initiate the Irish Literary Revival. The purpose of this revival, spearheaded by Yeats – which took place in a world that was, coincidentally, just beginning to understand how brands could provide a powerful means of differentiation – was to encourage writers and poets to indulge in boundless mythomaniac invention (Monagan 2004). It was hoped that this nostalgic vision, which looked back towards the "memory" of an ancient "Celtic race" (Kearney 1997), would begin both to de-Anglicize Ireland and to reposition the country, according to Terence Brown (2006: 57), as "a zone of Celtic spirituality, a territory of the imagination, scenic in the Romantic fashion: rural, primitive, wild and exotic". By actively opposing the stereotypes and prejudices prevalent in Ireland, the revivalists created an alternative space for the representation of a new Irish identity within which the "marginal and the oppressed can find expression" (McLoone 2000: 123). They challenged restrictive definitions of Irish culture through a radical revision of prevalent modes of representation, such as Joyce's playful subversion of the English language in *Finnegan's Wake* and Wilde's knack of challenging convention in literature and in life.

Against the backdrop of the Irish Literary Revival, Éamonn de Valéra played a key role in the creation of Ireland's national narrative and, indeed, was hugely influential in shaping the entire course of twentieth-century Irish history. A fierce patriot, he was one of the leaders of the unsuccessful Easter Rising of 1916, and in the wake of the martyrdom of his unfortunate fellow revolutionaries he chose to commemorate the event with a statue of Cú Chulainn, a mythic guerrilla fighter of fierce bravery. It came to symbolize both the emerging nationalist consciousness and the republican struggle (Cullen 2006) – a struggle that de Valéra took too far when, to show his scorn for the British at the end of World War II, upon hearing of Adolf Hitler's death, he rashly decided to pay his respects at the German embassy in Dublin (Skelly 2006). In 1926 he formed Fianna Fáil, which rose to power in 1932 on a protectionist ticket of inward industrial development. His nationalistic aim was to retain Irish production in Irish hands, provide employment, and diminish the constant emigration that was emptying the country. Even though such a strategy proved to be of limited economic worth, it served an important social purpose – the creation of a powerful national self-image that could help lift the darkness created by generations of colonization (Campbell 2005). From a postcolonial perspective, de Valéra's penchant for insular policies exemplifies Edward Said's (1994) term "affiliation" – the radical creation of one's own world and contexts and version of tradition. The limits of protectionism became widely accepted during the 1950s, when a new outward-looking strategy was created which in the main provided capital grants and tax concessions to boost export-oriented manufacturing.

This focus on a culture of resistance, which Irish writers and politicians knew to be absent from traditional history books, revised the history of Ireland, stimulated cultural pride, functioned as a means of community building, and ultimately began the long process that created contemporary Ireland. In conjunction with the fragile survival of the Gaelic language in certain parts of the country and the Emerald Isle's rich history of "impressive stone circles, megalithic ritual sites, solitary round towers, Middle Age monasteries, and romantic castles" (Olsen 2007: 61), the revival has served to emphasize and preserve the isolation and peculiarity of the Celtic tradition that constitutes much of what the Irish national narrative is all about. It was a further lucky twist of fate that the thrust of the

Celtic revival so perfectly tallied with the cornerstones of today's consumer appeal, particularly in the drinks market, where heritage, authenticity and tradition are highly prized (da Silva Lopes 2007).

Ireland's national appeal, then, is not a homogeneous entity. Instead, it is fractured, fluid and multidimensional. For the purposes of explication, though, three loose categories of its national narrative, which appeal to tourists on different levels, can be discerned – Generic-Ireland, Regional-Ireland and Ireland-Plus. These, it must be stressed, are not tightly delineated. The category boundaries outlined may change, or new ones may spring into being, as it continues to evolve.

Generic-Ireland

This construction of the Irish national narrative is essentially a set of stereotypes that view Ireland as a homogeneous entity. Here leprechauns and shamrocks are writ large, and tourists are perpetually sold the good time *craic* of the Emerald Isle. Some deem this the tackier side of Irish tourism, the one that is often condemned as superficial and patronizing (Bielenberg 2006; Courtney 2007) and that Crowley and Maclaughlin (1997) dub "Ireland Inc", wherein "Ireland itself has become a vast hotel and ethnic theme park – Eiredisney". Typical tourist offerings in this category of Irishness can be found in every airport souvenir shop in the country: the tea towels, the T-shirts, the oven-gloves – all the Paddywacked made-in-China memorabilia that Irish natives would rarely buy themselves. Among the most blatant attempts to cash in on Generic-Ireland was the launch of an Irish alcoholic drink by A & M Ferguson called The Craic.

Another prominent tourist asset in this category is offered for sale by the ubiquitous Irish theme pub chains which collectively tend to celebrate a form of kitsch "Oirishness". Although their heyday has well and truly passed, they are still in abundant supply. In the UK, O'Neill's, first developed by Bass but now owned by Mitchells and Butlers, is the single largest chain in the world, with eighty-two outlets as of 2009. Punch Taverns lags some way behind, with its thirty-nine Scruffy Murphy's. The Greenalls Group operates a chain of twelve individually named Irish themed pubs, including Shifty O'Shea's, Daisy O'Brien and O'Rafferty's, and Whitbread has followed suit with ten outlets under the sign of O'Hagan's and J. J. Murphy.

When they first entered the marketplace their prospects were not promising. Consider the story of Flanagan's Apple on Mathew Street in Liverpool, which first opened its doors in 1984. It was not the first Irish pub in England by any means, but it was one of the first Irish theme pubs. The pervading sentiment at the time suggested that it could never be the apple of England's eye. The British authorities, in particular, were extremely reluctant to grant the venue a pub licence. Nightly knee-capping, punishment beatings, exploding incendiary devices, and the everyday death of soldiers from Liverpool and Leeds on the streets of Northern Ireland had dubbed the era "The Troubles" and damaged the yet to flourish image of

Brand Ireland. To make matters worse, the bloodshed was beginning to seep across to the British mainland where, ironically, pubs, among other venues, were prime targets for IRA bombers. Consequently, Irishmen living in England were viewed through a veil of racial mysticism. Every Paddy or Mick had an evil glint in his eye and a heart as black as the pint of Guinness in his hand. Opening an Irish themed pub such as Flanagan's Apple, it was thought, might inflame sectarianism by acting as a rallying point and recruiting station for hard-line republican sympathizers, particularly in light of their historical involvement in the organization of "nationalist secret societies" (Reilly 1977: 571). The landlord's masterstroke was convincing the Liverpudlian police and local community that the pub could be successful, even though it was a potent symbol both of centuries of struggle between Ireland and England and of fervent Irish nationalism (Elson 2004). Needless to say, his charm offensive worked.

Today, Flanagan's, and other Irish pubs like it, is still a success not just because of its sandblasted bars or the dancing leprechauns in the stained-glass windows, but because claiming an association with Irish traits can complement a consumer's identity. As Delaney (2006) asserts, "It's about pretending that you're James Joyce or Shane MacGowan and that you're getting pissed to reconcile your intense masculinity with your deeply romantic soul. Rather than the fact that you're a weak, pathetic booze-hound who despises every detail of your hellish, pub-bound existence." Whether it is as pathetic a pursuit as Delaney asserts, such indulgence is part and parcel of what Negra (2001: 76) calls "the pleasures of white ethnic heritage". It allows white emigrants, not necessarily of Irish origin, to revel in a rich identity that would otherwise be unavailable to them and enables them to make poetic declarations:

> My mind keeps telling me I am an American. But I also feel that I'm a tiny part of a much larger story, perhaps a mere noun; but carrying with me all that hurt and passion, all that sacrifice that did not make a stone of the heart. I roam with Leopold Bloom. I bleed with Cuchulainn. I brandish the summit on a blasted hill and wave my defiance. I am dancing, wild and naked, under a crimson moon.
>
> (Patterson 2007: 139)

Regional-Ireland

Regional-Ireland recognizes difference within the construct of Irishness and usually focuses on a specific dimension of Irish heritage, especially a place name. It benefits from being able to draw on Ireland as a general construct and a specific place name that is attractive to both tourists and natives. Regional-Ireland tourist appeal therefore moves from the general to the specific. It profits first from the broad-sweeping characteristics associated with Ireland, invoking some of the associations that have already been discussed in this chapter and perhaps some others that have not yet been mentioned, such as the breathtaking landscapes, the glacier-carved valleys, the bleak and beautiful mountainous terrain and the unspoiled, green countryside. Ironically, this sparsely populated countryside now so celebrated by Bord Fáilte is the direct and still visual consequence of the famine caused so unnecessarily by Ireland's colonial masters (Foley and Fahey 2004). Regional Irish products garner further brand distinction by focusing on the specific – the particular local characteristics that make each product special. In the same way that the quirkiness of a person's accent can be endearing and interesting, that same regional variation can accentuate a product. Consider Tayto potato crisps, a popular Irish export favoured by tourists and migrants: it relies as much on the local story told on every pack as it does on the country of origin kudos it receives from Ireland's national narrative to bring its brand to life: "Set deep in the heart of the Ulster countryside is Tayto Castle where Tayto have been making . . .". The product is so sought after outside Ireland that it has a website entirely dedicated to cater for the international market.

A key aspect of regionalism concerns the different ways in which Irish tourism is rendered on either side of the border. Northern Ireland, for instance, might be saddled with a history of violence on its streets, but unlike the Republic it benefits from being able to employ a two-pronged strategy that allows it to sell itself as British in British friendly-tourist territories and Irish in Irish-friendly tourist markets (Dinnie 2007). How this schizophrenic dynamic affects the broader construction of Ireland's national narrative is still relatively uncharted. Furthermore, Henchion and McIntyre (2000), who conducted an interesting study of regional branding in Ireland, make the point that, although there are many regional brands – such as KerryGold, Coleraine Cheddar and Cookstown sausages – their relationship to the overall national Irish context and how they impact on Brand Ireland and tourism remains understudied, and is deserving of attention from marketing and tourism scholars.

Ireland-Plus

Further along the trail, tourist initiatives that can be characteried as Ireland-Plus have Generic-Ireland values at their core, but no longer explicitly promote these values in marketing communications, because tourists are generally well aware of the product's traditional Irish pedigree. These Irish goods are reluctant to roll out the clichéd images that Foley and Fahy (1994: 215) describe as "donkeys, turf baskets and smiling red-headed natives", since they are an unnecessary reminder of the postcolonial struggle that Ireland has endured and are quite simply overplayed. Tourist-favourite brands such as Guinness and Bailey's Irish Cream typify this category. The latter, for instance, relies to some extent on the traditional Irish national narrative of heritage and authenticity. It even prints the word "Original" twice on its front label: "Original Irish Cream" and "Bailey's the original". Nonetheless, it has moved on from courting purely Irish values, and instead has introduced new tropes in order to build a more sophisticated personality and reposition the brand away from the elderly consumers that until recently were its only customers (Kapferer 2008). It has put its ethnic component on ice, preferring instead to link its brand with the trope of "the lover", as in its "Bailey on Ice" campaign. To this end, it has sponsored shows such as *Sex and the City* and run saucy advertisements. Bailey's Ireland-Plus strategy sought to reposition its brand above and beyond the rural ideal Irish tropes. In this manner, by employing an Ireland-Plus strategy, more sophisticated tourists who are not swayed by the lure of sentimental nationalism as propagated by Generic-Ireland might also be persuaded to visit Ireland.

Conclusion

This chapter has demonstrated how the Irish national narrative has had a specifically anti-imperialist slant that has led to the accidental, but perfectly rendered, creation of a solid market for Irish tourism and the three incarnations of its national identity: Generic-Ireland, Regional-Ireland and Ireland-Plus. Ireland's competitive advantage is that, unlike many other countries, it does not pay homage to Anglo-American culture but strives instead to be an "expression of non-Western cultural identity" (Williams 2000: 10). Destination marketers with branding toolkits and tourism permanently on their minds could hardly have achieved more, but then Yeats and other poets of his generation who collectively wrote the Irish nation were, it has been contended, bonafide marketers armed with Celtic legend books and a romantic sensibility (Aherne 2000).

Nonetheless, complacency about Ireland's continuing cultural relevance to tourists should be avoided. Nation brands seeking to attract tourists, like all brands, can all too easily stagnate and even become reviled – as champions of a certain superpower, coping with rampant anti-Americanism, will all too readily attest (see Martin 2007). No one can deny that today we live in an era of "competitive postcolonialisms", where it is not necessarily the country that suffers the most at the hands of a colonial power that will succeed, but the country that can brand itself the best (Punter 2000: 76). In the *2007 Anholt Nation Brands Index*, Ireland ranks number 16 in the world – not a bad effort for such a small country, it might be argued – but, when considered against the knowledge that Belgium is just one place behind, one may begin to wonder if Ireland's potential to sustain tourism really is on the wane.

Many argue (Foley and Fahey 2004; Bielenberg 2006; Courtney 2007) that Ireland is out of touch with reality, that it is no longer oppressed by its colonial master, that postcolonialism has served its purpose, that the country's heritage and history is secure – so why keep selling the same old reified and imagined values to tourists? Perhaps the reluctance to let this popular portrayal of the Irish national narrative fall out of favour is because, in the main, it keeps bringing tourists to Ireland. It might be terribly unfashionable to suggest as much, but the essentialist conceptualization of Generic-Ireland detailed in this chapter has remained fairly consistent and virtually unchanged for decades. The feat perpetrated by the Irish government has been to present a seemingly refreshed national identity by tweaking the other more peripheral incarnations – Regional-Ireland and Ireland-Plus – while retaining a set of central tropes that remain anchored and in keeping with tourist expectations. It is this unique formula that will, it is hoped, keep tourists coming back to experience Ireland's national narrative for centuries to come.

References

Aherne, A. (2000) "Chronicles of the Celtic Marketing Circle, Part I: The Paradise Parchment", *Marketing Intelligence & Planning*, 18(6/7): 400–13.
Batey, M. (2008) *Brand Meaning*. London: Routledge.
Bielenberg, K. (2006) "Great Irish icons – 2006", *The Independent*, 6 May; www.independent.ie/unsorted/features/great-irish-icons-2006-96622.html.
Boland, E. (1996) "Imagining Ireland", in *Arguing at the Crossroads: Essays on a Changing Ireland*. Dublin: New Island Books.
Brown, S., and Patterson, A. (2000) "Knick-knack paddy-whack, give a pub a theme", *Journal of Marketing Management*, 16(6): 647–66.
Brown, T. (2006) "Anglo-Irish literature", in J. T. Koch (ed.) *Celtic Culture: A Historical Encyclopedia* (Vol. 1, pp. 55–8). Santa Barbara, CA: ABC-Clio.
Campbell, H. (2005) "Modern architecture and national identity", in J. Cleary and C. Connolly (eds) *Modern Irish Culture* (pp. 285–303). Cambridge: Cambridge University Press.
Carroll R. T. (2003) *The Skeptic's Dictionary: A Collection of Strange Beliefs, Amusing Deceptions, and Dangerous Delusions*. Hoboken, NJ: John Wiley.
Catey, A. S. (2008) "Reservation system", in J. H. Moore (ed.) *Encyclopedia of Race and Racism* (Vol. 2, pp. 499–503). London: Thomson Gale.
Courtney, K. (2007) "Cúl Hibernia?", *Irish Times*, 3 March; www.irishtimes.com/newspaper/magazine/2007/0317/1173880350835.html.
Cullen, P. (2006) "Cú Chulainn", in J. T. Koch (ed.) *Celtic Culture: A Historical Encyclopedia* (Vol. 2, pp. 119–20). Santa Barbara, CA: ABC-Clio.
Curtis-Wilson, K., McCain, G., and Ray, N. (2006) "The challenge of creating and maintaining respected country-of-origin assets: the Irish linen story", *Journal of Business Case Studies*, 2(3): 71–83.
da Silva Lopes, T. (2007) *Global Brands: The Evolution of Multinationals in Alcoholic Beverages*. Cambridge: Cambridge University Press.
Deegan, J., and Dineen, D. J. (2003) "The changing contribution of tourism in a dynamic economy: the case of Ireland", *Tourism Economics*, 9(2): 147–64.
Delaney, S. (2006) "The hard sell: Magners Irish Cider", *The Guardian*, The Guide, 29 April, p. 3.
Dinnie, K. (2007) *Nation Branding: Concepts, Issues, Practice*. London: Butterworth–Heinemann.
Ellis, J. C. (2000) "Man of Aran", in T. Pendercast and S. Pendercast (eds) *International Dictionary of Films and Filmmakers*, Vol. 1: Films (pp. 730–32). 4th edn, Detroit: St James Press.
Elson, P. (2004) "A clever blend of Englishness, Irishness and Liverpoolness", *Liverpool Post*, 17 March; http://icliverpool.icnetwork.co.uk/0100news/0100regionalnews/content_objectid=14060665_method=full_siteid=50061_headline=-A-clever-blend-of-Englishness--Irishness-and-Liverpoolness-name_page.html.

Ferriter, D. (2005) *The Transformation of Ireland 1900–2000*. London: Profile Books.

Foley, A., and Fahey, J. (2004) "Incongruity between expression and experience: the role of imagery in supporting the positioning of a tourism destination brand", *Brand Management*, 11(3): 209–17.

Foster R. F. (2002) *The Irish Story: Telling Tales and Making it up in Ireland*. Oxford: Oxford University Press.

Gibbons, L., Hopper, K., and Humphreys, G. (2002) *The Quiet Man*. Cork: Cork University Press.

Giddens, A. (1990) *The Consequences of Modernity*. Cambridge: Polity.

Henchion, M., and McIntyre, B. (2000) "Regional imagery and quality products: the Irish experience", *British Food Journal*, 102(8): 630–44.

Holt, D. B. (2004) *How Brands Become Icons: The Principles of Cultural Branding*. Boston: Harvard Business School Press.

Hooper, G. (2001) *The Tourist's Gaze: Travellers to Ireland*. Cork: Cork University Press.

Kapferer, J. N. (2008) *New Strategic Brand Management: Creating and Sustaining Brand Equity Long Term*. London: Kogan Page.

Kearney, R. (1997) *Postnationalist Ireland: Politics, Culture, Philosophy*. London: Routledge.

Kissane, N. (1995) *The Irish Famine: A Documentary History*. Dublin: National Library of Ireland.

Koch, J. T. (ed.) (2006) *Celtic Culture: A Historical Encyclopedia*. Santa Barbara, CA: ABC-Clio.

Lesinska, E. (2005) "Breakfast with Brontosaurus: an interview with Harold Bloom", *Eurozine*, 7 October, www.eurozine.com/articles/2005-10-07-bloom-en.html.

McLoone, M. (2000) *Irish Film: The Emergence of a Contemporary Cinema*. London: BFI.

Martin, M. (2007) *Rebuilding Brand America: What We Must Do to Restore our Reputation and Safeguard the Future of American Business Abroad*. New York: AMACOM.

Monagan, D. (2004) *Jaywalking with the Irish*. London: Lonely Planet.

Negra, D. (2001) "Consuming Ireland: lucky charms cereal, Irish spring soap and 1-800-shamrock", *Cultural Studies*, 15(1): 76–97.

Negra, D. (ed.) (2006) "Introduction", *The Irish in Us: Irishness, Performativity, and Popular Culture*. Durham, NC: Duke University Press.

O'Loughlin, D., and Szmigin, I. (2007) "Exploring the use of dichotomy in marketing: Celt versus Saxon revisited", *Irish Marketing Review*, 19(2): 19–25.

Olsen, B. (2007) *Sacred Places Europe: 108 Destinations*. San Francisco: Consortium of Collective Consciousness.

O'Toole, F. (1994) *Black Hole, Green Card: The Disappearance of Ireland*. Dublin: New Island Books.

O'Toole, F. (1997) *The Lie of the Land: Irish Identities*. London: Verso.

Patterson, A. (2007) "Inventing the theme pubs of Ireland: the importance of being post-colonial", PhD thesis, University of Ulster.

Patterson, A., and Brown, S. (2007) "Inventing the pubs of Ireland: the importance of being postcolonial", *Journal of Strategic Marketing*, 15(1): 41–51.

Paul, D. B. (2008) "History of eugenics", in J. H. Moore (ed.) *Encyclopedia of Race and Racism* (Vol. 1, pp. 441–7). London: Thomson Gale.

Punter, P. (2000) *Postcolonial Imaginings: Fictions of a New World Order*. Edinburgh: Edinburgh University Press.

Reilly, J. (1977) "The American bar and the Irish pub: a study in comparisons and contrasts", *Journal of Popular Culture*, 34(2): 571–8.

Said, E. (1994) *Culture and Imperialism*. London: Vintage.

Schroeder, J. E., and and Salzer-Mörling, M. (2006) *Brand Culture*. London: Routledge.

Skelly, J. (2006) "De Valera", in J. T. Koch (ed.) *Celtic Culture: A Historical Encyclopedia*, Vol. 1, pp. 463–4). Santa Barbara, CA: ABC-Clio.

Smyth, G. (2001) *Space and the Irish Cultural Imagination*. London: Palgrave Macmillan.

Steingart, G. (2008) *War for Wealth: The True Story of Globalization, or Why the Flat World is Broken*. London: McGraw-Hill.

Williams, G. (2000) *Branded?* London: Victoria and Albert Museum.

Witoszek, N., and Sheeran P. (1998) *Talking to the Dead: A Study of Irish Funerary Traditions*. Amsterdam: Rodopi.

4 National identity construction and tourism in Hungary

A multi-level approach

Melanie Smith and László Puczkó

Introduction

This chapter proposes a multi-level approach to identity creation and tourism promotion, based on a combination of Hungary's colonial heritage, socialist heritage, Europeanness, regional characteristics, global culture, and unique national and local cultural attributes. It will draw on visitor perception research data, the content analysis of national tourism promotion, and personal observations of long-term residents of Hungary. The aim is to convey the complexity of national identity creation while providing a solution to some seemingly irresolvable dilemmas.

The question of national identity has been especially significant in the post-socialist countries of Central and Eastern Europe (hereafter CEE) since 1989, the year when these countries were liberated from Soviet rule. Before that, national identities had been suppressed for almost fifty years as a result of the imposition and enforcement of Soviet systems, language and culture; tourism development was extremely limited as few visitors were allowed in or out of the country. However, after 1989, the curiosity of foreign visitors about life behind the "iron curtain" forced a representation of socialist heritage, while at the same time these countries were trying to cast off the shackles of political oppression, to assert their "Europeanness" by joining the EU, and to present themselves as dynamic, modern and cosmopolitan (Hall 2004). During the socialist period, Hungary (especially its capital city, Budapest) was seen as being the most Western of the Eastern countries (Jancsik 1999). The main reason for this was that Hungary's socialist system was not quite as rigid as that in some of the other countries in the region. Because of its relatively benign form of state socialism, sometimes referred to as "goulash communism", Hungary was often referred to in the West as "the Happiest Barracks". Before the socialist period (1867–1945), it flourished during the Austro-Hungarian monarchy. However, the country has rarely been free of colonial occupation (for example, 150 years of Turkish rule from 1526), meaning that true Hungarian identity has seldom been freely established. It is therefore difficult to know which aspects of culture should be presented, as the dissonant legacies of colonialism and political oppression are an integral part of the country's past but not necessarily what it would wish to promote. It is also important to establish which aspects of its identity are uniquely Hungarian, especially given the growing competition for tourism within the region and internationally.

Multiple identity construction in Central and Eastern Europe

The countries of CEE spent almost half a century within an imposed ideological bloc which restricted their freedom to create national and regional identities. The occupying Soviets instead imposed a unified identity across the whole region consisting of a socialist/communist political system with its very specific social and cultural implications, including the suppression of religion and the enforced learning of the Russian language. Following independence in 1989, it was sometimes a struggle for the CEE countries to (re)develop and promote their national identities. Tourism was also limited during socialist times, so the challenge of identity construction, as well as heritage interpretation and cultural representation, was needed in tourism marketing. However, it is difficult to know which aspects of history and culture should be presented, especially in countries where the political systems suppressed cultural expression for many decades.

Many new nation-states emerged in the post-communist era, not only the former Soviet states but also those in the former Yugoslavia. Political, cultural and tourism agencies are faced with the challenging task of deciding how to redefine their nation and present a new image to the outside world. Many CEE countries are still relatively unknown outside the region. For example, Olins (2004: 23) asks of countries like Slovenia and Slovakia, "How many people know where they are or the significant differences between them?" He notes that Romania and Bulgaria, Bucharest and Budapest, are often confused by foreigners.

Countries usually feel obliged to display their socialist history and heritage as it is of considerable interest to international visitors. Young and Light (2006) also suggest that some form of nostalgia for the socialist era tends to exist in most CEE countries, and it is certainly true in Hungary that many of the older generation often feel that life was "easier" under the socialist regime (Politics.hu 2008). However, Young and Light conclude that "the use of the socialist past as a heritage resource allows the past to re-emerge and potentially disrupt efforts at post-socialist identity construction" (2006: 256). It is also true to say that, for many residents in CEE countries, the socialist heritage is dissonant and serves as a reminder of difficult times which they would rather forget. For this reason, most of the icons, statues and memorabilia associated with the socialist era have been removed from the streets and placed in museums, and many names of roads or buildings have been changed. However, it is important to note that, in recent years, the unique selling proposition of socialist heritage has started to wane. This is because cities in particular have become increasingly "cosmopolitan" as a result of new developments and foreign investment (Andrusz 2004), and first-time "curiosity" visitor numbers are decreasing (Rátz 2004).

Therefore, rather than focusing on socialism, new narratives of place identity may choose to invoke an idealised "Golden Age" which is pre-socialist and often later nineteenth century (Young and Light 2006). Following accession to the EU of many CEE countries, there is often a desire to promote those characteristics which are deemed typically European or reflect the common heritage. An aspiration to be thought of as globally competitive will also drive most countries' identity formation and image projection through tourism or other means. This results in a complex multi-layering of identity construction which can generate conflict. However, it is also an inevitable process of re-establishing national identity in countries which lost their individual freedom for almost fifty years.

Hall (2004) notes some of the ongoing problems with branding countries in CEE on account of international perceptions of regional instability, poor service, infrastructure and the general quality of public facilities. Romania and Bulgaria failed to meet the criteria for EU accession in the first round in 2004 for economic and political reasons. Many of the newly independent CEE countries have also been relatively slow to develop tourism, often because of the poor state of their infrastructure following decades of neglect and lack of government investment. In some cases – for example, Romania – many of the original heritage buildings were even destroyed by political leaders for "ideological" reasons.

The advent of low-budget airlines has had a significant effect on many CEE destinations, extending and transforming the market, if not always in the direction of positive destination image and identity construction. This is because many visitors are not especially knowledgeable about or interested in the specific characteristics of the destination, but merely visit because it is perceived as cheap (TOB 2006). Thus, relatively undesirable forms of tourism, such as "stag and hen" drinking weekends or mass cultural tourism, may emerge in cities such as Prague, Kraków and Tallinn. Many CEE cities are inherently cultural and historic and therefore inevitably promote their monuments, museums and galleries. Richards (2001) notes that there has been a fall in the local consumption of "high" culture in many Eastern countries since 1989, mainly because of a lack of state subsidy and declining incomes. Thus foreign tourism can provide the boost that is needed for many flagging cultural attractions.

Like all successful destinations, CEE countries need to promote a distinctive product, which may be based on the uniqueness of their heritage and culture. They may choose to capitalise on their former history, even if it is of a dissonant nature (e.g. socialist or other occupational legacies). On the other hand, these countries also want to be seen as modern, cosmopolitan and progressive, especially as the majority of visitors expect (and are used to) relatively high levels of comfort and services. This complex blend of elements is essential if they want to become competitive in the global tourism market and establish a positive identity.

EU accession and identity

The role of tourism and culture in the process of national and European identity construction is of considerable importance. For example, Hughes and Allen describe how "Both culture and tourism have been utilised to display a break with the past, to promote particular national identities and to demonstrate a new openness and willingness and eagerness to embrace a wider European identity" (2005: 175). The often stated role of the EU in the context of identity construction is to support "unity in diversity". This implies that common aspects of European heritage, as well as aspects of national, regional, local or ethnic identities, should be celebrated and promoted. The concept of European integration is difficult for many Western European countries such as Denmark and Britain, but it is even harder for CEE countries, which have only just been liberated from the tyranny of an "integrated" system. The definition of national values and identities remains more important than embarking on any European projects related to a common identity (Javrova 2005). Other barriers also exist, namely the need in the EU for collaborative working, which is fundamental to integration and cross-cultural exchange. Such ways of working are unfamiliar in many CEE countries and may also be undesirable, as they are reminiscent of past structures. For example, Farkas (2005) notes that, in Hungary during the socialist era, many citizens spent their time devising ways to avoid political and social networks.

European cultural or tourism strategies may clash with national priorities, and there is an ongoing question within the new accession countries of the EU as to how far they should promote their national and regional identities as opposed to their "Europeanness" – that is, their common heritage. For the newer accession countries (Hungary joined in 2004), the assertion of their "Europeanness" is seemingly of foremost importance (Hall 2004; Smith and Hall 2006). This might be because of the heritage of previous centuries and civilisations, many of which, such as the Roman Empire or the widespread cultural movements of Art Nouveau or Jugendstil, are common to other European citizens. For example, Light (2006) discusses the way in which the promotion of Romania harks back to eras which precede socialism, and instead represents its historical and cultural ties with Western Europe.

The European Holocaust and its legacy is commonly viewed as being almost beyond interpretation because of its enormity and sensitive nature. Similar emotive (albeit smaller) debates ensued about the interpretation and representation of the European socialist or communist heritage and its legacy. In the early 1990s, displaced symbols of communism in the form of architecture or statues "littered" the landscape. Debates arose as to whether they should be removed or simply converted. Museums and galleries often had to rethink the presentation of their collections, and it was not uncommon for them to remain closed temporarily while curators considered reinterpretation (Smith 2003). It was important to consider for whom and for what those heritage sites, museums and galleries were created. Were they simply there as memorials or reminders of the past, so that European societies could learn from them in the future, or were they vehicles through which "new" nations could explore and display their identities? Clearly, no country wants to be permanently associated with a legacy of oppression and terror, especially if they have recently gained or hope to gain EU status.

A positive initiative would be to promote the cultures of diverse ethnic groups in accordance with the EU's "unity in diversity" slogan. However, many minority groups (e.g. Jews, Roma) were persecuted under socialist and other political regimes. Unfortunately, there has also been a recent resurgence of nationalism in Europe, and particularly in CEE countries, including Hungary, which are largely intolerant of ethnic minorities (DEMOS Hungary 2007). For tourism purposes, the celebration of cultures can be a way of increasing the positive image of minority groups in society. Gipsy folk music and Jewish klezmer are particularly popular in CEE, and so can be promoted to visitors. This has worked well in Poland, where the Jewish quarter of Kracόw has become a major visitor attraction. On the other hand, care must be taken that such developments are not appropriated by those from outside the ethnic group, as they have been in Kracόw (Smith 2009), as this can ultimately lead to the standardisation or misrepresentation of ethnic identities.

Globalisation and the erosion of identity

Globalisation is clearly not a new concept for Europeans, for whom history has always been a series of shifting hegemonic powers and occupations (internal and external). Some parts of Europe, with their many empires and colonies scattered throughout the world, have played a central role in global trading. Others, like those in CEE, have been the victims of foreign invasion throughout history – in the case of Hungary, it has been occupied by the Romans, Turks, Austrians (Habsburgs) and Russians. In fact, its first period of true independence for several centuries began in 1989.

As mentioned earlier, many destinations in CEE, especially cities, are keen to be seen as dynamic, modern and cosmopolitan (Hall 2004). Andrusz (2004) highlights the difficulties for post-socialist cities of retaining their heritage and cultural identity at the same time as developing new facilities that meet the needs of global business investors and tourists.

Tourists generally desire certain levels of service quality and familiar brands, and the challenge then becomes to provide that service but within a localised cultural context (e.g. drawing on domestic hospitality rather than importing it from elsewhere).

Despite numerous theories about globalisation, Europeanisation and the apparent death of the nation-state, Olins (2004) suggests that the interest in branding nations is actually rising, no doubt partly as a form of cultural protectionism. Many countries in CEE (as in France and Britain) may fear the loss of their unique cultural identity or language and are therefore keen to increase measures which protect it. By developing heritage sites, memorials, museums or cultural centres which may also be attractive to tourists (domestic and international), countries have a guaranteed platform for cultural protection and promotion. Morgan and Pritchard (1998) note that the relationship between tourism promotion and the projection of national identity in the former socialist countries is particularly significant. However, the establishment of a clear and distinctive brand image is still a challenge in a competitive global market. Some CEE cities are moving towards the model that has been established in many Western countries, whereby extensive regeneration strategies are being implemented (Smith 2007). These are increasingly taking into consideration the notion of the "experience economy" (Pine and Gilmore 1999), which is based on a number of factors relating to the character and authenticity of destinations, as well as entertaining, creative and spectacular products and events. "Flagship" or "mega" events can help to create a lasting legacy and identity for a destination, whereas one-off or short-term activities or events can contribute to animation and atmosphere, and thus enhance image. However, care must be taken in regeneration not to standardise the character and atmosphere of a destination overmuch (e.g. through copycat schemes which resemble those of other successful locations), or it will lose its unique identity.

National identity construction in Hungary

Anholt (2004) suggests that branding a country is not just related to tourism; it must also take into consideration other factors – climate, politics, people, business – which are often beyond the control of marketing agencies. It is further determined as much if not more by the consumer and the marketplace. Anholt believes that the tourism image of a country can sometimes be at odds with the overall image. For example, Hungary's unique cultural asset may be its local folk cultures, but quaint customs and traditions are not in the least attractive to international business and real-estate investors. On the other hand, creative and technological industries make a country seem modern and dynamic in business, but they are usually so globalised that they represent little of national or local culture.

Hungary has had an especially difficult history – not just during the socialist era – and so narratives of oppression and occupation cannot easily be avoided in the process of heritage representation and identity creation. The inclusion of socialist heritage attractions in its product development and marketing has seemed to be necessary because of foreign visitor curiosity and the need for national remembrance and memorial. Although many Hungarians were happy to see the statues of their former socialist leaders placed in a statue park outside the city (which most Hungarians never visit), it is important that memorials or museums serve as reminders of the past and educate future generations. However, like many CEE countries, Hungary has somewhat reluctantly capitalised on the socialist past in the process of tourism development. It is of course difficult to promote the disproportionate impact of just half a century of socialism on the country's international or even its internal image. It is important to reiterate that domestic perceptions of Hungary differ fairly radically from those of foreign visitors. The majority of domestic tourists clearly had little or no interest in their socialist heritage, which merely became a reminder of an unpopular era. A good example is that of the 2006 Hungarian National Tourism Office (HNTO) campaign, which was named the "Winter Invasion". This provided a witty and ironic reference to previous invasions and periods of occupation: "After 400 years of the Romans, 150 years of the Ottomans and 45 years of the Soviets, you'll be the first who's welcome to stay longer, so have an extra night on us!" (HNTO 2006). However, the name of the campaign was later changed to "Winter Invitation", as it was thought that the slogan might be considered too insensitive or even offensive to the general population.

The marketing of Hungary between 1990 and 2010 has been focused on re-establishing the country as a tourist destination and familiarising visitors with the main attractions and icons, namely the built heritage, culture and spas. The main aim was to put the country back on the world tourism map and to create a positive image and identity. In the early 1990s the country's political and organisational framework, including the tourist boards and marketing agencies, was restructured. The Tourist Office of Budapest (TOB) was created in 1996, but before this the National Tourism Office was responsible for communication, and many tourism industry members did not believe that Budapest deserved greater attention than the rest of the country. The marketing of the capital city was therefore fairly limited until about 1996, when a World Expo was expected to be staged there, but this was cancelled because of lack of funding and changed priorities. The slogan created for the city with the Expo in mind was "The Bridge between Two Europes". The only other international events promoted at this time were the Spring Festival (mainly a performing arts festival) and the Formula 1 Grand Prix.

In 2000, when Hungary's EU accession was confirmed for 2004, the HNTO inaugurated a series of studies aimed at collecting information and data about the perception of the country. This research aimed to analyse the tourism image, which cannot easily be separated from the more general country image. The studies involved both qualitative and quantitative data collection methods, such as desktop research, in-depth interviews with representatives of major tour operators and travel media, focus group discussions with those who had and those who had not yet been to Hungary, and personal or computer-assisted telephone interviews with a representative sample of the population. Data collection took place in both Hungary and other countries.

The results confirmed results that, apart from Austria and Germany, the general image of and knowledge about Hungary in EU member countries was either based on stereotypes or was rather limited. Non-image was a problem among several (especially Western) nationalities, who knew very little about Hungary, except perhaps the capital city Budapest. The research results confirmed that a little over 50 per cent of all foreign tourists visit Budapest, which is the most important destination (Rátz *et al.* 2008). Some nationalities (e.g. the Italians, Spanish and British) imagined Hungary to be "grey" and "cold". However, most visitors were "pleasantly surprised", suggesting that their experiences exceeded their expectations. Most of the negative associations were related to infrastructure and the insufficient quality and quantity of services, accommodation establishments and events (HNTO 2004), which echoes Hall's (2004) comments about the perceptions of CEE countries more generally. Hughes and Allen's (2005) research showed that

Hungary's product was focused mainly on Budapest because that was the place that most visitors had heard of, but that the tourist boards were keen to educate the general public that there is more to Hungary than the capital (HNTO 2004). Therefore, the Ministry of National Cultural Heritage, together with the HNTO, was spurred into action by the results of the image studies and started to organise special events in selected countries (notably France, Netherlands, Italy and the United Kingdom) under the title "The Year of Hungarian Culture". The rich cultural programme of this series of events resulted in greater numbers of tourists and, it was hoped, a modification of the national image.

As a direct positive impact of EU accession, Hungary's image among EU members was expected to improve further, leading to an increase in the number of visitors from both old and new member countries. One of the major direct impacts of EU membership was the growing number of budget airlines entering the Hungarian market. The Tourist Office of Budapest (2006) conducted a budget airline study, which confirmed that the majority of visitors, especially from Northern countries, had little or no image of Hungary or Budapest, but were motivated by the cheap airfares and relatively cheap prices (TOB 2006). All in all, three main factors appeared to influence a visit to Hungary: recommendation by people who had already visited the city, cheap air fares and low(er) prices.

However, the research data also indicated that there are differences in the characteristics and motivation among budget airline visitors, which can be attributed directly or indirectly to certain image factors or to the lack of a distinctive image of Hungary in the sender countries. Visitors from Scandinavia were motivated mainly by the cheap prices. The French and Swiss came to visit cultural sites and events. Curiosity was the main stimulation for the British, and the Germans were nostalgic about historical connections and either wanted to return or dreamt of visiting the country for the first time (before reunification, when it was impossible to cross the Berlin Wall, many East and West Germans used to meet at Lake Balaton).

Overall, most of the positive perceptions about Hungary tend to relate to culture. For example, those from Austria, France, Italy, Spain and Poland mentioned the historic buildings, architecture, spas, museums and café culture (HNTO 2002). Hungary is a country where cultural tourism development has always been extremely important, partly on account of the lack of a coastline and mountains, but also because the country has a distinctive culture and language, quite different from those of its mainly Slavic neighbours. Indeed, Hughes and Allen (2005) suggest that cultural tourism in Hungary is almost inseparable from tourism in general. Cultural tourism has been the focus of Budapest's marketing strategies for the past fifteen years or more, with the built heritage being the major selling point. In 2008, in preparation for the themed "Year of Cultural Tourism" in 2009, the HNTO carried out a series of surveys about perceptions of cultural tourism in Hungary. It was clear from the surveys that there was a very high awareness of the built heritage among all tourists. It therefore made more sense for an awareness-raising campaign to focus on less well-known aspects of culture. Based on the survey and focus group research, five main cultural themes or pillars were identified: wine and gastronomy, living traditions, festivals, cultural events, and twenty-first-century culture and contemporary arts (HNTO 2008).

Creating local distinctiveness

Overall, most first-time international tourists visit Budapest. Although the city is quintessentially Hungarian in terms of its culture and heritage, it is also the only truly global space in the country. For example, the majority of global companies have their local headquarters in Budapest, all national institutions are located there, and only three internationally branded hotels can be found elsewhere in the country (Puczkó *et al.* 2007). However, the majority of domestic tourists are not always attracted to Budapest, even though it is considered by Hungarians to be the most multicultural city (Gyáni 2005). The capital is viewed by Hungarians as being cosmopolitan, elegant and modern, but also polluted, crowded, dangerous, expensive and alienating (Kajner 2002). Hungarians, of course, know far more about the rest of the country, which is virtually unknown to many foreign visitors.

There is considerable competition and conflict between Budapest and the rest of Hungary. Although it is a magnet and a gateway for tourists, there is a general belief among governmental and other agencies that Budapest has been over-marketed by the HNTO. The Tourist Office of Budapest has argued that other regions and destinations should find ways to attract those tourists who are already in the capital. However, there is little doubt that, in the future, tourists, especially repeat visitors, need to be encouraged to visit other parts of the country. The National Development Plan (2007–13) has made this a priority by extending and developing the mix of attractions.

For several years, Hungary has been running various "Years of . . ." marketing campaigns to promote the specialisms of the whole country. These have included Gastronomy (2006), Ecotourism (2007), Waters (2008), Cultural Tourism (2009), Festival Tourism (2010) and Health Tourism (2011). Their success has not been generally researched and the campaigns are designed mainly for domestic tourists. The full potential of such initiatives in improving the image and identity of the different regions of Hungary is therefore not fully realised and the impacts are unknown. The city of Pécs in the south, close to the Croatian border, was European Cultural Capital in 2010, which, it is hoped, helped to raise its European and even international profile as a destination. It originally competed against other cities in Hungary, including Budapest, to win this status. Many cities in Europe have used this initiative to create new images and identities through cultural developments, regeneration and tourism. One of the most quoted examples is Glasgow (1990), which transformed itself from an industrial to a cultural city, and now even competes for tourists with the Scottish capital, Edinburgh.

There are some current discussions in Hungary about improving the "Hungarian Towns of Culture" initiative, which started in 2005. Towns can bid according to a set of established criteria and are judged on what they can offer in the way of contemporary, youth and lifestyle-based culture and creative industries, as well as more traditional forms of culture and heritage. Unfortunately, however, many of the towns do not use the initiative effectively in their communications and tourism strategies. The slogans they employ do not give a sense of their specific Hungarian regional or local identity and could apply to towns almost anywhere; indeed, many of them convey a connection to other parts of Europe. However, they offer a good starting point for differentiating between various towns in Hungary and could be useful for future marketing and branding strategies. Rátz (2008) undertook research on the image and profile of a number of places, including Pécs and two "Hungarian Towns of Culture", Székesfehérvár and Miskolc, and suggested a number of slogans by which the towns could be identified: Debrecen – a "Calvinist Rome"; Eger – a "Hungarian Athens"; Pécs – "Gateway to the Balkans"; Sopron – "City of wines"; Szeged – "Gateway to Europe"; Székesfehérvár – "City of Kings"; Veszprém – "City of Queens"; Győr – "Baroque City"; and Miskolc – "70,000-year-old living history museum".

A national campaign in 2008 featured the image of Hungary as a kind of "Mini Mundus" mosaic with the slogan "Love for Life". This has been questioned by several experts from the tourism industry (including the researchers), as it arguably misrepresents the Hungarian attitude to life, which is not overly optimistic. Slightly more understandable is the 2009 slogan "Garden of Wellbeing", referring to Hungary's many spas and health tourism facilities, although it should be noted that the country is better known for medical than for wellness tourism.

Budapest appears to have few problems creating its own identity independently from the rest of the country. In 2008 the Municipality of Budapest developed a branding strategy which went beyond tourism and addressed wider image issues, as can be seen from the induced values summarised in Table 4.1 (MOB 2008). Here, there is a clear juxtaposition between heritage and contemporary everyday life. Socialist-realist architecture is mentioned as part of the built heritage, as well as the House of Terror (a museum dedicated to communist/socialist heritage in Hungary). Some references are made to the city's ethnic groups (e.g. Roma and Jewish communities) as well as the gay subculture. Contemporary culture features quite prominently in the form of film, cinema, photography, modern art, contemporary dance and rock music (such as the Sziget Festival, a five-day annual rock music festival). The promotion of the creative industries is a ubiquitous trend in Europe and the United States, but one which Hungary, and in particular Budapest, has only recently started to embrace (Ságvári and Lengyel 2008; Smith 2008). The marketing slogan for 2008, "City of Senses", also implied a more experiential form of tourism. A campaign created in 2009, "Budapest Adventure", identified six different segments: party and fun, art and design, relax and enjoy, love and romance, festivals and events, and summer adventures.

These examples of marketing campaigns suggest that Budapest is trying to create a balance between the traditional and the contemporary, the global and the local, the European and the national. Whether this will be a successful strategy remains to be seen, but it certainly represents a more ambitious and

Table 4.1 Budapest branding strategy, 2008

Organic values	Induced values
• The cityscape • The Danube • Built heritage • Cultural vibrancy • Spas, baths and Budapest waters • Music • Budapest lifestyle	• Dynamic economic and business centre • Education • Creative industries

Table 4.2 A multi-level analysis of Hungary's identity

Global	European	Regional (CEE)	National	Local
• International festivals • Business and conference tourism • Shopping • Nightlife • International museum collections • Creative industries (e.g. media, design)	• Roman heritage • Baroque architecture • Art Nouveau • Jewish heritage • Café culture	• Socialist heritage • Spas • Danube • Coffee houses • Roma/gipsy culture	• Heritage • Gastronomy • Classical music • Folk culture • Language • Currency	• Village tourism • Arts and crafts • Local festivals • Wine regions • Historic towns

representative multi-layering of image and identity from which the rest of the country could perhaps learn. However, it is applicable more to cities that may already have both a good blend of heritage attractions from previous eras and a greater number of contemporary cultural or arts developments (e.g. Pécs, European Capital of Culture in 2010). Rural areas may instead promote their particular landscapes (e.g. the wine-producing areas of Hungary), "Hungaricums" (unique and protected Hungarian products such as Tokaj wine) or the folk cultures of local people (dance, crafts, costumes, music). In these areas, a single regional or local identity may be more appropriate than a European or global one. The important point is that nations, regions and localities should try to emphasise what is distinctive about their resources, people and culture, rather than copying other destinations or developing standardised attractions.

Table 4.2 suggests some of the features which could be used to create an identity and image for Hungary in future tourism marketing and branding strategies. Clearly, the combination of elements would need to be carefully selected in order to appeal to different target segments, but it provides a useful starting point for a complex, multi-level identity construction in a typical post-socialist country.

Conclusion

It is clearly difficult for CEE countries such as Hungary to create a new national identity while at the same time remaining globally competitive and locally unique. Although a global and cosmopolitan identity may seem attractive in the short term, the long-term consequences are likely to be an erosion of distinctiveness and individual character. Identity construction is further complicated by the desire to embrace Europeanness in terms of recognising common heritage, promoting cultural diversity and meeting EU economic standards. Furthermore, the socialist political heritage of the region can be contentious in terms of interpretation and representation, especially for local residents and domestic visitors. However, like other historical legacies which tend to be the consequences of occupation or invasion (the Austro-Hungarian, Turkish or Roman heritage), socialism played an extremely important role in shaping the country's recent identity and should be acknowledged.

A diversification of Hungary's identity clearly requires increasing the knowledge of foreign visitors or potential visitors about the country in general, but more especially the towns and regions outside Budapest. The HNTO has been working on this issue for several years but, clearly, more needs to be done. The major challenge is to encourage first-time visitors but, more especially, to persuade repeat visitors to venture outside Budapest. There is also a need to consider the different interests of various nationalities as well as domestic tourists. It was noted that Hungary should try to develop an individual and distinctive identity, rather than always positioning itself in opposition to its main competitors (Prague and Vienna).

There is a need to redefine the way in which hotels and the tourism industry in general are created in order to establish a new identity and to answer new challenges. One way could be to create networks in which sectors work together – for example, culture, gastronomy, hospitality and architecture. As mentioned earlier, integrated ways of working are somewhat new for CEE countries, but this could help to create a more holistic and coherent sense of identity. In 2009, in response to this challenge, a National Brand Committee was established which is endeavouring to create a national identity. The ongoing complexities of this process are not to be underestimated, but this is clearly a step in the right direction.

References

Andrusz, G. (2004) "From wall to mall", address at the conference "Winds of Societal Change: Remaking Postcommunist Cities", University of Illinois, Urbana-Champaign, 18–19 June.

Anholt, S. (2004) "Nation-brands and the value of provenance", in N. Morgan, A. Pritchard and R. Pride (eds) *Destination Branding: Creating the Unique Destination Proposition* (pp. 26–39). Oxford: Butterworth–Heinemann.

DEMOS (Hungary (2007) *Hungary's Strategic Audit 2007*. Budapest: DEMOS Hungary.

Farkas, B. (2005) "Panel debate", session at conference "The Readiness of Hungarian Society for European Unification", Budapest, 6 April.

Gyáni, G. (2005) "Budapest túl jón és rosszon", *Beszélő: Politikai és kulturális folyóirat*, http://beszelo.c3.hu/node/274/print (accessed 14 June 2006).

Hall, D. (2004) "Branding and national identity: the case of Central and Eastern Europe", in N. Morgan, A. Pritchard and R. Pride (eds) *Destination Branding: Creating the Unique Destination Proposition* (pp. 111–27). Oxford: Butterworth–Heinemann.

HNTO (Hungarian National Tourist Office) (2002) *Summary of Visitor Perceptions Surveys*. Budapest: HNTO.

HNTO (Hungarian National Tourist Office) (2004) *Marketing Plan*. Budapest: HNTO.

HNTO (Hungarian National Tourist Office) (2006) *Winter Invasion Campaign*. Budapest: HNTO.

HNTO (Hungarian National Tourist Office) (2008) "Kultúra és turizmus utazásra motiváló kulturalis látnivalók és programok", *Turizmus Bulletin*, 12(3): 20–28.

Hughes, H., and Allen, D. (2005) "Cultural tourism in Central and Eastern Europe: the views of 'induced image formation agents'", *Tourism Management*, 26(2): 173–83.

Jancsik, A. (1999) "Turisztikai bevételek és kiadások Magyarországon, valamint ezek várható alakulása az Európai Unióhoz való csatlakozás után", *Turizmus Bulletin*, 3(1): 10–18.

Javrova, Z. (2005) "European integration is hard work", presentation given at "Europe: Challenges, Examples and Opportunities: The European Union Approach to Culture", Euclid Seminar Series, London, 7 March.

Kajner, P. (ed.) (2002) *Növekedés vagy fejlődés? Állásfoglalás Budapest jövőjéről*. Budapest: Védegylet.

Light, D. (2006) "Romania: national identity, tourism promotion and European integration", in D. Hall, M. K Smith and B. Marciszewska (eds) *Tourism in the New Europe: The Challenges and Opportunities of EU Enlargement* (pp. 256–69). Wallingford: CABI.

Morgan, N., and Pritchard, A. (1998) *Tourism, Promotion and Power: Creating Images, Creating Identities*. Chichester: John Wiley & Sons.

MOB (Municipality of Budapest) (2008) *Budapest Branding Strategy*. Budapest: MOB.

Olins, W. (2004) "Branding the nation: the historical context", in N. Morgan, A. Pritchard and R. Pride (eds) *Destination Branding: Creating the Unique Destination Proposition* (pp. 17–25). Oxford: Butterworth–Heinemann.

Pine, B. J., and Gilmore, J. H. (1999) *The Experience Economy: Work is Theatre and Everyday Business a Stage*. Boston: Harvard Business School Press.

Politics.hu (2008) "Poll shows majority of Hungarians feel life was better under communism", 21 May, www.politics.hu/20080521/poll-shows-majority-of-hungarians-feel-life-was-better-under-communism (accessed 21 October 2009).

Puczkó, L., Rátz, T., and Smith, M. (2007) "Old city, new image: perception, positioning and promotion of Budapest", *Journal of Travel and Tourism Marketing*, 22(3/4): 21–34.

Rátz, T. (2004) *European Tourism*. Székesfehérvár: Kodolányi János University College.

Rátz, T. (2008) "A Magyar Athén és a kálvinista Róma – kulturális üzenetek megjelenése magyar városok észlet imázsban", *Turizmus Bulletin*, 12(3): 41–51.

Rátz, T., Smith, M., and Michalkó, G. (2008) "New places in old spaces: mapping tourism and regeneration in Budapest", *Tourism Geographies*, 10: 429–51.

Richards, G. (ed.) (2001) *Cultural Attractions and European Tourism*. Wallingford: CAB International.

Ságvári, B., and Lengyel, B. (2008) *Kreatív Atlasz*. Budapest: DEMOS Hungary.

Smith, M. K. (2003) *Issues in Cultural Tourism Studies*. London: Routledge.

Smith, M. K. (2007) *Tourism, Culture and Regeneration*. Wallingford: CABI.

Smith, M. K. (2008) *Putting the "C" back into the Cultural and Creative Industries: Implications for Hungary*. Budapest: DEMOS Hungary.

Smith, M. K. (2009) *Issues in Cultural Tourism Studies*. 2nd edn, London: Routledge.
Smith, M. K., and Hall, D. (2006) "Enlargement implications for European tourism", in D. Hall, M. K. Smith and B. Marciszewska (eds) *Tourism in the New Europe: The Challenges and Opportunities of EU Enlargement* (pp. 32–43). Wallingford: CABI.
TOB (Tourist Office of Budapest) (2006) *10 years Anniversary of the Tourism Office of Budapest*. Budapest: TOB.
Young, C., and Light, D. (2006) "Communist heritage tourism: between economic development and European integration", in D. Hassenpflug, B. Kolbmüller and S. Schröder-Esch (eds) *Heritage and Media in Europe: Contributing towards Integration and Regional Development* (pp. 249–63). Weimar: Bauhaus Universität.

5   Wizards everywhere?

Film tourism and the imagining of national identity in New Zealand

Anne Buchmann and Warwick Frost

Introduction

Film, as a key driver of tourism, sets expectations about the experiences tourists will have, the people they will meet and the national identities with which they will interact (Beeton 2005). Much of the research into tourism generated by film and television ("film tourism") has concerned the marketing of destinations, particularly through the projection of attractive scenery and iconic images.

This chapter will extend the discussion in two ways. First, it will examine how both tourism and film validates national identity. This occurs through tourist visitation and audience viewing of films, demonstrating that a country is worthy and interesting to outsiders. Such validation by outsiders might be constructed as objective, for they are not from the country and do not have to live there, but have chosen to express interest in it, presumably for its intrinsic attractive qualities. Film and tourism provide that validation separately, but in some cases they do so in combination. Furthermore, national governments build attractions and promote destinations with the view that they will tell national stories to both domestic and international audiences (Pitchford 2008; see also Frost and Hall 2009; Park 2010; Pretes 2003; Stanly 2002).

Secondly, the chapter will discuss how film tourism mediates or reimagines national identity. Many films project images that are somewhat different to those which communities and governments would wish to disseminate. The English, it is said, like to see themselves as epitomised by James Bond, whereas the rest of the world sees them as Mr Bean. Dracula, for example, is a national hero in Romania, but, to the consternation of the authorities, Western tourists, through cinema, imagine him as a supernatural villain (Light 2007). Through films such as *The Quiet Man* (1952) and *Brigadoon* (1954), Ireland and Scotland are portrayed as intensely rural and old-fashioned, and these become the images of the "real" country that tourists desire to experience (Beeton 2005). Films shot in the Australian outback project it as a frontier, a magical landscape with promises that it will provide life-changing experiences for those who visit it (Frost 2010).

Similarly, for years New Zealand tourism campaigns have successfully used the image of "unspoilt" natural environments to promote the whole of the country as "clean and green" (Heaton 1996). This image has been based on romantic roots

(Heaton 1996; Payne 1999) and its rhetoric proves strong (Macnaghten and Urry 2001). Despite it being one of the most developed countries in the world, and notwithstanding the less than pristine state of its environment (Becken 2002), New Zealand still has a "green" image that is heavily used for promotional purposes – for example, in the "New Zealand 100% Pure" campaign. This campaign has been running for over ten years, and its "message is a simple one. It encapsulates all that is unique about New Zealand as a destination: our landscapes, our people, and the stories that link the two" (Tourism New Zealand 2010). The campaign was controversial in the beginning but is now considered to be one of the most successful cases of national branding. In other cases there is "locational dissonance", whereby films are set in one place but actually shot in a different country (Frost 2009: 86).

How, then, do host communities feel and react when tourists come with expectations of a completely different country? In order to examine this issue the chapter presents a case study of New Zealand and how the success of *The Lord of the Rings* films altered perceptions of national identity.

The Lord of the Rings

New Zealand has produced feature-length films since 1914 (*Hinemoa*) and soon attracted British tourists who were looking for the mystical "Maoriland". The country has also been utilised by foreign filmmakers as a production site for nearly the same length of time, starting in 1916 with *A Maori Maid's Love* and *The Mutiny on the Bounty*. More recently, Jane Campion's *The Piano* (1993) drew domestic and international tourists to the featured Karekare Beach, and, with this, contemporary film tourism became a widely recognised phenomenon. In the new millennium, *The Lord of the Rings* (hereafter abbreviated to *LotR*) trilogy (2001, 2002, 2003) lifted film tourism to a new level, which has now extended to such diverse productions as *Whale Rider* (2002), *The Last Samurai* (2004), *The World's Fastest Indian* (2005), *King Kong* (2005), *The Chronicles of Narnia* (2005), *River Queen* (2006), *Sione's Wedding* (2006), *The Lovely Bones* (2009) and *Avatar* (2009).

LotR stands out as the main driver of film tourism in New Zealand. There are more than thirty-five operators offering over fifty film-related tours of varying lengths, visiting a single place or a range of locations (Buchmann 2006). While most of these concentrate on *LotR*, other films have found their way into the narratives of the tourism industry. It is somewhat surprising that the majority of tours were established in response to requests by potential tourists, a situation where industry followed the market rather than trialling a speculative venture. Furthermore, many within the industry thought that the tours would be a passing phase and continue to be surprised by their ongoing strength nearly ten years after the first *LotR* film was released.

It is paradoxical that *LotR* is so closely associated with New Zealand. Tolkien, a South African-born Englishman, set his book in the fictional "Middle-earth", based on a mixture of England, Italy and the Balkans. In the UK, a number of sites have been identified as inspiring locations for the book and accordingly attract tourists. For example, Tolkien's Two Towers have been linked with Perrott's Folly and the Edgbaston Waterworks Tower, both near his home town of Sarehole (Rose 2002). Similarly, the Hobbiton Mill can be found close to the Birmingham house once owned by Tolkien (Buchmann, personal observation, 2005). The films – American-German productions with an international cast and a New Zealand landscape heavily modified through computer effects – quickly developed into a "national tourism product" that both reinforced the existing ideal identity of a green, clean and safe country with spectacular scenery and also created a new identity. This new identity saw New Zealand as a creative and clever country, modern and both technologically and culturally sophisticated. Furthermore, the "Kiwi" character of the production and the "authentic" props and relationships it produced were embraced by media and public alike. These elements were consequently used heavily in the promotion of the films and in film tourism.

Buchmann (2010) demonstrated that *LotR* film tourists want to experience both the "real" New Zealand and the more fantastical Middle-earth. Furthermore, they anticipate an authentic and sincere experience. Such sincerity takes place when there are genuine encounters between tourists and guides: "rather than seeing value as the emanation of an 'authentic object', the moment of interaction may become the site in which value is generated" (Taylor 2001). This shift from objectification towards negotiation can deepen our understanding of the perception of authenticity in the tourism experience.

Many tourists are influenced by pre-tour images provided by *LotR* film clips and still images showing the "green and clean" New Zealand and the "magical" Middle-earth in the films, the novel and "behind the scenes" documentaries. The demonstration of camaraderie among staff working on the films also proved crucial for the formation of tourist expectations.

A 100% pure New Zealand landscape

New Zealand has traditionally been marketed in terms of its natural landscapes, national parks and adventure tourism (Croy and Buchmann 2009; Frost and Hall 2009; McClure 2004). Film has added a new dimension: most film tourists see a strong connection between *LotR* and New Zealand, whose scenery was heavily featured and provided an important and reoccurring element in the storylines. All those surveyed perceived the locations as a fair presentation of the Middle-earth described in the novel. For this chapter respondents were surveyed and interviewed. Journal notes were also kept of tours. Indeed, most film tourists connected the novel, films and country as motivational drivers for their travel: "The movies will be my favourite for eternity . . . [and] without the books, the movies wouldn't exist and I wouldn't be in New Zealand right now" (questionnaire 76).

Despite knowing that Tolkien had conceived Middle-Earth in Europe, many film tourists emotionally perceived the New Zealand setting as authentic and worth visiting. As New Zealand film director John O'Shea pointed out, the country's national identity "became fused with the look of the land. The rolling hills, the wide open spaces, yet so much of it rugged and craggy" (O'Shea 1999: 126). And while most of its citizens live in urban areas, film usually portrays a different reality: "Yet any moving image that comes from New Zealand is likely to be stamped with the inevitable flavour of – strangely enough – the country-side" (ibid.). Many films about New Zealand, even when made through overseas locations and directors, were set in the time of early settlement. Māori featured – if at all – as simple and picturesque people for exoticism (Simmons 1999) and romance (Conrich and Davy 1997; Ward 1990). And, while early European set-tlers showed ambivalent behaviour when keeping wilderness at bay and creating new domestic space (Pawson and Brooking 2002; Simmons 1999), most films reduced the country itself "to the status of the scenery, albeit exotically shot, for a story worthy of universal and hence European significance" (Jones 1999: 16).

Indeed it is striking that many of the "natural" landscapes of Central Otago used in the *LotR* films are the product of recent environmental degradation – the result of the region being the site of a major Gold Rush in the 1860s – which somewhat contradicts the image of a "green and clean" New Zealand. This is particularly so in river valleys, where gravel banks and terraces have been sluiced. Later pastoral expansion has been characterised by the clearance of native vegetation (Frost 2005; Pawson and Brooking 2002). It is intriguing to watch *LotR* and realise that many iconic scenes take place in greatly modified landscapes, including sites which were clearly heavily mined during the Gold Rush and pastoral settings (such as Hobbiton) which are completely lacking in native New Zealand trees.

A mythic land

Along with this mystification of landscape, films often featured storylines of the man alone (Dennis and Bieringa 1992) showing the traditional male gaze (Simmons 1999). New Zealand directors such as Geoff Murphy often examined the themes of masculinity, nationality and identity (Rayner 1999). Many films portrayed "places of isolation, remote or distinctively rural, delayed industrial-ism, individuals trapped in 'alive' landscapes dwarfed by the power of land, characters are fragile, eccentric or disturbed" (Conrich and Davy 1997: 7). More generally, the identity of Central Otago has often been built on the rugged masculine individual, particularly the iconic "Southern man" utilized to advertise Speights beer (Croy and Buchmann 2009).

While it is true that nature is simply part of New Zealand's heritage and culture (Schöllmann *et al.* 1998), the country is also seen as sporting inherent mythical qualities. Jones (1999) argued that it has often been misunderstood and frequently been idealised overseas as the exotic other, and that its films at best attract an aware-ness for New Zealand film culture. More often, they have been read in ways mean-ingful to the receptive culture while ignoring any other messages (Jones 1999).

A case in point is the reception of *Once Were Warriors*, whose theme the American audience read as interracial violence while New Zealanders correctly decoded the problematic issue of domestic violence.

We have already shown how film has helped shape New Zealand's image. It is telling to reflect on the reception of the *LotR* films. Downie (2004) pointed out the similarities between New Zealand and Middle-earth, where "the constructed events and incidental details springing from the three films' production were feeding into what has for a long time been part of the constructed New Zealand imaginary". The films were treated as an authentic New Zealand project; furthermore, "national authenticity is based on claiming the trilogy as a local 'New Zealand' product, a unique expression of the legacy of national identity" (Jones and Smith 2005). A vital element of the New Zealand claim to the films was that the director himself was a "Kiwi": "The image of Jackson's creativity, entrepreneurship, patriotism and 'Kiwi' character represents in an intense form the themes of creative and national authenticity" (ibid.).

Altogether, the various myths of the making of the films, their Kiwi character and the "authentic" props and relationships they produced were embraced and used for strengthening the national identity of New Zealand as well as both domestic and international branding. Thus, to understand fully the impact of the *LotR* phenomenon, it is necessary to look at its creative and national meaning. In this it becomes understandable why the project was embraced so willingly by most of New Zealand's people, even the government, and the worldwide audience.

The willingness to believe the image says much about the longing for myths in modern times. The concept of the outback as a magical life-changing place is central to Australian film tourism (Frost 2010), and this can be extended to New Zealand. Furthermore, many of the film tourists clearly projected extraordinary and fantastic elements onto New Zealand and were only too willing to immerse themselves in this mythical world: "It's almost like we tune out reality and become engrossed in the magic. In some ways it's rather sad having to come back to the reality" (interview 8). Such a dreamlike journey was facilitated by mythical elements and stories that seemed to merge flawlessly with the geographical reality of New Zealand. In consequence, film tourists were actively re-creating their experience as one that merged real and fantastical elements.

The many readings of New Zealand

Intrigued by the many and varied readings of New Zealand, we inquired into the kind of relationship film tourists had with both the fantasy and the geography, and in particular how their relationship to both had changed. Most enjoyed experiencing New Zealand: "it gave me an opportunity to see special places" (questionnaire 12), and both New Zealand and its *LotR* connection were important: "as well as seeing *Lord of the Rings* sites you also see different towns, sites, cultures and tourist sports" (questionnaire 102); "we got to see *Lord of the Rings* locations, do shopping and to see New Zealand and make friends" (questionnaire 83). Some commented that "this was a fabulous tour of both New Zealand and *Lord of the Rings* sites" (questionnaire 96) or that they were "very happy and satisfied as a *Lord of the Rings* fan and as a tourist to New Zealand. Best trip ever" (questionnaire 84).

Overall, for many film tourists it seemed the merging was facilitated by New Zealand's range of exciting and unique environments. They rarely perceived these environments as similar (journal 3, 17 and 18). While this is true in some cases, in places the landscape of New Zealand is not that different from that in, for example, Oregon, USA, or the United Kingdom. Yet even film tourists from these countries often perceived New Zealand as having mythical qualities (journal 18; questionnaire 71).

In such narratives, these tourists revealed more about their own point of view than the actual visited country (Bhattacharyya 1997). In this case, New Zealand was representing the exotic "other". This perception is well established, partly on account of the country's geographical isolation and distance from Europe, and has influenced the reception of New Zealand films for a long time (Jones 1999; Simmons 1999). Both the films of *LotR* and the "making ofs" documentaries further promote these exotic and mythical qualities – qualities that were also used in the official "100% Pure" tourism campaign: New Zealand was portrayed as an exotic and faraway country that is green, clean, exciting and yet safe, without major civil or military conflicts. Thus the image created by *LotR* and the official New Zealand image are very similar in their promotion of mythical elements. As a consequence, most film tourists had expectations of their own holiday experience that included such elements. New Zealand was seen as hosting a range of ecosystems and spectacular scenery and at the same time as being a safe and relaxing destination with a somewhat familiar culture. Consequently, most film tourists continued to construct their experience to fit their expectations. And many revealed an antagonistic understanding of nature/uninhabited places and culture/inhabited places. As a result, most preferred the largely uninhabited South Island over the North Island: "I think it's more of a magical thing . . . there's a whole kind of mythological, magic feeling in the whole place . . . I guess the scenery's got a lot to do with it, and especially the locations . . . the South Island of New Zealand really feels magical and mysterious to me" (interview 61).

This constructed binary opposition of natural (good) and urban (bad) environments is common in Western societies (Engelhardt 1994; Rabelt 1994). Interestingly, this also links to Tolkien's work, where the author sets the idyllic Hobbiton against the industrialised landscape of the terrorising wizard. This theme continues to be popular and partly explains the success of the books within the counterculture of the 1960s and 1970s (Carpenter 1977). However, any strict distinction between nature and culture is a cultural construction and tells us more about how people see or want to see their own position in the world than what that position really is (Faulstich-Wieland 1998). As stated above, most film tourists revealed a longing for the exotic other: "Well, for me, Edoras was like magic. When you get to Wellington you're in a city and I live in a city . . . cities I find a little bit boring" (interview 65). Clearly many film tourists seeking to experience the "real New Zealand" are less enthused about the reality of dealing with the urbanised majority of New Zealanders. The "magic", and indeed the national icons, are to be found elsewhere, away from the cultural centres of the cities and their familiar globalised appearance. Instead the fictive ideal prevails of the hard-working and yet social and friendly Southern man and his rugged landscape.

The role of authenticity and sincerity

Such an enthusiastic embrace of both reality and myth has been found in other forms of tourism and led to an ongoing debate into the importance of such notions as authenticity and sincerity – a debate that has been especially prominent in film tourism research (Buchmann *et al.* 2010; Frost 2009). In *LotR* tourism, the significance of authenticity is reflected not only in the quality of the relationships but also in the process of making films and props as close as possible to historical artefacts and Tolkien's words (Sibley 2002). This was duly embraced by most film tourists: "they're talking about the props and the fact that they're not stage props, they are realistic" (interview 57). And, even more, according to the production designer, Peter Jackson's goal was described as making "Middle-earth look like it was shot on location" (Grant 1999). The attention paid to every detail of the filmmaking was discussed often: "they're talking about the Elven costumes . . . and each layer is absolutely perfect. It's never actually seen on camera but it's properly made" (interview 57). Such retelling shows the high value many film tourists placed on these often mentioned aspects of authenticity. Overall, the "authenticity of the artefacts was central to this faithfulness to Tolkien's world" (Jones and Smith 2005) by the filmmakers that ultimately validated the achievement of the production. In short, while the concept of authenticity seems questionable in connection with film tourism, the very term presents a crucial part of the overall experience.

A reality of hyperreality and simulacra

Eco introduced the term "hyperreality" to describe how, in modern times, the boundaries between copy and original have broken down; consequently "authen-ticity" can no longer exist (Eco 1983). Baudrillard used the term "simulacrum" to describe the same phenomenon – a world where fantasy and reality are fused and no more originals exist (Baudrillard 1983). The worlds one sees on the big screen are such simulacra: places that never existed but seem to have been based on real locations. Indeed, real and hyperreal experiences were at times merged in the narratives of film tourists, who spoke about the history and mythology of Middle-earth and New Zealand. One participant saw the fictional Middle-earth mythol-ogy as complementary to New Zealand in the same way as Hellenic cultural heritage is to Greece (interview 63). Overall, the evidence seems to suggest that reality and hyperreality evoke the same emotions. Couldry's (1998) study of the *Coronation Street* set showed how the simulation of a street became its own reality through its signification as a film set: the fictional setting is considered authentic. But how can film sets become so real? The answer may lie partly in the medium of film itself, in the way films are produced and their images perceived (Couldry 1998; Frost 2009).

An instructive example of this is how the monument in Stirling of the Scottish hero William Wallace became an economically successful tourist attraction after the release of *Braveheart* in 1995, followed by the creation of a statue resembling actor Mel Gibson (Beeton 2005). However, the film was shot primarily in Ireland. Such "runaway" productions (where a film is not shot in the location that it portrays) are quite common, and New Zealand is one of the main producers of such films (Buchmann 2010; Frost 2009).

The very production of film requires considerable organisation and results in a highly de-fragmented product. There are numerous examples of films set and shot in New Zealand but financed overseas (e.g. *The Piano*), films shot overseas but with a New Zealand financial background and production (*A Soldier's Tale*) and films shot in New Zealand but without any significant New Zealand input (*The Frighteners* and *King Kong*). This questions the very use of the term "authenticity" in connection with film: "in terms of 'authenticity', on location sites are not necessarily authentic, in that many places are filmed in such a way that they appear quite different from 'real life' (larger, smaller or more extensive, for example)" (Beeton 2005: 174). So why does the term "authenticity" remain at the centre of the film tourism experience?

The consequences for film tourism

In this study of film tourism, as in the case of literary tourism studied by Herbert, "issues of authenticity were evident though rarely in explicit forms" (Herbert 2001). However, it was also shown how significant the authenticity concept has been in relation to the making and promotion of *LotR*. The analysis of data showed repeatedly the importance of perceived authenticity. In other words, film tourists sought a hyperreality and accepted it as reality. As Herbert noted in the case of literary tourism, "the visit needed to be pleasurable and the 'package' was not being scrutinized in any detailed way to test its authenticity" (ibid.). An example of this occurred when a *LotR* actor accompanied the tour for a few hours, when his (inauthentic) costume was well received: the "appearance of authenticity" – and the effort and acknowledgment of its importance signified through the attempts made to "be" authentic *did* matter (Halewood and Hannam 2001). Also, most film tourists could not remember the actor's name or the exact form of his involvement with the film a few hours later, yet they continued to value his participation as something very special (Buchmann, personal observation, 2005, 2006). The event was valued on account of its perceived and, in the film tourists' frame of reference, actual authenticity, the encounter being understood as sincere (Taylor 2001). Similarly, the supposed Kiwiness of certain foods (such as Hokey Pokey and Pavlova) and icons (untouched wilderness and being a "young" country) was never questioned, and with this the proposed national identity accepted (this will be discussed further).

While the debate over the nature of tourism authenticity is ongoing (Selwyn 1996), Wang (1999) showed that the tourism industry has already reacted to the longing of tourists by offering "authentic" experiences. However, it can only offer commodified authenticity packaged as a product that can be bought (Halewood and Hannam 2001), and tourists do not want to see too many contradictions to such performed authenticity. Thus one faces the contradiction of both the importance and the impossibility of authenticity. Many academics have argued for a wider understanding of the term. Bruner understood culture as continually changing and thus that there is no one single authentic culture, since "there are no originals" (Bruner 2005: 93). Consequently, Bruner also rejected notions of hyperreality, simulacra and the like, seeing these as a Eurocentric bias against American culture. Wang (1999) and Kim and Jamal (2007) have argued that both the bodily presence of the tourist and the trials the tourist undergoes create an individual "existential" authenticity (Buchmann *et al*. 2010). Such an "existential authenticity, unlike [the] object-related version, can often have nothing to do with the issue of whether toured objects are real" (Wang 1999). What matters is that the tourists perceive the object and/or experience as authentic.

Similarly, Poria, Butler and Airey suggested that tourist perception is important in understanding visitation patterns, as the meaning and not so much the artefact itself is crucial (Poria *et al*. 2006). Only such an approach can explain such comments as: "I am now sold completely on the concept of visiting a strange country with a theme, as you get to see the real country, not the tourist trap illusions" (journal 17). In the similar case of *Shangri-La*, Cater showed how tourists had internalised their expectations and consequently toured an imaginative geography (Cater 2001). The journey was meaningful and authentic in the participants' perception, despite its many "staged authenticities". In a sense, the authenticity was judged by how well it managed to sustain the myths. One participant was also well aware of how myths are created in modern times: "what most Scots think happened in Scottish history has very little to do with the reality. I think *Braveheart* . . . you see, that's where fact and fiction become mixed" (interview 19). The same process, of course, takes place in New Zealand.

Conclusion

Interviews with tourists indicate that embodiment, sincerity and authenticity are important in the film tourism experience. For example, as one respondent stated, "for me to be able to walk onto those fields is magical because I keep turning around looking for Gandalf or Frodo . . . and yet at the same time I'm able to bend down and touch the grass" (interview 8). Ultimately, the authenticity and sincerity of the experience is co-constructed by the tourists within the existing discourse that exists around the authenticity of the making of the film (Buchmann *et al*. 2010). This discourse also explains why the film tourist came to New Zealand instead of journeying to the original locations that inspired Tolkien's Middle-earth, such as Birmingham or the European Alps.

What is seen instead is that the former colony of New Zealand used the essentially English story to create its own Middle-earth and, while doing so, to reaffirm its own Pākehā (the Māori term for New Zealanders who are not of Māori bloodline) national identity. Or, as one tourist put it: "This [New Zealand] is Middle-earth" (interview 34). What is surprising is how many people agree with this reading of New Zealand, indicating a will to believe in mythical images even in modern "rational" times: "It is wild, it is primitive, it is remote, it is geologically young. Very 'Middle-earth' here. I like it" (journal 1). Both Middle-earth and New Zealand are constructed as a pre-modern paradise, idealised and sentimentalised; and the hardships of the filming process and ultimately the triumph of the Kiwi film team further strengthened this image, which is now used for tourism purposes. Such a reimagining excludes parts of New Zealand's real past, most powerfully ignoring the Māori heritage, but also the Gold Rush that was such a strong influence on Central Otago's landscape and culture.

More complicating is the fact that other films add to this imagined picture: "It's almost like *Lord of the Rings* and *Whale Rider* add to the scenery of the country . . . that would stimulate general tourism. You know, people say 'That's an incredible country, I've always wanted to go. Let's go'" (interview, staff of Te Papa national museum, 2004). However, the tourist's gaze rarely acknowledges the significance of pre-white settlement and continuation of Māori culture in Aotearoa New Zealand – as the "Land of the Long White Cloud" is correctly named in acknowledgement of its Māori and Pākehā identity. Instead, a single night of "Māori" dance performance followed by a traditional feast ("*hangi*") proved sufficient for many film tourists (interview 64): "I don't miss the maybe, lack of native Māori culture . . . because . . . I think that the experience is so rich as it is" (interview 104). This distinguishes *LotR* tourism from *Whale Rider* tourism.

Again, the images of New Zealand used in promoting the country as a whole and the images used in *Whale Rider* (2002) are similar, though in the latter case they include coastal scenery, a rural Māori community and, of course, the part real and part mythical story of the Whale Rider. Nowadays tourists come for both the film and its historical reality:

> Some people just want to go out and see the film set and say, "Oh yes, I stood here where Keisha [the lead actress in *Whale Rider*] stood, and I touched the whales, and I looked at the *waka*, and I walked along the beach." Others are really wanting to go out and learn more about the story, more about how the story actually fits into real Māori culture, whether it's the type of story that could possibly happen in real life. And others just want to learn more about Māori culture in itself.
>
> (Interview with visitor information centre staff, 2005)

Both cases of film tourism reflect an idealistic image; however, as one *LotR* film tourist put it: "*Whale Rider*, of course, was New Zealand. *Whale Rider* was really New Zealand" (interview 63). Such a statement is somewhat at odds with the usual "New Zealand is Middle-earth" paradigm and indicates an awareness of the limitations of such an approach to the readings of Aotearoa New Zealand as a "real country". Still, most tourists acknowledge and take an active part in this construction of modern New Zealand and its mainly Pākehā national identity. There is hope that an increase in the diversity of film directors might eventually not only challenge but overcome the hegemonic non-inclusive reading (Conrich and Davy 1997; Dennis and Bieringa 1992; O'Shea 1999).

Modern tourism is about myths and myth-making (Selwyn 1996) – a process that is similar, and in some regard identical, to that of making films and the imagining of a national identity. This chapter has shown how film and tourism can imagine and continue to create and thus validate a chosen national identity. Furthermore, the narratives of the film tourists' perception of the destination revealed more about their own point of view than of the actual visited country: "New Zealand is Middle-earth." Such a statement denies a wider reading of New Zealand (or should that be Aotearoa New Zealand?) and its complex history. Despite its seemingly harmless "playfulness", a powerful statement is made that clearly signals a want to project a simplistic image onto a diverse and contradictory reality. What is interesting is how media and tourists welcomed such a fantastical reading of New Zealand, and how easily this image could be blended with the overall promotional image of the country. At least for the time being, Māori and Pākehā cultures are considered "complementary" to the overall tourism experience and image and the national identity and not yet as essential. Thus issues of commodification have to be discussed, and incorporating Māori principles such as "*manaakitanga*" (hospitality) in the tourism industry does not necessarily address the fundamental imbalance the ethnic groups are still experiencing. The future will show if films such as *Sione's Wedding* (2006) and *No. 2* (2006) eventually transform the antiquated image(s) to create instead a more inclusive national identity of Aotearoa New Zealand.

References

Baudrillard, J. (1983) *Simulations*. New York: Semiotext(e).
Becken, S. (2002) "Energy use in the New Zealand tourism sector", doctoral thesis, Lincoln University, New Zealand.
Beeton, S. (2005) *Film-Induced Tourism*. Clevedon: Channel View.
Bhattacharyya, D. P. (1997) "Mediating India: an analysis of a guidebook", *Annals of Tourism Research*, 24(2): 371–89.
Bruner, E. M. (2005) *Culture on Tour*. Chicago: University of Chicago Press.
Buchmann, A. (2006) "From Erewhon to Edoras: tourism and myths in New Zealand", *Tourism, Culture & Communication*, 6(3): 181–9.
Buchmann, A. (2008) "The myth of the Elvish speaking film tourist: a case study of the multiple-day guided Lord of the Rings tourists in Aotearoa New Zealand", in *Proceedings*

of the New Zealand Tourism and Hospitality Research Conference, Hanmer Springs, New Zealand.

Buchmann, A. (2010) "Developments in the contemporary film tourism industry: a case study of the New Zealand experience", *Tourism and Hospitality Planning & Development*, 7(1): 77–84.

Buchmann, A., Moore, K., and Fisher, D. (2010) "Experiencing film tourism: authenticity & fellowship", *Annals of Tourism Research*, 37(1): 229–48.

Carpenter, H. (1977) *Tolkien: A Biography*. New York: Ballantine Books.

Cater, E. (2001) "The space of the dream: a case of mis-taken identity?" *Area*, 33(1): 47–54.

Conrich, I., and Davy, S. (1997) *Views from the Edge of the World: New Zealand Film*. London: Kakapo Books.

Couldry, N. (1983) "The view from inside the 'simulacrum': visitors' tales from the set of *Coronation Street*", *Leisure Studies*, 17: 94–107.

Croy, W. G., and Buchmann, A. (2009) "Film-induced tourism in the high country: recreation and contest", *Tourism Review International*, 13(2): 147–55.

Dennis, J., and Bieringa, J. (eds) (1992) *Film in Aotearoa New Zealand*. Wellington: Victoria University Press.

Downie, J. (2004) "Cyclones, seduction, and the middle mind – *Lord of the Rings: The Return of the King*", *Illusions*, no. 36.

Eco, U. (1983) *Travels in Hyperreality*. San Diego: Harcourt Brace Jovanovitch.

Engelhardt, E. (1994) "Sind Frauen die besseren Naturschützerinnen?", in J. Buchen, K. Buchholz, E. Hoffmann, S. Hofmeister, R. Kutzner, R. Olbrich and P. V. Rüth (eds) *Das Umweltproblem ist nicht geschlechtsneutral: Feministische Perspektiven* (pp. 16–33). Bielefeld: Kleine.

Faulstich-Wieland, H. (1998) "Perspektiven der Frauenforschung", in R.V. Bardeleben and P. Plummer (eds) *Perspektiven der Frauenforschung: Ausgewählte Beiträge der 1. Fachtagung Frauen- Gender-Forschung in Rheinland-Pfalz* (pp. 1–13). Tübingen: Stauffenburg.

Frost, W. (2005) "Making an edgier interpretation of the Gold Rushes: contrasting perspectives from Australia and New Zealand", *International Journal of Heritage Studies*, 11(3): 235–50.

Frost, W. (2009) "From backlot to runaway production: exploring location and authenticity in film-induced tourism", *Tourism Review International*, 13(2): 85–92.

Frost, W. (2010) "Life changing experiences: tourists and film in the Australian outback", *Annals of Tourism Research*, 37(3): 707–26.

Frost, W., and Hall, C. M. (2009) "National parks, national identity and tourism", in W. Frost and C. M. Hall (eds), *Tourism and National Parks: International Perspectives on Development, Histories and Change* (pp. 63–77). London and New York: Routledge.

Grant, B. K. (1999) *A Cultural Assault: The New Zealand Films of Peter Jackson*. Nottingham: Kakapo Books.

Halewood, C., and Hannam, K. (2001) "Viking heritage tourism: authenticity and commodification", *Annals of Tourism Research*, 28: 565–80.

Heaton, E. (1996) "Green and unique? A study of environment and promotion in New Zealand", thesis, Lincoln University, New Zealand.

Herbert, D. (2001) "Literary places, tourism and the heritage experience", *Annals of Tourism Research*, 28(1): 312–33.

Jones, D., and Smith, K. (2005) "Middle-earth meets New Zealand: authenticity and location in the making of *The Lord of the Rings*", *Journal of Management Studies*, 42(5): 923–45.

Jones, S. (1999) *Projecting a Nation: New Zealand Film and its Reception in Germany*. Nottingham: Kakapo Books.

Kim, H., and Jamal, T. (2007) "Touristic quest for existential authenticity", *Annals of Tourism Research*, 34(1): 181–201.

Light, D. (2007) "Dracula tourism in Romania: cultural identity and the state", *Annals of Tourism Research*, 34(3): 746–65.

McClure, M. (2004) *The Wonder Country: Making New Zealand Tourism*. Auckland: Auckland University Press.

Macnaghten, P., and Urry, J. (2001) *Bodies of Nature*. London: Sage.

O'Shea, J. (1999) *Don't Let it Get You: Memories – Documents*. Wellington: Victoria University Press.

Park, H. (2010) "Heritage tourism: emotional journeys into nationhood", *Annals of Tourism Research*, 37(1): 116–35.

Pawson, E., and Brooking, T. (eds) (2002) *Environmental Histories of New Zealand*. Melbourne: Oxford University Press.

Payne, S. (1999) *The Study of Literary Tourism*. Toronto: York University, Department of Geography.

Pitchford, S. (2008) *Identity Tourism: Imaging and Imagining the Nation*. Bingley: Emerald.

Poria, Y., Butler, R. W., and Airey, D. (2006) "Tourist perceptions of heritage exhibits: a comparative study from Israel", *Journal of Heritage Tourism*, 1(1): 1–22.

Pretes, M. (2003) "Tourism and nationalism", *Annals of Tourism Research*, 30(1): 125–42.

Rabelt, V. (1994) "Von der Weltformel zum Widerspruch: über mein Verhältnis nur Naturwissenschaft aus feministischer Sicht", in J. Buchen, K. Buchholz, E. Hoffmann, S. Hofmeister, R. Kutzner, R. Olbrich and P. V. Rüth (eds) *Das Umweltproblem ist nicht geschlechtsneutral: Feministische Perspektiven* (pp. 34–48). Bielefeld: Kleine.

Rayner, J. (1999) *Cinema Journeys of the Man Alone: The New Zealand and American Films of Geoff Murphy*. Nottingham: Kakapo Books.

Rose, S. (2002) "The Two Towers: A J. R. R. Tolkien museum trail", www.culture24.org.uk (accessed 11 January 2010).

Schöllmann, A., Perkins, H., and Moore, K. (1998) "Fantastic mountains on our doorsteps: touristic place promotion and urban identity in Christchurch", paper presented at the Third New Zealand Tourism and Hospitality Research Conference.

Selwyn, T. (ed.) (1996) *The Tourist Image: Myths and Myth Making in Tourism*. Chichester: Wiley.

Sibley, B. (2002) *Lord of the Rings: The Making of the Movie Trilogy*. London: HarperCollins.

Simmons, L. (1999) "Distance looks our way: imagining New Zealand on film", in D. Verhoeven (ed.) *Twin Peaks: Australian and New Zealand Feature Films* (pp. 39–49). Melbourne: Damned Publications.

Stanly, N. (2002) "Chinese theme parks and national identity", in T. Young and R. Riley (eds) *Theme Park Landscapes: Antecedents and Variations* (pp. 269–89). Washington, DC: Dumbarton Oaks.

Taylor, J. P. (2001) "Authenticity and sincerity in tourism", *Annals of Tourism Research*, 28(1): 7–26.

Tourism New Zealand (2010) "100% Pure New Zealand", www.tourismnewzealand.com/campaigns (accessed 11 January 2010).

Wang, N. (1999) "Rethinking authenticity in tourism experience", *Annals of Tourism Research*, 26(2): 349–70.

Ward, V. (1990) *Edge of the Earth: Stories and Images from the Antipodes*. Auckland: Heinemann Reed.

6 The role of the horse in Australian tourism and national identity

Leanne White

Introduction

The fundamental role and powerful mythology of the horse in the Australian tourism and leisure industries will be explored in this chapter. The majesty of the horse conjures up evocative thoughts of its crucial position in the development of Australian identity, culture and society – in particular, in Banjo Paterson's famous 1895 bush ballad "The Man from Snowy River" and the Melbourne Cup champions Carbine, Phar Lap and Makybe Diva. The chapter will examine how the horse and the notion of horsemanship have helped to form the Australian national identity, and especially the ways in which key tourism and leisure industries deliberately work to manufacture and sustain the myth. It will closely analyse the way in which the horse has been imagined, created, replicated and relayed (often for commercial purposes) in Australian culture and sport – two significant tourism-related industries.

The grace and power of the horse has fascinated humans for many thousands of years. Around 17,000 years ago, images of horses were painted on the walls of caves such as at Lascaux in France. The Assyrians were also fascinated by the horse and recruited the animal for the purposes of war, hunting and sport. The horse was introduced into Egypt around 1600 BC and was soon displayed in art. Horsemanship was depicted on the frieze of the Parthenon around 450 BC, exhibiting the special connection between the Greeks and the noble animal. And knights riding their horses in the Norman Conquest are distinctively represented in the well-known Bayeux Tapestry.

In the 1860s the French artist Manet captured the excitement of the racecourse with *The Races at Longchamp*; Degas painted *Racehorses before the Stands* in the 1870s; while Gauguin's *The White Horse* (1898) is another commanding painting of the powerful animal. Among Australian paintings which illustrate the horse are Adam Lindsay Gordon's *Steeplechasing at Flemington* (1868), Tom Roberts's *A Break Away!* (1891) and Sidney Nolan's *Death of Constable Scanlon* (1946).

Horses have also played a unique role in popular culture. Famous film horses have included Black Beauty, the Lone Ranger's mount Silver and Roy Rogers's faithful companion Trigger. On the small screen, the *Mr Ed* theme song written by Jay Livingston and Ray Evans, beginning with the words "A horse is a horse, of course, of course . . . " is known to many. Between 1961 and 1966, 144 episodes of the famous show about the special relationship between Wilbur and his talking horse were produced.

Horses operate as significant tourist attractions in many countries. In Canada the world-famous red-coated Royal Canadian Mounted Police are a considerable draw-card for travellers and locals. Both the maple leaf and the "mountie" are iconic signi-fiers of the picturesque country. In England, the annual "Trooping the Colour" has attracted large crowds since 1755. The event now takes place on the queen's birth-day and helps the country maintain its meticulous pageantry, pomp and ceremony.

In Australia, horses are bred for a wide range of activities, such as mustering cattle, racing, show-jumping, agricultural shows, riding and rodeos. Horses have played an important role in a wide range of industries in this country since the first seven horses arrived on Australian soil with the First Fleet in 1788. Horse-racing's popularity in Australia may partly be explained by the English origins of the first settlers. As David Mosler explains, "Sport in colonial society was intimately bound up with Englishness: hunting, horse racing, bowls and riding were transported from the home country and maintained English identity in a strange land" (Mosler 2002: 98). Champion horse trainer Bart Cummings argues that "the love of horses is something inherent in most Australians" (Cavanough and Davies 1971: vii).

The horse industry is one of Australia's largest recreational and entertainment industries (Pilkington and Wilson 1993: 86). Pilkington and Wilson argue that the "cultural and historical significance of the horse in Australian society" ensures a high participation rate in horse-related activities. The horse is an animal with which many form a special bond from a very early age, as shown by the delight and wonder of the merry-go-round (see Figure 6.1). The significant influence of the horse and related mythology on Australia's national identity is the focus of this chapter, first with an examination of its presence in Australian arts and culture and then with an exploration of its role in sport.

The horse in Australian arts and culture: "The Man from Snowy River"

The majesty of the horse conjures up evocative thoughts of its crucial role in the development of Australian culture and society – including Banjo Paterson's "The Man from Snowy River". As examined in further detail elsewhere, numerous interpretations of "The Man" have played a key role in keeping the famous Australian bush myth firmly fixed in the national consciousness (White 2009). This chapter builds upon earlier research and attempts to broaden the discussion to explore how and why the horse is so significant in Australia's national identity.

The story of "The Man" has played a central role in the Australian national consciousness. Manufacturers of products associated with the legend in its numerous textual forms benefit from the overt association with Andrew Barton Paterson's ballad, which was first published in 1895. It has been relentlessly told and retold for a range of commercial purposes in the leisure and tourism industries (White 2009). The popular poem has also sparked a host of other narrative forms, including a television series, a novel, an annual bush festival in the Victorian

Figure 6.1 The merry-go-round with horses holds a special appeal for the young.

country town of Corryong and an "Arena Spectacular", and it featured at the very beginning of the opening ceremony of the 2000 Olympic Games in Sydney.

Some argue that the poem was based on a man named Jack Riley, whom Paterson visited in 1890. Indeed, the headstone of Riley's grave in Corryong proclaims him to be "The Man from Snowy River". The reality is that Paterson created a character with whom many readily associated. A few years before his death the poet explained:

> I felt sure that there must have been a Man from Snowy River and I was right. They have turned up all over the mountain districts – men who did exactly the same ride and could give you chapter and verse for every mile they descended and every creek they crossed. It was no small satisfaction that there really had been a Man from Snowy River – more than one of them.
>
> (Semmler 1982: 17)

The original idea for the 1982 feature film *The Man from Snowy River* came from Paterson's poem. "The Man" is described in the third of the thirteen stanzas as "a stripling on a small and weedy beast". The skilled rider, audacious and persevering, has come to symbolise for Australians the rugged individualism and determination of the bushman. The film received an Australian Film Institute award for the powerful musical score, written by Bruce Rowland – music that helps explain much of the popularity of the film. While some argue that Paterson's original story has already been sufficiently exploited, Rowland firmly believes that the story of "The Man" could be "a very big money spinner for Australia" if it was successfully exported (Dennis 2002). The sequel *Return to Snowy River* (also known as *The Man from Snowy River II*) was released in 1988 – the year of Australia's Bicentenary.

The television series *Snowy River: The MacGregor Saga* was first aired on Australian television in 1993. Three series were produced, with such actors as Andrew Clarke, Wendy Hughes, Guy Pearce and Brett Climo; famous Australians, including Olivia Newton John and Charles "Bud" Tingwell, also made guest appearances. Reflecting the genre of "The Man" films, some of the names of the episodes were "Comeback", "Black Sheep", "The Lovers", "The Claimant" and "Difficult Times".

Neither the films nor the television series were filmed in the Snowy Mountains region where Banjo Paterson's myth was created. What mattered most to the producers was the aesthetic beauty of the Australian bush setting chosen and how it would translate to the screen. The television series was in fact filmed in the town of Trentham in Victoria, perhaps because of various incentives offered at the time by the local shire.

The 2000 Olympic Games in Sydney represented the biggest event ever held in Australia (Tomlinson 2004: 160) and the opening ceremony was the most watched television event in history. It was broadcast to a global television audience of 3.7 billion in 220 countries – a record at the time (Loland 2004: 189) – and official ratings figures recorded that 10,436,000 Australians tuned in (Warneke 2000: 6). These figures are even more impressive when one considers that they do not take into account those people who watched the event on giant outdoor screens and in pubs and clubs. Additionally, a local audience of almost 110,000 witnessed the spectacle live in Stadium Australia, having paid up to $1,400 for a ticket (Tomlinson 2004: 156).

Those who planned the opening ceremony were very much aware that the international success of the film *The Man from Snowy River* would enable its commanding score to work as a powerful signifier for rural Australia. The "welcome" sequence commenced with a horseman entering the arena, followed by other stockmen and women riding to the theme music from the film. It was the largest "musical ride" (where horses and riders perform to music) ever staged. Kym Johnson, one of the participants, explained, "It all started with an ad in several horse magazines, newspapers, newsletters and of course word of mouth" that "very special riders were needed for an Olympic event" (Smith 2001: 67).

The performance was designed to highlight Australia's rich equestrian background (Vergoulis and Cho 2000). All 120 riders in the "bush cavalry" entered the arena carrying a white flag, with the five Olympic rings displayed in the aqua blue colour of the sea – a colour selected because the sea unites all nations of the world and occupies two-thirds of the planet. The Olympic colours of red, blue, green, yellow and black were represented by the riders' scarves. Five teams of twenty-four horses and riders formed a long line, rode across the dirt-covered arena, then peeled off to the sides and eventually circled the perimeter of the performance area. The next formation was the five Olympic rings, then five crosses, symbolising the main stars of the Southern Cross constellation. Channel 7 announcer Garry Wilkinson began the official commentary by emphasising the Australian imagery and symbolism of the horse-riding spectacle: "From the outback and from the mountains to the sea, Sydney and this pioneering land Australia welcome the world to the Games of the XXVIIth Olympiad in a real Aussie way."

When the rider who performed the role of "The Man" entered Stadium Australia, he was deliberately portrayed as "small and weedy" (echoing Paterson's poem) by the television cameras. He was instantly dwarfed by the huge size of the arena and the camera angles carefully selected by Peter Faiman, the director in charge of the mammoth telecast. The national significance of this particular image may also have suggested to some that a small country like Australia was about to take on the weighty responsibilities entrusted to it by the International Olympic Committee in staging the 2000 Olympic Games. The welcome sequence included impressive displays of riding in formation by horses and riders, a stirring fanfare and the national anthem.

The epic saga "The Man from Snowy River" has played a central role in the Australian consciousness in so many ways. The popular live performance of "The Man" which began the Sydney Olympic Games has been reproduced in a number of live forms – most recently in an ongoing production performed since 2006 on Queensland's Gold Coast which goes by the name of "Australian Outback Spectacular". In 2001, a similar performance to that of the opening ceremony was staged at Sydney's Royal Easter Show.

When Australia hosted the Asia Pacific Economic Cooperation in 2007, twenty-one world leaders were paraded on the steps of the Sydney Opera House for the traditional summit "class photograph" sporting Driza-Bone coats – the popular weather-proof coat worn mainly by those who live in rural and regional Australia. The coats were trimmed in the colours of mustard yellow, red ochre, slate blue or eucalyptus green, representing Australia's sun and sandy beaches, outback, sky and bush respectively. To reinforce Australian culture, along with dining on the best food and wine, the leaders and their spouses were presented with Akubra hats, Australian art, folders made from kangaroo skin, and black opals.

The R. M. Williams name has come for many to represent good-quality boots (colloquially known as "RMs"; see Figure 6.2). Reginald Murray Williams (1908–2003) has become part of Australian folklore. In 1932 he made a pair of boots for himself, and then quickly produced a range of tough clothes and horse-riding equipment. He soon established a mail-order business to meet the increasing demand for his products, and the RM annual catalogues remain a key aspect of the company's success to this day. Not surprisingly, the organisation boasts a long and proud equestrian heritage. Williams played a prominent role in forming the Equestrian Federation of Australia (which boasts around 14,000 members, more than 28,000 horses and 500 affiliated clubs) and the Australian Stock Horse Society (with more than 100,000 registered stock horses). He also founded the Australian Rough Riders' Association and played a vital role in the creation of the Stockman's Hall of Fame, the National Horse Trail and the Bicentennial

Figure 6.2 A well-worn pair of R. M. Williams boots – colloquially referred to as "RMs".

Cattle Drive. Apart from the Australian Outback Spectacular, the company sponsors the Outback Stockman's Show and the annual Longreach Muster. In the late 1940s, the R. M. Williams magazine *Hoof and Horns* spread the corporate message, while today the *Outback* magazine performs the same role.

In 2001, R. M. Williams launched a travelling retail store, the "Longhorn Express", which makes its way from country music events to bush festivals and local agricultural shows. This distinctive store is a custom-made prime mover which converts into a shop. In 2004 the company moved more overtly into the tourism business by developing Wrotham Park Lodge, a 600,000-head working cattle station and exclusive resort on the Mitchell River in the far north of Queensland. Its chief executive officer, Hamish Turner, explained that moving into tourism made sense for the company, because "international tourism makes up 30 per cent of total retail sales. They see it as buying a piece of Australia and taking it with them" (Tarrant 2004: 14). Significant amounts of company memorabilia and seventy-fifth anniversary editions of the boot were produced in 2008.

There is no doubt that various texts of "The Man from Snowy River" hold a special place in the Australian national psyche. Countless commercial operators have profited from the inherent drama of Paterson's legend, whether it be through its numerous mediated forms, events, fashion labels or equestrian experiences aimed squarely at the paying tourist. While the story of "The Man" in its many incarnations has been part of Australian culture for over a century, it shows no sign of losing momentum and remains Australia's favourite and most influential bush legend. The magnificence of the horse and extraordinary skills of the rider that

Figure 6.3 Some impressive wrought-iron work at the Flemington racecourse winning post.

accompany this prominent myth have earned special places in the Australian national identity.

The horse in Australian sport: "the race that stops a nation"

Horse-racing is often referred to as "the sport of kings". The horse industry is one of Australia's largest, and racing in particular is only marginally smaller than the largest service enterprise – that of pubs, clubs and restaurants (Pilkington and Wilson 1993: 86). "The track" is a significant recreational space for many Australians. Racing is valued at more than $7.7 billion a year and employs around 250,000 people (Nicholson 2005: 16). In Victoria it generates around $2 billion annually and employs more than 64,000 people. The Spring Racing Carnival, with the Melbourne Cup, is the main event on the racing calendar and plays a central role in tourism in the state.

Australia's first race meeting was held at Sydney's Hyde Park in 1810 and the first Melbourne Cup took place just over fifty years later, in 1861, at Flemington racecourse (see Figure 6.3). The cup awarded to the winner, known as the "loving cup", was first presented in 1919. With a total prize pool of around $6 million in 2010, the 3,200-metre race is generally considered the most prestigious handicap in the world. Known as "the *race* that stops a nation", it is considered an Australian institution and is run on the first Tuesday of November each year, when most Australians stop what they are doing in order to watch or listen.

As for many years the race has regularly attracted more than 100,000 people, the Victorian Racing Club now pre-sells a set number of tickets. Unlike other countries, Australia holds public holidays to allow people to celebrate its leading horse-racing days (Ward 2010: 18), and in the home state the day was declared a public holiday as early as 1875. The event is known just as much as a corporate hospitality and fashion event as it is for excessive betting. On Cup Day gambling is elevated to something of an art form, and the race attracts thousands of people who do not bet at any other time during the year. As the Melbourne Cup is a handicap race, the heavily backed favourite does not normally win. On this day almost everyone in the country suddenly becomes an expert punter and the reasons for picking a winner are many and varied.

Melbourne Cup Day has become a tradition, a carnival, and a time for families and friends to get together and celebrate with parties and sparkling wine. The Spring Racing Carnival (marketed as "the *celebration* that stops a nation") takes place over fifty days from early October to late November and attracts the world's best horses and jockeys. While the focus of the Spring Carnival is firmly on Flemington racecourse, the carnival involves thirteen metropolitan and sixty-nine country race days and generates more than $600 million for the economy in Victoria (Racing Victoria 2007: 6–7). Flemington is one of the world's great horse-racing venues and was added to the National Heritage List in 2006. Around the same time, the racecourse received a $25 million makeover, with a new track comprising almost half the renovation bill. On the ceiling of the hill stand is Australia's largest and most detailed mural, with a simple yet all-encompassing title, *The History of Racing*. The mural, commissioned by the Victoria Racing Club for Australia's Bicentenary in 1988, comprises seven panels and is the work of the artist Harold Freedman.

In the glamorous world of Australian racing, a number of horses, trainers, jockeys and owners have earned a special place in popular culture. The most famous horse is undoubtedly the chestnut gelding Phar Lap – ironically a New Zealand-born horse. Phar Lap (the name means "lightning") was known as "Australia's Wonder Horse" and the "Red Terror", and was considered the people's champion in a similar way to the Australian cricket legend Don Bradman – partly because he became a symbol of hope to many during the Great Depression. However, in more recent times, the importance of this legendary horse to the Australian people has been called into question by at least one historian (Lemon 2010).

Phar Lap had won almost every major race in Australia – and many of them on more than one occasion. As a result, he was not popular with some – particularly bookies. In 1930, a gunman in a passing car attempted to shoot the iconic horse when he was being taken for a walk near Caulfield racecourse in Melbourne. Two years later, at the height of his international career, Phar Lap died under mysterious circumstances in San Francisco, having won the prestigious Agua Caliente Handicap in Mexico a few weeks earlier. In June 2008 forensic tests finally confirmed the long-standing rumour that the champion horse had died as a result of arsenic poisoning. While it had long been suspected that he had been killed by

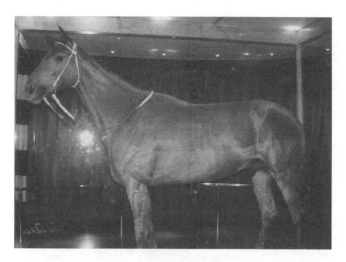

Figure 6.4 Phar Lap now takes pride of place in a glass cabinet at the Melbourne Museum.

Americans, it would appear that Phar Lap was most likely accidentally killed by his trainer Tommy Woodcock (Dale 2006: 66).

Phar Lap's remains are scattered across the Tasman. His skeleton is displayed at the Museum of New Zealand, while his 14-pound heart can be viewed at the National Museum of Australia in Canberra. Phar Lap's stuffed hide takes pride of place in a large glass cabinet in a red-curtained room at the Melbourne Museum (see Figure 6.4), where it has been the most popular exhibit since 1933. In 1981, the horse and cabinet were even "trotted out" to Flemington racecourse, though curators no longer dare to move it. Numerous books, songs and movies have been written about this well-known and much-loved horse. In 1983, the film *Phar Lap* was a box-office success, with $9 million in ticket sales.

In the domain of Australian sport, comparisons are often made between legends, even if these appear rather futile – and that has certainly been the case with Phar Lap and the champion Olympic swimmer Ian Thorpe. Thorpe's body size and shape also generated a fair share of interest in the media, much being made of his size 17 shoes. Ironically, Phar Lap was an impressive 17 hands tall. Thorpe's intriguing feet enhance his legendary status: "maybe his feet are a little too large, but that just adds to the legend and mystique of the man . . . a little bit like Phar Lap with his XOS heart". In an article in the *Herald Sun*, the swimmer is again compared with the famous horse, as "Big Foot versus Big Red" (Brundrett 2002: 19).

Before Phar Lap, the stallion Carbine was considered to be Australia's greatest thoroughbred horse (Pierce and Kirkwood 1994: 39). Known fondly as "Old Jack", Carbine, the great-great grandfather of Phar Lap, won the 1889 and 1890 Melbourne Cup races and was probably Australia's first hero of the turf. In the

Figure 6.5 A statue at Flemington racecourse honours Makybe Diva's three successive cup
wins.

1890 race, he beat a field of thirty-nine starters (the largest ever assembled) while
carrying a phenomenal 65 kilograms (a record weight). On account of careful
breeding, Carbine's powerful pedigree lived on in a large proportion of Melbourne
Cup champions in the twentieth century.

Between 2003 and 2005, the mare Makybe Diva (see Figure 6.5) made racing
history when she became the first horse to win three successive Melbourne Cup
races. After her thrilling win in 2005, when she carried 58 kilograms, her owner
Tony Santic announced that, having performed above and beyond everyone's
expectations, the "people's horse" should be immediately retired (Rolfe 2008:
365). A new and seemingly impossible benchmark had now been set.

One particular trainer who has developed a special affinity with the Australian
public is James Bartholomew Cummings. As Les Carlyon explained in the fore-
word to Cummings's autobiography, "No one in Australian sport is as Australian
as he is" (Cummings 2009: vii). He has trained twelve Melbourne Cup winners –
more than twice as many as any other trainer. Bart, as he is affectionately known,
had his first winner in 1965 with the horse Light Fingers, and his most recent win
with Viewed in 2008. He has also trained nine placegetters and seventy-eight Cup
runners since 1958 (ibid.: 373). At eighty-three years of age, Bart shows no signs
of slowing down and plans to continue working with horses for as long as he is
able. Michael Lynch explains that, if single-name status is the measure of achiev-
ing significant cultural status, "Bart is already there". He adds that Australian
children will learn "the roll call of Bart's dynamic dozen . . . just as readily as
they learn the national anthem" (Lynch 2009: 12). Cummings was made a

Figure 6.6 A statue at Flemington racecourse honours "Cups King" Bart Cummings.

Member of the Order of Australia in 1982, named one of Australia's Living Treasures in 1997, inducted into the Racing Hall of Fame in 2001, and had a stamp issued in his honour by Australia Post in 2007. Despite the many awards, Cummings remains humble and jokes that the statue made in his honour (see Figure 6.6) is a great attraction for the pigeons at Flemington.

Conclusion

The Melbourne Cup and "The Man from Snowy River" now hold special places in the Australian psyche, their fascinating stories having been part of Australian culture for over a century and certainly showing no sign of losing momentum. Both have successfully crossed the urban/rural divide and the generational divide and have formed deep and enduring roots in the Australian national identity.

As Banjo Paterson wrote his ballad in 1895, the laws of copyright cannot prevent those who choose to copy, create, cultivate and commercially benefit from the telling and retelling of the story in a variety of forms. "The Man from Snowy River" has stood the test of time as an inexhaustible media phenomenon, the source of an essential part of Australia's national costume, and an indispensable tourist attraction into the twenty-first century.

The central role of the horse on the most important day in the Australian sporting calendar cannot be underestimated. On the first Tuesday of each November, Melbourne Cup champions are celebrated in Australia and across the world. "The Cup" is much more than the most anticipated race of the year – it is Australia's biggest social event. In 1895 the American author Mark Twain claimed: "The Melbourne Cup is the Australasian National Day. It would be difficult to overstate its importance" (Cavanough *et al.* 2001: 5).

References

Brundrett, R. (2002) "Bradman of the Pool", *Herald Sun*, 6 August, p. 19.

Cavanough, M., and Davies, M. (1971) *The Melbourne Cup: Complete History and Statistics*. Sydney: Pollard.

Cavanough, M., Kirkwood, R., and Meldrum, B. (2001) *The Melbourne Cup, 1861–2000*. Melbourne: Crown Content.

Cummings, J. B. (2009) *Bart: My Life*. Sydney: Macmillan.

Dale, D. (2006) *Who We Are: A Miscellany of the New Australia*, Crows Nest, NSW: Allen & Unwin.

Dennis, A. (2002) "Just can't get enough of 'The Man'", *Sydney Morning Herald*, 18 June.

Lemon, A. (2010) *The History of Australian Thoroughbred Racing*, Vol. 3: *In Our Time: 1939 to 2007*. Melbourne: Hardie Grant Books.

Loland, S. (2004) "The vulnerability thesis and its consequences: a critique of specialization in Olympic sport", in J. Bale and M. Krogh Christensen (eds) *Post-Olympism? Questioning Sport in the Twenty-First Century* (pp. 189–99). New York: Berg.

Lynch, M. (2009) "View from on high", *The Age* (Sport supplement), 18 October, p. 12.

Mosler, D. (2002) *Australia: The Recreational Society*. Westport, CT: Praeger.

Nicholson, R. (2005) *The Track: Australian Racing's Hall of Fame*. Southbank, Vic.: News Custom Publishing.

Pierce, P., and Kirkwood, R. (1994) *From Go to Whoa: A Compendium of the Australian Turf*. East Melbourne: Crossbow.

Pilkington, M., and Wilson, G. (1993) *Australian Horses as a Primary Industry: Numbers, Organisation and Research Needs*. Canberra: Australian Government Publishing Service.

Racing Victoria (2007) *2007 Spring Racing Carnival Guide*. Melbourne: Racing Victoria Limited.

Rolfe, C. (2008) *Winners of the Melbourne Cup: Stories that Stopped a Nation*. Fitzroy, Vic.: Red Dog.

Semmler, C. (1982) "Introduction", in D. Parker (ed.) *A Tribute to the Man from Snowy River*. Sydney: Angus & Robertson.

Smith, L. (2001) *Living is Giving: The Volunteer Experience*. Sydney: Playright.

Tarrant, D. (2004) "Riding with R. M. Williams", *Business Express*, June, pp. 11–14.

Tomlinson, A. (2004) "The Disneyfication of the Olympics? Theme parks and freak-shows of the body", in J. Bale and M. Krogh Christensen (eds) *Post-Olympism? Questioning Sport in the Twenty-First Century* (pp. 147–63). New York: Berg.

Vergoulis, J., and Cho, J. (2000) "Games info: the who's who and what's what of the opening ceremony", www.gamesinfo.com.au/of/ar/arofoc.html (accessed 18 April 2007).

Ward, T. (2010) *Sport in Australian National Identity: Kicking Goals*. London: Routledge.

Warneke, R. (2000) "Games win gold", *The Age* (Green Guide supplement), 28 September, p. 6.

White, L. (2009) "The Man from Snowy River: Australia's bush legend and commercial nationalism", *Tourism Review International*, 13(2): 139–46.

Part II
Culture and community

7 Tourism's role in the national identity formulation of the United Kingdom's Pakistani diaspora

Nazia Ali and Andrew Holden

Introduction

This chapter examines the role played by the "myth of return" in the making and remaking of a diasporic Pakistani national identity in the context of diaspora tourism – the return visit of UK Pakistanis to their ancestral homeland. The premise is to illustrate the importance of diaspora tourism in preserving the "myth of return" in the minds of the UK Pakistani community, which subsequently contributes to the (re-)creation of a national identity. The chapter contributes to the existing debate on the "myth of return" in post-migration tourism (see Ali and Holden 2006) and the "ways in which individuals experience identity *through* tourism" (Palmer 2005: 7). Importantly, the discussion further develops Benedict Anderson's (1983) concept of "imagined communities" by recognising tourism – intertwined with the "myth of return" – as an emblem of a (diasporic) Pakistani national identity, which is of equal significance to a flag, a national anthem and the homeland in the minds of migrant communities. Thus, this manifestation of the "myth of return" in tourism is recognised as imperative to comprehending such aspects of an "imagined community" as nation, nationalism and national identity. The current work emphasises the preservation of the "myth of return" many years after migration to Britain, which continues to shadow the articulation of a Pakistani national identity. The fieldwork is based upon an interpretive ethnographic study with the Pakistani community of Bury Park in Luton.

The "myth of return"

Definitions of the word "myth" are wide and varied and, as Segal (2004) notes, there is no consensus across disciplines upon an agreed meaning. Several understandings centre upon narratives of the past (Bascom 1965), stories/tales deemed to be true (Kirk 1984), stereotyping (Sardar 1998) and communication of meanings (Giles and Middleton 2008). Barthes (1973: 143), in his seminal text *Mythologies*, notes that the concept of myth "organises a world" for human beings, which provides justifications and explanations for actions that might otherwise remain incomprehensible. Giles and Middleton (2008: 114) build on Barthes's meaning to highlight the relationship between myths and historical happenings in ordering a collective consciousness. Moreover, they assert: "We cannot simply dismiss myth as falsehood, lies, fiction. Instead, we need to engage with the ways in which myth interacts with everyday life to produce certain behaviours and understandings of the world at a specific moment" (2008: 116).

The intention here is not to present a transdisciplinary review of definitions of myth but to identify a suitable explanation of the concept in the context of national identity and diaspora tourism. Therefore, the understanding of both Barthes (1973) and Giles and Middleton (2008) have relevance to the current work because their comprehension draws attention to the continuation of myths long after a historical event, such as migration, has occurred.

As a type of myth, the "myth of return", or what Brah (1996: 16) refers to as an "ideology of return", is common among many migrant communities arriving in host societies, whether as a consequence of forced or of voluntary migration (Stopes-Roe and Cochrane 1990; Al-Rasheed 1994; Cohen and Gold 1997; Kershen 2005). In conceptualising this, Cohen and Gold highlight the illusionary dimension of the term:

> The two words, myth (usually a fantasy) and return (maybe a reality), connote a wishful fantasy, or belief, of immigrants that, in an unspecified date in the future, they will return permanently to their homeland. While aspirations to return are not regarded by the migrants as a myth, they become a social myth because they never materialise despite the fact that they are commonly expressed by many migrants of different ethnic origins.
>
> Cohen and Gold (1997: 375)

However, some migrants do transform the fantasy into reality by returning to live permanently in their homelands. For example, Kulu and Tammaru (2000) observe the return of Estonians from Russia following the break-up of the Soviet Union, while Portuguese (and Turkish) migrants to Germany fulfilled the myth by resettling in their native countries in the mid-1980s (Klimt 2000); similarly, Ramji (2006) observed the return "home" of retired British-Hindu Guajarati Indians to Gujarat.

Imagined communities, imagined homelands

Just as the notion of the "myth of return" may be important to those in the diaspora in their connection with the homeland, mythical bonds are critical for maintaining this relationship. As Billig (1995: 74) comments: "a nation is more than an imagined community of people, for a place – a homeland – also has to be imagined". A "homeland myth" fuels the imaginary creation of the natal nation, consequently influencing the sense of national identities of people living in a diaspora (Rahemtullah 2009). Thus the maintenance of mediums such as storytelling, photographs and interaction with elders is critical for a connection to the homeland. As Butler (2001: 200) observes, an ethos of diaspora is based upon "shared memories and myths around which this unique type of imagined community is built". For example, language, cultural symbols and shared biographies are important to the maintenance of a sense of Israeli identity among the diaspora in Toronto (Cohen and Gold 1997).

Travel also has a role to play in the maintenance of the relationship with the homeland, a common pattern being to visit family and relatives and to maintain cultural links. Tourism studies investigations reveal that diasporic communities regularly travel or return to countries reflective of their national identity through participating in diaspora tourism, a form of tourism that is "primarily produced, consumed and experienced by diasporic communities" (Coles and Timothy 2004: 1).

Those who may be labelled as participating in diaspora tourism are individuals and groups who share a "myth of return" and wish to travel to their place of origin to reaffirm their national identity (Nguyen *et al.* 2003; Duval 2004; Hall and Duval 2004; Stephenson 2004a, 2004b; Ali and Holden 2006). Hollinshead (2004: 46), employing Bhabha's (1994) postcolonial perspective, recognises diaspora tourism as "discursive spaces of identity-making and identity-projection for 'restless' diasporic people with hybrid identities". This draws attention to the role of diaspora tourism, which functions to bind the "multiple ties" (social, cultural and national) to the homeland (Duval 2004: 58). Diaspora tourism is particularly relevant to understanding the extent to which tourism is formulated to have potential influences on constructions of national identity and to comprehend the role of tourism in reforging links with the ancestral homeland to sustain "imagined communities" and to preserve the illusion of return.

However, returning to one's place of origin is sometimes rooted in sentiments of ambivalence and discontentment (King 1984; Yocum 1996; Ramji 2006). Returnees may be confronted by places that are largely unrecognisable as a consequence of social-economic changes, particularly if they have delayed their visit for several years, presenting them with what King (1984: 162) refers to as "a kind of culture shock". The consequent feeling of unfamiliarity with where they came from may lead to subsequent difficulties in the articulation of their "authentic" national identity, which is shadowed by pre-migration conceptions (Ramji 2006). The resulting challenges that are faced by individuals in a diaspora in locating their national identity, especially with the passage of time, are aptly summarised in the postcolonial narrative of Salman Rushdie:

> all migrants leave their pasts behind, although some try to place it into bundles and boxes – but on the journey something seeps put of the treasured mementoes and old photographs, until even their owners fail to recognise them, because it is the fate of migrants to be stripped of history, to stand naked amidst the scorn of strangers.
>
> (1983: 63)

The Pakistani diaspora and the "myth of return"

The focus of this chapter is the influence of travel and tourism to the homeland on the identity of the Pakistani diaspora in England. The emigration of thousands of Pakistanis to Britain, or the "promised land", began in the late 1950s and early 1960s. The common motive of migration was economic, to accumulate enough wealth in order to return to Pakistan and attain a higher standard of living (Ballard 1994) – the emphasis being upon a return to the homeland. The migrants settled in the industrial areas of England, typically working in the textile, construction and manufacturing industries (Shaw 1988; Werbner 1990). However, while they were originally encouraged to migrate to the United Kingdom as "guest workers" to fill gaps in the workforce, and always had the intention of returning to Pakistan, on account of the economic opportunities on offer they progressively became "settlers" (Khan 1977). So, "although many Pakistanis continue to hope that they will return home to Pakistan, most of them are in Britain for good . . . their stay in Britain has been prolonged indefinitely" (Werbner 1990: 152).

The act of returning to Pakistan on a permanent basis weakened organisations developed to facilitate links and ties between the diaspora and the homeland. Such organisations were termed by Khan (1977) the "institutions of migration" and included travel agents and national airlines. Their importance in facilitating links to the homeland continues, according to Stopes-Roe and Cochrane (1990: 192), to influence the mindset of the Pakistani diaspora in England: "a purposeful desire to return might be expected to have an effect in preserving customs, traditions and relationships that would be considered essential for renewed living in the country of origin". Although this statement was made twenty years ago, the "myth of return" among the UK Pakistani diaspora has been noted as being in a state of revival following 9/11 and the "war on terror", which has marginalised many British Pakistanis. Subsequently, as Bolognani (2007: 65), comments: "an imaginary homeland is the antidote to frustration: if things are not good here for younger transnationals, they need to believe that elsewhere there is a place where working towards personal well-being is possible."

The Pakistani diaspora and national identity

The first-generation Pakistani migrants, who arrived in the United Kingdom in the late 1950s, identify strongly with their place of birth (Modood *et al.* 1994). For second-generation Pakistanis, the majority of whom were born in Britain or experienced virtually all of their schooling here, the formation of identity is more complex, as it is a synthesis of the "old" and the "new" (Anwar 1998). Within the diaspora, the "old" facets of a Pakistani national identity are often being "hyphenated" to "new" national identities that emerge through interactions and contact with British society. A common theme in social research is that, in contrast to the original migrants, successive generations of Pakistanis born in the UK more readily recognise an association with the British nation (Ellis 1991; Knott and Khokher 1993; Husain and O'Brien 2000; Runnymede Trust 2000; Werbner 2000; Ansari 2002; Thompson 2002). Pakistani national identity in this chapter is therefore considered in a diasporic context which recognises the hybrid nature of nationalistic attachments both with and beyond the ancestral nation.

Research setting and methodological issues

The Pakistani diasporic community in Luton in the UK has since 1971 been the largest group of immigrants in the town (Luton Borough Council 2003) and in 2001 constituted 9.2 per cent of the population (National Statistics 2001). Major reasons for settling in Luton were the employment opportunities available in such large industrial companies as Electrolux, Vauxhall and Skefko (Luton Borough Council 2003). The community is now into its third generation. However, despite this legacy of settlement, events in the first decade of the twenty-first century have challenged perceptions of national identity. Apart from the global ramifications of the attacks of 11 September 2001, British-born Pakistanis were involved in race riots in the towns of Oldham, Leeds, Burnley and Bradford. The riots provided a disconcerting image of race relations in Britain and the frustration among British-born Pakistanis concerning their status and access to opportunities in society (Kundnani 2001; Bagguley and Hussain 2003a, 2003b; Hussain and Bagguley 2005). This was aptly captured by Kundnani (2001: 105), who commented that these "race" riots depicted Britain as a nation "fragmented by colour lines, class lines and police lines. It was the violence of hopelessness." The questioning of identity was reinforced by the suicide bombings in London on 7 July 2005 carried out by British-born Pakistani Muslims (Anon 2005).

It was against this background that the main fieldwork for this chapter took place, involving four Pakistani families and a local Asian women's group during 2004 and 2005. Framed in an interpretive ethnographic approach, utilising semi-structured interviews, focus groups and participant observations, rich data was sought to aid understanding. The sample comprised twenty-four informants: ten were first-generation Pakistanis born in Pakistan, twelve were second-generation Pakistanis whose parents had been born in the UK, and two were third-generation Pakistanis. Here we draw upon the data collected from three of the four families, as the informants' responses relate closely to tourism and national identity: Mr and Mrs Khalid and their daughter Shazia; Mrs Salim and her son Nasir and daughter Tabassum; and Mrs Shafi, a second-generation Pakistani, married with two children. Three second-generation research participants, Mina, Rubina and Shenaz from the women's group, are also referred to in the results. Pseudonyms have been given to all informants to protect their identity.

At the heart of the conduct of study was the interpretive philosophical perspective, central to interpreting the meanings Pakistanis attach to their tourism journeys. Hughes (1990: 89) argues that fieldworkers adopting an interpretive philosophical stance are an essential part in the construction of meanings, because "experiences of others can be grasped through the apprehension of their inner meaning". To develop interpretive practice, our work drew upon Geertz's (1973) anthropological theory on the "interpretation of cultures". The central premise in Geertz's theory is that culture is transmitted through such symbols as speech, art, text or music, which, as public displays of cultural practices, can be observed, recorded and analysed. Interpretations of culture should consist of "thick descriptions" of human behaviours discovered through "peeling" away strips of reality. According to Geertz (1973: 37): "as one analyses man [*sic*], one peels of layer after layer, each such layer being complete and irreducible in itself, revealing another, quite different sort of layer underneath." Therefore interpretive research philosophy contributes to examining the meanings and experiences of tourism among the Pakistani community, in association with such related characteristics of national identity as ethnicity, culture, diaspora and migration.

"Thematic analysis" was used to examine the data collected. Thematic analysis is a means of generating thick descriptions of human behaviour in ethnographic studies and of organising data for interpretive scrutiny (Holliday 2002). In ethnographic conduct, it involves "indexing the data into categories and themes" (Brewer 2000: 109). In tourism research, Stephenson (2002) and Duval (2003) carried out thematic analysis of their interpretive ethnographic data to produce interpretively rich texts. The two main themes were selected for this investigation in order to examine their interrelationships: tourism participation and identity. In order to comprehend tourism's role in national identity formulation for the UK Pakistani diaspora, we examined (i) visits to Pakistan and national identity; (ii) British Pakistanis and the "myth of return"; and (iii) the future impact of the "myth of return" upon national identity.

Visiting the "homeland" and national identity

Within the community, tourism is predominantly understood as visiting the ancestral homeland, and definitions and understandings were typically discussed in the context of returning to Pakistan. For the first generation it featured as an essential component in understanding and negotiating a diasporic national identity. Similarly, the second generation referred to their parents' natal country to substantiate the meanings of their national identity. For the first generation, the return home for a minimum of six weeks was an opportunity to reconnect with their roots. The desire to "relive" the past and provoke memories of life before migration was a common theme among informants. Visits also served the purpose of reducing levels of discontent associated with not returning for permanent settlement. When first-generation informants were asked to define their identity, the natal nation and pre-migration lives were symbolically significant in the responses:

Mr Khalid: I am a Pakistani . . . Pakistan is my homeland, that is where I was born, but brought up here [Britain] . . . Just the way of life there . . . you know . . . it is just the love of Pakistan really . . . my homeland really. It symbolises me . . . yes, my background. I mean I have been brought up here since I was eight but will always call myself a Pakistani really . . . because that is where I was born . . . the culture

... the way of life there [Pakistan] I prefer that ... I have to live here not out of my choice. I just have to.

Mrs Khalid: The real thing I am is Pakistani ... I have British nationality ... but in my mind I don't feel British, I still see myself as Pakistani ... I was born in Pakistan, my mum, dad are there ... I was brought up there [Pakistan] ... I have never really thought of myself as British ... for me, I just want to go to Pakistan ... We always say when we go we will settle [in Pakistan] with the children, we haven't been able to ... The culture is different, especially for my children, who are very different.

Mrs Salim: [I am] Pakistani ... I was born in Pakistan ... I went to school there, I made swings with my friends, and playing in the fields it was so nice ... If I wasn't born there that would be another story ... that is where I come from. I remember a lot about Pakistan ... I like going to Pakistan ... no, I love going to Pakistan.

In contrast, the second-generation Pakistanis recognised themselves as being both British and Pakistani, or British-Pakistani. They were adamant in not overlooking their attachments to both nations, the dual identification being an amalgamation of their hybrid past, present and future. There was a desire to preserve their Pakistani identity in recognition of their parents' histories. Learning about their ancestral roots contributes to the maintenance of bonds with the homeland and socialises the second generation into following their parents' patterns of tourism. Examples of the aspirations of the second generation are shown in the following responses.

Tabassum: I am Pakistani ... [long pause] ... Pakistani because my parents are from Pakistan ... I go to Pakistan for my holidays and my grandparents are from Pakistan ... My history is in Pakistan ... it is the way I have been brought up, to accept I am Pakistani as well [as British].

Nasir: Going to Pakistan, to find out about being Pakistani ... it is OK to say I am Pakistani ... that is easy ... It is harder trying to find out about this ... I mean, I am not the same as the Pakistanis in Pakistan ... It does feel like I don't fit in because there will always be this British sign on my head ... which means I have to try harder to fit in ... It is OK for my parents and grandparents because they were born in Pakistan, grew up in Pakistan, they have nothing to prove about being Pakistani – instantly they are connected.

Shazia: [I am] Pakistani ... I feel really funny when I say Pakistani ... but then again I don't have that strong feeling like my parents have ... I think us new generation varies ... I think going back to Pakistan nourishes you again, because it reminds you obviously that is where you are from, that is me, that is my background.

The second generation were typically keen to use tourism as a means of reconstructing the Pakistani element of their dual national identity. This process is similar to Baldassar's observations of second-generation Italians in Australia who were planning to visit Italy. She notes: "the second generation see their visits as transformative, as important to their sense of ethnic identity" (Baldassar 2001: 10). Furthermore, second-generation Pakistanis were generally eager to travel to Pakistan as a measure to preserve a diasporic national identity because the ancestral nation was a central determinant of their transnational attachments. Nguyen and King (2004) found a similar outcome in their study of tourism patterns of the Vietnamese diaspora in Australia, stressing that the preservation of their identity is the central "push factor" for instigating a return to Vietnam.

Negotiating diasporic national identities

Tourism to the homeland, shadowed by the "myth of return", is a double-edged sword in terms of the making and remaking of a national identity. The Pakistani travellers, especially those of the second generation, understood the "myth of return" as offering not only an assurance but also spaces of ambivalence. The "myth of return" is utilised by the first generation as a means of strengthening the Pakistani identity of their British-born children. They have a fear that the younger generation may have a weaker attachment to Pakistan following their integration into British society, and so journeys are encouraged to maintain the ties to their roots.

Mr Khalid: I would take my children anytime to Pakistan and then take them to Pakistan again and again, because that is where our roots are, and as much as I can take them there they would know about their culture and religion.

Mrs Khalid: How I kept them [the children] since they were younger matters when they are older . . . They will know how their parents have lived and taught them . . . they will do the same. My children go with our culture, my culture, they understand my culture . . . they go as I tell them. I told them when they were younger, this is how I am living, going to Pakistan, this is how you should live . . . They got used to it, it is not difficult for them.

Mrs Salim: I remember everything when I go back to Pakistan, and I show my children these things as well . . . they should know so one day they can tell their children.

However, the second generation often experienced a sense of ambivalence towards their identity when visiting Pakistan. They were conscious of relatives there analysing their identity for traits of Britishness. Because they were not born in Pakistan, they felt they were being treated as "guest visitors", while their parents seemed to be accepted as part of the extended family. Thus, second-generation Pakistanis could not escape the hyphen in their identity, as they were always considered British-Pakistanis. The following statements highlight these sentiments.

Mrs Shafi: I don't feel like I entirely fit in with life in Pakistan . . . Relatives accept my parents more because they were born in Pakistan . . . With me, my husband and children, it is another story . . . we are British . . . we are seen as just Pakistani by name, not by heart.

Mina: Yeah, we [my brother and I] were still seen as the others – the way we hold ourselves, the way we walk, the way we talk . . . it was kind of, like, "Um, they are British", and we didn't feel we belonged . . . That is why I say this [Britain] is my country.

Rubina: OK, I am Pakistani . . . Travelling to Pakistan won't make me any more Pakistani . . . You see, they [relatives] still see you as British . . . the outsider . . . People stare like you have fallen out of space . . . watching you so closely.

This experience of being treated like a "guest" by kin in Pakistan gave rise to feelings of "unbelonging", even though their time was spent with people who were generally perceived to share a similar national identity. Tourism opens up what Bhabha (1994) refers to as a "third space" within which identity is negotiated. The identities of the second generation in the third space can be considered as endlessly "shifting" and "splitting". These Bhabhian concepts are applied by Hollinshead (1998: 148) to highlight the intervening role of tourism in the production of cultural hybridity. In these "chaordic spaces" (Werbner 2002) of national identity, participation in diaspora tourism is an indicator of the continued importance of the ancestral homeland on national identity formation, demonstrating the ability of second-generation Pakistanis to transmit aspects of their identity between societies.

The future of the "myth of return"

Tourism performs a pivotal role in the survival of the "myth of return" in the post-migration lives and imaginations of the Pakistani diaspora. It is through its embodiment in tourism that notions of self- and collective diasporic Pakistani national identity can be understood. Thus, the "myth of return" is a defining feature of what it means to be Pakistani and performs a functional role in maintaining attachments to the ancestral nation. It influences the travel patterns of second-generation Pakistanis, as indicated in the following statements.

Tabassum: It is not so bad going to Pakistan, because it shows relatives in Pakistan we haven't forgotten where we come from and we are not completely British.

Nasir: So far I have always gone with my parents to Pakistan . . . my parents use to go with their parents . . . It is like a family thing [travelling to Pakistan] . . . something passed down to the next generation.

Shenaz: Yes, yes, I follow their [parents'] patterns of tourism . . . I would like my children as well to keep going back to Pakistan, their country to where they belong . . . their culture, where their family is from.

However, they viewed Britain as their natal homeland and also as their "home". Travel movements shadowed by the "myth of return" tended to reiterate a sense of belonging "here" in the United Kingdom rather than "there" in Pakistan.

Nasir: It [England] is my homeland . . . this [Luton] is my home . . . I have lived here all my life . . . Everything I know is in Britain, I don't feel lost . . . when I am in Pakistan, home is Britain, this is where I come to.

Mrs Shafi: This [Britain] is my country, my homeland . . . I was born in this country . . . I was bred in this country . . . I can't take that out of my system . . . I say my ethnic origin is Pakistani but my nationality is British . . . Being British gives me a place in this world . . . I don't feel like I entirely fit in with the life in Pakistan . . . Relatives accept my parents more because they were born in Pakistan.

Mina: I would definitely say I am British Pakistani . . . British Pakistani . . . Well, where I was born, where I was brought up . . . my way of life . . . it is where my identity has been formed in this country [England] and a lot of identity is based around the British culture but there are hints of Pakistani . . . But that is why I empathise with British because that is where I am heavily attached to, but Pakistani because I think it is very important to be aware of your culture, your heritage, where your parents came from, where your grandparents came from, where your great-great grandparents came from . . . You know, going back the ancestral lines, it is important where you come from and that is very important part of your way of life as well.

Similarly, Qureshi, in her study of young British Pakistanis, found "cognitive conflicts" over not "fitting in" and the questioning of their identity during visits to Pakistan. One respondent, Zubeda, states she was considered "as British luggage from London" (Qureshi 2006: 221). Thus these cognitive conflicts challenge the survival of the "myth of return", as Britain as "home" for the second generation carries the emotional significance that Pakistan does as "home" for first generation. Despite a sometimes hostile social and political climate, the second generation expressed a greater affinity for life in Britain than in Pakistan and the aspiration to remain in the United Kingdom. However, the work of Bolognani (2007) challenges this finding, emphasising a strained relationship with mainstream British society post 9/11 that promotes allegiance to Pakistan. Based upon the results of this research, it is argued that tourism in the form of travel to Pakistan leads the second generation to have closer ties with Britain.

Conclusion

"Diaspora tourism" based upon return travel to Pakistan is important in formulating identity. While for the first generation it helps to perpetuate the "myth of return", for the second generation it leads to a questioning of association with the "homeland" of Pakistan, a sense that they are different. There exists a feeling of restlessness, arising from living in between a dual national identity – British by birth and Pakistani in origin.

Confusion over a sense of national identity when visiting Pakistan is characterised for the second generation by sentiments of ambivalence, as well as ambiguities and antagonism. They found that their sense of attachment to Pakistan was overshadowed by their British nationality and led to their feeling different to the indigenous population and their parents, making it difficult to integrate into the Pakistani host society. British-born Pakistanis are disenchanted to find that their relatives in Pakistan give precedence to the British component of their national identity, despite their engagement with the "myth of return" as a reflection of their diasporic identity. It is evident that such encounters give rise to new and different narratives of belonging, reinforcing the British component of national identity and challenging the perceived notion of the second generation's identity being defined by their parents' country of birth.

Based on this ethnography of the Pakistani community in Bury Park, Luton, it is evident that tourism and travel to the homeland has a significant influence on national identity. As global migration increases and diasporic communities diversify, the role of tourism in the formulation of identity is likely to be increasingly prominent. However, at present, research into these effects on the identity and behaviour of tourists is sparse. It is argued that understanding the experiences of different generations is a crucial component in attaining a more holistic understanding of the relationship between diaspora and national identity.

References

Ali, N., and Holden, A. (2006) "Post-colonial Pakistani mobilities: the embodiment of the 'myth of return' in tourism", *Mobilities*, 1(2): 217–42.

Al-Rasheed, M. (1994) "The myth of return: Iraqi Arab and Assyrian refugees in London", *Journal of Refugee Studies*, 7(2/3): 199–219.

Anderson, B. (1983) *Imagined Communities*. London: Verso.

Anon (2005) "Lahore to Leeds", *The Guardian*, 16 July [leader article], www.guardian.co.uk/uk/2005/jul/16/july7.pakistan (accessed 22 October 2010).

Ansari, H. (2002) *Muslims in Britain*. London: Minority Rights Group International.

Anwar, M. (1998) *Between Cultures: Continuity and Change in the Lives of Young Asians*. London: Routledge.

Bagguley, P., and Hussain, Y. (2003a) "The Bradford 'riot' of 2001: a preliminary analysis", paper presented at the ninth Alternative Futures and Popular Protest conference, Manchester, April.

Bagguley, P., and Hussain, Y. (2003b) "Conflict and cohesion: official constructions of 'community' around the 2001 'riots' in Britain", paper presented at the Communities Conference, Leeds, September.

Baldassar, L. (2001) *Visits Home: Migration Experiences between Italy and Australia*. Victoria: Melbourne University Press.

Ballard, R. (1994) "Introduction: The emergence of *desh pardesh*", in R. Ballard (ed.) *Desh Pardesh: The South Asian Presence in Britain*. London: Hurst.

Barthes, R. (1973) *Mythologies*. London: Granada.

Bascom, W. (1965) "The forms of folklore: prose narratives", *Journal of American Folklore*, 78(307): 3–20; www.jstor.org/stable/538099?seq=2 (accessed 7 June 2010).

Bhabha, H. K. (1994) *The Location of Culture*. London: Routledge.

Billig, M. (1995) *Banal Nationalism*. London: Sage.

Bolognani, M. (2007) "The myth of return: dismissal, survival or revival? A Bradford example of transnationalism as a political instrument", *Journal of Ethnic and Migration Studies*, 33(1): 59–76.

Brah, A. (1996) *Cartographies of Diaspora: Contesting Identities*. London: Routledge.

Brewer, J. D. (2000) *Ethnography*. Buckingham: Open University Press.

Butler, K. D. (2001) "Defining diaspora, refining discourse", *Diaspora*, 10(2): 189–218.

Cohen, R., and Gold, G. (1997) "Constructing ethnicity: myth of return and modes of exclusion among Israelis in Toronto", *International Migration*, 35(3): 373–94.

Coles, T. L., and Timothy, D. J. (2004) "My field is the world: conceptualizing diasporas, travel and tourism", in T. L. Coles and D. J. Timothy (eds) *Tourism, Diasporas and Space: Travels to the Promised Lands*. London: Routledge.

Duval, D. T. (2002) "The return visit–return migration connection", in C. M. Hall and A. M. Williams (eds), *Tourism and Migration*. Dordrecht: Kluwer Academic.

Duval, D. T. (2003) "When hosts become guests: return visits and diasporic identities in a Commonwealth Eastern Caribbean community", *Current Issues in Tourism*, 6(4): 267–308.

Duval, D. T. (2004) "Conceptualizing return visits: a transnational perspective", in T. L. Coles and D. J. Timothy (eds) *Tourism, Diasporas and Space: Travels to the Promised Lands*. London: Routledge.

Ellis, J. (1991) "Local government and community needs: a case study of Muslims in Coventry", *New Community*, 17(3): 359–76.

Geertz, C. (1973) *The Interpretation of Cultures*. London: Fontana.

Giles, J., and Middleton, T. (2008) *Studying Culture: A Practical Introduction*. 2nd edn, Oxford: Blackwell.

Hall, M. C., and Duval, D. T. (2004) "Linking diaspora and tourism: transnational mobilities of Pacific Islanders resident in New Zealand", in T. L. Coles and D. J. Timothy (eds) *Tourism, Diasporas and Space: Travels to the Promised Lands*. London: Routledge.

Holliday, A. (2002) *Doing and Writing Qualitative Research*. London: Sage.

Hollinshead, K. (1998) "Tourism, hybridity, and ambiguity: the relevance of Bhabha's 'third space' cultures", *Journal of Leisure Research*, 30(1): 121–56.

Hollinshead, K. (2004) "Tourism and third space populations: the restless motion of diaspora peoples", in T. L. Coles and D. J. Timothy (eds) *Tourism, Diasporas and Space: Travels to the Promised Lands*. London: Routledge.

Hughes, J. A. (1990) *The Philosophy of Social Research*. London: Longman.

Husain, F., and O'Brien, M. (2000) "Muslim communities in Europe: reconstruction and transformation", *Current Sociology*, 48(4): 1–13.

Hussain, Y., and Bagguley, P. (2005) "Citizenship, ethnicity and identity: British Pakistanis after the 2001 'riots'", *Sociology*, 39(3): 407–25.

Kershen, A. J. (2005) *Strangers, Aliens and Asians: Huguenots, Jews and Bangladeshis in Spitalfields 1660–2000*. London: Routledge.

Khan, V. S. (1977) "The Pakistani Mirpuri villagers at home and in Bradford", in J. L. Watson (ed.) *Between Two Cultures: Migrants and Minorities in Britain*. Oxford: Blackwell.

King, R. (1984) "Population mobility: emigration, return migration and internal migration", in A. Williams (ed.) *Southern Europe Transformed: Political and Economic Change in Greece, Italy, Portugal and Spain*. London: Harper & Row.

Kirk, G. S. (1984) "On defining myths", in A. Dundes (ed.) *Sacred Narrative: Readings in the Theory of Myth*. Berkeley: University of California Press.

Klimt, A. (2000) "European spaces: Portuguese migrants' notions of home and belonging", *Diaspora*, 9(2): 259–84.

Knott, K., and Khokher, S. (1993) "Religious and ethnic identity amongst Muslim women in Bradford", *New Community*, 19(4): 593–610.

Kulu, H., and Tammaru, T. (2000) "Ethnic return migration from the East and the West: the case of Estonia in the 1990s", *Europe–Asia Studies*, 52(2): 349–69.

Kundnani, A. (2001) "From Oldham to Bradford: the violence of the violated", *Race and Class*, 43(2): 105–31.

Luton Borough Council (2003) *Sticking Together: Embracing Diversity in Luton*. Luton: Community Cohesion Scrutiny Panel.

Modood, T., Beishon, S., and Virdee, S. (1994) *Changing Ethnic Identities*. London: Policy Studies Institute.

National Statistics (2001) "Census 2001", www.statistics.gov.uk (accessed 5 March 2004).

Nguyen, T. H., and King, B. (2004) "The culture of tourism in the diaspora: the case of the Vietnamese community in Australia", in T. L. Coles and D. J. Timothy (eds) *Tourism, Diasporas and Space: Travels to the Promised Lands*. London: Routledge.

Nguyen, T. H., King, B., and Turner, L. (2003) "Travel behaviour and migrant cultures: the Vietnamese in Australia", *Tourism Culture and Communication*, 4(2): 95–107.

Palmer, C. (2005) "An ethnography of Englishness: experiencing identity through tourism", *Annals of Tourism Research*, 32(1): 7–27.

Qureshi, K. (2006) "Trans-boundary spaces: Scottish Pakistanis and trans-local/national identities", *International Journal of Cultural Studies*, 9(2): 207–26.

Rahemtullah, O.-S. (2009) "Interrogating "Indianness": identity and diasporic consciousness among twice migrants", *Anthurium: A Caribbean Studies Journal*, 7(1/2); http://anthurium.miami.edu/volume_7/issue_1/rahemtullah-interrogatingindianness.html (accessed 22 October 2010).

Ramji, H (2006) "British Indians 'returning home': an exploration of transnational belongings", *Sociology*, 40(4): 645–62.

Runnymede Trust (2000) *The Future of Multi-Ethnic Britain: The Parekh Report*. London: Profile Books.

Rushdie, S. (1983) *Shame*. London: Vintage.

Sardar, Z. (1998) *Postmodernism and the Other*. London: Pluto Press.

Segal, R. A. (2004) *Myth: A Very Short Introduction*. Oxford: Oxford University Press.

Shaw, A. (1988) *A Pakistani Community in Britain*. Oxford: Blackwell.

Stephenson, M. L. (2002) "Travelling to the ancestral homelands: the aspirations and experiences of a UK Caribbean community", *Current Issues in Tourism*, 5(5): 378–425.

Stephenson, M. L. (2004a) "Tourism, racism and the UK Afro-Caribbean diaspora", in T. L. Coles and D. J. Timothy (eds) *Tourism, Diasporas and Space: Travels to the Promised Lands*. London: Routledge.

Stephenson, M. L. (2004b) "Tourism and racialised territories in Europe", paper presented at the conference "Borderless Frontiers and the Implications for Tourism in the New Enlarged European Union", Nicosia, Cyprus, December.

Stopes-Roe, M., and Cochrane, R. (1990) *Citizens of this Country: The Asian-British*, Clevedon: Multilingual Matters.

Thompson, K. (2002) "Border crossing and diasporic identities: media use and leisure practices of an ethnic minority", *Qualitative Sociology*, 25(3): 409–18.

Werbner, P. (1990) *The Migration Process: Capital, Gifts and Offerings amongst British Pakistanis*. Oxford: Berg.

Werbner, P. (2000) "Divided loyalties, empowered citizenship? Muslims in Britain", *Citizenship Studies*, 4(3): 307–24.

Werbner, P. (2002) "The place which is diaspora: citizenship, religion and gender in the making of chaordic transnationalism", *Journal of Ethnic and Migration Studies*, 28(1): 119–33.

Yocum, D. (1996) "Some troubled homecomings", in I. Chambers and L. Curtis (eds) *The Post-Colonial Question: Common Skies and Divided Horizons*. London: Routledge.

8 The 2008 Beijing Olympic Games and China's national identity

A host community perspective

Fang Meng and Xiang Li

Introduction

The modern Olympic Games, as one of the most important and popular hallmark events in the world, generates tremendous positive impacts for host cities and countries in terms of improved facilities and infrastructure, urban revival, international media attention, and increased business development opportunities (Hall 1987; French and Disher 1997; Weed 2007). Tourism growth and an enhanced national identity showcased to the world within and beyond the duration of the event are arguably the primary economic and social legacies sought by host cities and countries (Kang and Perdue 1994; Teigland 1999; Chalip 2000). Therefore, hosting the games may serve as a strategic tool to uplift and promote national image and identity on a large scale.

Globalization has provided growing international interconnections among societies, economies and cultures. The Olympics receive high-profile worldwide media attention not only while they are in progress, but also beforehand and afterwards. The constant media exposure can last around ten to twelve years, from a decision to bid for host status until the games become "a fading memory" (Weed 2007). The Olympic Games serve as a strategic tool to develop a global awareness of host cities and countries over a long period of time. The so-called Olympic opportunity includes a short-term boom in international tourism as well as the chance to uplift or reposition the overall image of the host destination in the long run (Chalip 2000). It has been revealed that countries such as Greece and Spain are still repositioning themselves through the Olympics (Quelch and Jocz 2005). Weed (2007) suggested that the pre-games tourism is derived from perceptions about the future of the event, whereas afterwards it is significantly affected by the perception of the games through attendees and media. It is therefore essential for the host cities and countries to build, enhance or reposition their national identity and image via the Olympic opportunity.

China's tourism industry has enjoyed fast growth over the past two decades. The Beijing Olympic Games, held between 8 and 24 August 2008, undoubtedly provided a tremendous opportunity for the country's tourism and for the projection of its national identity to the world community, and it marked "a watershed in China's continued long march toward a modernized, unified, and internationalized nation in the global community of nations" (Xu 2006: 91). More than 11,000 athletes from 204 countries competed in twenty-eight sports (Anet 2008). Over 4.7 billion viewers, or 70 percent of the world's population, watched the games, the largest audience ever (Nielsen 2008). Within China, the Beijing Olympics received tremendous public support (Tang 2001), and 94 percent of Chinese TV viewers tuned in to the coverage (Nielsen 2008). At the closing ceremony, Jacques Rogge, president of the International Olympic Committee, declared that the event was a "truly exceptional games" (Rogge 2008).

Starting from Beijing's first bid, for the 2000 Olympics, China was determined to turn the games into "the celebration of a Chinese renaissance and the harmonization of world civilizations" in an era of globalization (Xu 2006). Chinese people have traditionally linked sport with national salvation (Brownell 1995), and the very idea of "transform[ing] the 'sick man of East Asia' (*Dong Ya bingfu*) into a strong and modern nation respected by the world" has motivated generations of Chinese athletes (Xu 2006: 92). As such, hosting a highly successful Olympic Games, with Chinese athletes performing well, has been strongly associated with national pride and spirit. Further, the themes of "Green Olympics, High-tech Olympics, and People's Olympics" reflect the recently redefined national strategy based on the notion of "development for people" (*yi min wei ben*) and "building a 'harmonious socialist society' through the 'scientific and sustainable pursuit' of China's development" (ibid.: 97). China attached great political and symbolic significance to the Beijing Olympics "in terms of constructing national identity and pursuing international primacy" (ibid.: 104). The tourism industry in Beijing, as well as in the rest of China, also hoped to benefit from the Olympic Games. The China National Tourism Administration (CNTA) launched a multifaceted campaign built around the promotional theme "2008 China Olympic Tourism Year" (CNTA 2008) in order to broaden the influence of this mega-event.

As part of the strategy to establish and promote Beijing as a "global city," the hosting of the 2008 Olympic Games was listed by both the central national government of China and the municipal government of Beijing as one of the four themes of city development (Wei and Yu 2006). A key goal of the government was to display to the world a new image through promoting the traditional Chinese culture, history and development of Beijing, as well as the friendliness and hospitality of the Chinese people (BOCOG 2003). As Ritchard (2004) pointed out,

> Beijing 2008 will be the source of many "first impressions." The Games will be the most comprehensive [and nicely packaged] up-close look at China in half a century, and history will judge the event as the vehicle for demystifying the world's image of the country.
>
> (Ritchard 2004: 3)

Despite the impact of the Olympic Games in establishing the image and national identity of a country, empirical research is still lacking on how this mega-event influences the host country's national identity as perceived by its own people. This chapter attempts to provide an insight into the impact of the 2008 Beijing Olympic Games on the local community. The specific research objective is to examine the influences of the games on local Beijing residents' perceptions of national belonging and national identity construction.

The Olympic Games and its impact on the local community

Researchers have examined the impacts of events such as the Olympic Games on host cities and countries from different approaches – for example, the economic impact (Hall 1987; Kang and Perdue 1994; Kirkup and Major 2006; Madden 2002; Hiller 1998; Kasimati 2003); the social impact (Waitt 2001, 2003); environmental implications (May 1995); country image (Quelch and Jocz 2005); and the perception of the host country/residents (Ritchie and Lyons 1987, 1990; Ritchie and Aitken 1984, 1985; Ritchie and Smith 1991; Jeong and Faulkner 1996; Mihalik and Simonetta 1999; Deccio and Baloglu 2002). Increased employment opportunities, business investment and tourism revenues are perceived benefits of holding the Olympic Games (Jeong and Faulkner 1996; Ritchie and Lyons 1990). Negative impacts include price inflation, tax burdens, and the mismanagement of public funds or expenditures by organizers (Ritchie and Aitken 1984). The Olympics can impact on the local community by providing improved infrastructure and public facilities and better public transportation, while at the same time bringing greater traffic congestion, overcrowding and disruption to local residents' lives (Waitt 2001, 2003; May 1995).

Social exchange theory is commonly used in examining the residents' perceptions of the impacts of tourism (Ap 1992; Jurowski *et al.* 1997; Perdue *et al.* 1990, 1999; Waitt 2003). The theory accounts for divergent evaluations, primarily in terms of experiential or psychological outcomes (Waitt 2003). Feelings, perceptions or psychological states result from the experiences conveyed "symbolically through the objects exchanged, the functions performed by the exchange, or the meanings attributed to the exchange" (Bagozzi 1975: 38). The theory suggests that local residents perceive or evaluate tourism/events as having either positive or negative outcomes in terms of the expected benefits or costs.

Waitt (2003) provided a detailed explanation of the "antecedent conditions" of residents' positive or negative evaluations proposed in Searle's work (1991): rationality, the satisficing (a combination of satisfying and sufficing) of benefits, reciprocity, and the justice principle. In the tourism setting, rationality indicates that residents who perceive the rewards of maintaining and/or improving their social and economic well-being are likely to evaluate the event positively (Ap 1992). The satisficing of benefits implies that residents who perceive the positive aspects as outweighing the costs are likely to accept tourism even though they are aware of the negative effects. So, in the social exchange relationship, residents tend to seek a satisfactory, reasonable or acceptable level of benefits rather than the maximum advantages. Reciprocity proposes that the perceived rewards should equate to the residents' willingness both to carry the costs, burdens and inconveniences and to extend friendliness and hospitality to tourists. The justice principle indicates that the exchange ensures that residents receive reasonably fair and equal return for their support or participation.

Exchange relationships can differ in their individual and collective forms (Faulkner and Tideswell 1997). Therefore, residents' evaluations of tourism or events could vary depending on such intrinsic factors as their proximity to attractions and could be further readjusted by altruistic surplus in that an individual puts group interests ahead of his/her own. At the same time, extrinsic factors such as the stage of the development, the ratio of tourists to residents and the cultural differences between hosts and guests could also influence perceptions in social exchange relationships.

National identity and its connection with the Olympic Games

Although hosting an Olympic event may bring substantial benefits to a country/ city, some benefits (such as economic benefits) may remain debatable (ETOA 2006, 2008; Martin 2008). However, consensus has generally been reached that hosting the Olympic Games can help enhance community pride and promote the host country/city's culture and image (Brown *et al.* 2004; Long and Ma 2004; Ritchie 1989; Ritchie and Smith 1991; Waitt 2003; Mihalik and Simonetta 1999).

Brownell (1995: 314) suggested that today's Olympic Games have become "the world's largest single event for the production of national culture for international consumption." As such, their impact, as well as that of other international sporting events, on host country's national identity has long received multidisciplinary research attention (Hargreaves and Ferrando 1997; Hogan 2003; King 2000; Tervo 2002; Tomlinson and Young 2006; Wamsley and Heine 1996). For instance, Hargreaves and Ferrando (1997) conducted a political analysis of the impact of the 1992 Barcelona Olympic Games on Spain's national integration and national identity and concluded that they polarized relations between Catalonia and Spain. Hogan (2003), from a sociological perspective, analyzed the opening ceremonies of the games in Nagano (1998), Sydney (2000) and Salt Lake City (2002). She argued that the Olympics are "commercialized discourses of national identity," serving "not only as an affirmation of national identity but also as an extended advertisement for the host nation and an opportunity to promote tourism, international corporate investment, trade, and political ideologies." Most recently, Xu (2006) provided an insightful discussion on the socio-political implications of the 2008 Beijing Olympics on China's identity politics and international image and relations.

It has been suggested that nowadays national identity has become "vulnerable to the new supremacy of global information flows, and the power of increasingly multinational grids of investment, production and marketing" (Comer and Harvey 1991: 45). Indeed, part of the reason the Olympics have been frequently associated with national identity research is their role in promoting both universalism and nationalism, both tradition and change (Hogan 2003). The commitment of the Olympic Games, as an international event, is to stage a celebration of globalization and humanity, where people from all over the world join together as a family regardless of their differences. Nevertheless, rarely can one find more intense competition between nations. This is particularly true of the host country, which utilizes the games as a unique opportunity to present its national culture and promote its national pride to the world. Tradition and change present yet another "ideological tension" (ibid.: 104) inherent in the Olympics. Host countries always face the challenge of showcasing simultaneously their history and their socio-economic progress. The 2008 Beijing Olympics exemplified all these challenges and paradoxes.

Results and discussion

The empirical results of the study here come from a larger project examining the social, cultural and economic impacts of the Beijing Olympics on the local community, defined as the residents of Beijing who stayed in the city during the games. Data were collected three months after the games ended. Phone surveys took place by proportionate sampling through a random digit-dialing system to all the eight administrative districts of the Beijing city area. This method was chosen partly because it was fast and economical but also because of its generally higher response rate and the ability to minimize incomplete answers (Waitt 2001).

Trained interviewers used the computer-assisted telephone interviewing system to call the households identified and then asked to speak to the person there, over the age of eighteen, whose birthday was closest to 1 January. This method ensured the randomness of the selection process (Mihalik and Simonetta 1999). The phone calls were made between 9 a.m. and 9 p.m. on weekdays as well as at weekends to ensure that people of various ages and occupations would participate. A call-back procedure was adopted to minimize non-response biases that might result from residents not being at home. Each interview lasted twenty to twenty-five minutes. As a result, a sample of 800 responses was collected during a two-week period. The overall response rate of 15 percent was calculated by using the number of completed interviews divided by the number of completed interviews plus the number of refusals and the number of uncompleted calls.

The survey recorded perceptions of the economic and social impact of the games on the local community; residents' overall attitude toward and satisfaction with the games; residents' sports attachment and involvement; and the demographic and socio-economic characteristics of the respondents – age, gender, education, income and occupation. Gender and age group were carefully monitored to generate a balanced dataset. Both structured and unstructured questions were included in the survey.

The findings of this study are presented below, along with an attempt to capture local residents' perceptions of national belonging and identity. One question was phrased as follows: "Judging the success of the Beijing 2008 Olympic Games, which one of the following is the most important criterion to measure the success of this event?" The choice of answers was adapted from Ritchie and Aitken's (1984) Olympulse research: (1) economic benefits, (2) national spirit enhancement,

Table 8.1 The most important criteria in measuring the success of the Beijing Olympic Games (N=800)

Variable	Percentage
Economic benefits	6.6
National spirit enhancement	20.6
Performance of the Chinese athletes	12.4
China's capability, social/culture values shown to the world	54.9
All attendees good experience in Beijing	4.1
Other/not sure	1.3

(3) the performance of the Chinese athletes, (4) China's capability, culture and social values shown to the world, and (5) all attendees having a good experience. The majority of respondents (54.9 percent) reported that the most important measure of the success of hosting the event was China's capability, culture and social values shown to the world, followed by national recognition and spirit (20.6 percent) and the performance of the Chinese athletes (12.4 percent). Only 6.6 percent considered economic benefits to be the most important criterion (see Table 8.1). This clearly indicates that the local residents had a strong sense of national belonging, and that they gave the highest priority to national identity and the enhancement of international recognition.

In terms of support for the games, 92.2 percent of the respondents chose either "strongly support" (59.1 percent) or "support" (33.1 percent) as their answer. Only 5.6 percent reported that they were "neutral," and 2.1 percent indicated that they either opposed or strongly opposed hosting the games (see Table 8.2). When asked whether they had suffered any inconvenience on account of the games, only 19.2 percent reported that they had. Among these respondents, 25.3 percent indicated that they were "willing" or "very willing" to cope with the inconvenience – about the same number as those who were unwilling to do so. The primary reasons for their willingness to cope with the inconvenience, once again, were associated with the establishment of national identity and spirit and the sense of national belonging and pride in hosting this great event. The short-term inconvenience for many respondents (38.5 percent) was perceived as being offset by the new resources for city rejuvenation and development in the long term. Economic benefits, comparatively, were the least important reason for coping with the inconvenience (see Table 8.3).

Similarly, analysis of the open questions provided insights into local residents' viewpoints of hosting the Beijing games. From their responses it appears that one of the most important outcomes should be that China has a new and positive image in the world. Among such assertions were: "I hoped that, through hosting the Olympic Games, Beijing's new image would be promoted to the world; and China as a country would receive a positive identity and become more influential in the world" and "the Olympic Games is a showcase to a global audience for what China really is and what it can achieve; therefore I care most about the positive feedback from the world as a result of hosting this event." Others

Table 8.2 Residents' support for hosting the 2008 Olympic Games in Beijing (N=800)

Variable	Percentage
Strongly oppose	1.2
Oppose	0.9
Neutral (neither oppose nor support)	5.6
Support	33.1
Strongly support	59.1

Table 8.3 The primary reason for being willing to cope with the inconvenience during the Olympic Games (N=154)

Variable	Percentage
National spirit enhancement	23.1
Economic benefit	12.8
Pride of hosting the event in Beijing	25.6
Long-term city rejuvenation	38.5
Other/not sure	0.0

commented that they gave most consideration to Chinese athletes winning gold medals. These perceived outcomes reflected the host residents' attention to China's international recognition and identity in the wider global community.

The results suggest respondents' support for the Beijing Olympic Games was also associated with their willingness to make economic and individual life sacrifices. When asked about the negative aspects of hosting the games, points included inflated prices on goods and housing, increased traffic controls/restrictions, and higher general costs of living. However, most people either seemed unconcerned about the overall cost issue of hosting the event or believed that the gains outweighed the costs. They perceived greater social and economic benefits deriving directly from the games, such as better infrastructure and a more pleasant environment in the city, more convenient public transportation, and improved business opportunities. More importantly, when respondents were asked how the event had affected their lives, three altruistic themes were revealed: "community and national spirit," "international recognition of China" and "overall improvement of Beijing city."

The frequent recurrence of the theme "community and national spirit" indicates that, among many respondents, patriotism was given a high priority in the list of perceived benefits. Some expressed opinions included "enhancement of national pride," "inspired morale and spirit of the Chinese people," and "the Games made Chinese people more closely united and full of pride." Others mentioned the improved social responsibility and sense of honor among the local residents: "[I felt] amazed by the community spirit through volunteerism and the local social support network before and during the Olympic Games. People paid more attention to the etiquette, manners and city civilization, which promoted a harmonious society." In other words, a community and national spirit emerged and was further enhanced by the unique opportunity of hosting this worldwide hallmark event.

"International recognition of China" proved to be another significant outcome of hosting the 2008 Olympic Games. Compared with Greece or Australia, China might appear to be an unfamiliar, distant country and so not be perceived as psychologically "safe" or physically convenient/comfortable (Weed 2007). Furthermore, Chinese society remains strikingly at odds with Western liberal views (Wei and Yu 2006), and there were some reservations among the international community and negative media coverage in relation to human rights issues (Weed 2007). The Chinese need to overcome these difficulties to present to the world a country that is an increasingly important member of the global economic and political community. The respondents showed the desire to promote Beijing and China to the world and believed that hosting the Olympic Games would enhance the recognition and influence of their country. They indicated that the most important benefits were "to display China and Chinese culture to the world and let the world understand China," "to increase China's international influence and prestige," "to provide the world a brand new view of China," and "to make the country more prosperous and powerful." Some connected the international recognition of China with the success of hosting the games and the performance of the Chinese athletes. For example, a few people thought that "the successful Beijing Olympic Games and Chinese athletes' gold medals won glory for the country and showed China's increasing advances through sports achievement." It can therefore be concluded that respondents believed that important outcomes of hosting the Olympic Games were national and community pride among the citizens and a greater international profile for China. They also perceived "the overall improvement of Beijing city" as a significant reward: "more convenient public transportation and traffic conditions," "better environment on the overall city appearance and air quality," "improved infrastructure," "better quality of life in Beijing," and "accelerated city development of Beijing." Hosting the Olympic Games was perceived as a remarkable component in upgrading all aspects of city development and in helping the promotion of Beijing as a first-class, modern global city.

Conclusion

The Olympic Games, as one of the most significant international mega-events, brings valuable opportunities in development, business investment and tourism, which ultimately increases the international profile and recognition of the host cities and countries. This study contributes to the literature examining the enhancement of national identity-building through the Olympic Games from the host community's perspective.

The results of the survey undertaken revealed that the majority of the respondents either supported or strongly supported hosting the Olympic Games in Beijing, and perceived "China's capability, culture and social values shown to the world" and "national recognition and spirit" as the most important criteria to measure the success of hosting the event. The three major themes that emerged were "community and national spirit," "the international recognition of China" and "the overall improvement of Beijing city." Although some negative aspects did emerge, respondents were willing to make sacrifices and believed in the wider social and economic benefits that had been generated. Those who were inconvenienced by the games had been willing to cope with it, mostly on account of the sense of national belonging and pride in hosting this event. It can be concluded that the residents attached a significant symbolic meaning to the Olympic Games in constructing national identity and international recognition.

According to social exchange theory, residents' support in hosting such a mega-event has to do with the issues of rationality, satisfaction, reciprocity and social justice (Waitt 2003). In this study, it is suggested that the host community's feelings of patriotism and national belonging and pride, along with the majority of positive reactions, occurred when the perceived social benefits outweighed the costs in the exchange relationship between the event and the individual. Apparently, the majority of Beijing residents believed that hosting the 2008 Olympic Games would bring enormous economic and social returns. Compared to what the city and the whole country gained from hosting this event, the associated cost – the additional tax burden and some inconvenience to daily life – were considered to be acceptable. It should be noted that the residents' strong sense of community spirit, and the desire to establish and enhance the international recognition and national identity of their country through the Olympic Games, are aspects that have been reported in other Olympic impact research (Ritchie and Aitken 1984, 1985; Ritchie and Lyons 1990; Ritchie and Smith 1991; Waitt 2003) and in this case may originate in China's collectivist culture (Hofstede 1980, 2001). In a typical collectivist society, people are integrated into strong, cohesive groups and value the sense of group belonging and loyalty. To the Chinese people, the pursuit of a more united, harmonious society, a strong national identity, and the country's international recognition and influence are particularly desirable. The success of hosting the 2008 Olympic Games was a symbolic achievement representing China's overall national strength. The games brought a unique opportunity to construct and enhance a new and positive national image of the country in the global community. As the largest developing country in the world, China will benefit both economically and socially in the long term from hosting the Olympic Games.

References

Anet (2008) "The Beijing 2008 summer Olympic Games: statistics and summary," www.associatedcontent.com/article/979500/the_beijing_2008_summer_olympic_games.html (accessed 29 December 2009).
Ap, J. (1992) "Residents' perceptions on tourism impacts," *Annals of Tourism Research*, 19: 665–90.

Bagozzi, R. (1975) "Marketing as exchange," *Journal of marketing*, 39: 32–9.

BOCOG (Beijing Organizing Committee for the Olympic Games) (2003) *Beijing Olympic Action Plan*. Beijing: BOCOG.

Brown, G., Chalip, L., Jago, L., and Mules, T. (2004) "The Sydney Olympics and brand Australia," in N. Morgan, A. Pritchard and R. Pride (eds) *Destination Branding: Creating the Unique Destination Proposition* (pp. 163–85). 2nd edn, London: Elsevier Butterworth–Heinemann.

Brownell, S. (1995) *Training the Body for China: Sports in the Moral Order of the People's Republic*. Chicago: University of Chicago Press.

Chalip, L. (2000) *Leveraging the Sydney Olympics for Tourism*. Barcelona: Centre d'Estudis Olímpics i de l'Esport; http://olympicstudies.uab.es/pdf/wp096_eng.pdf (accessed 18 December 2007).

CNTA (China National Tourism Administration) (2008) "Zhong guo ao yun lv you nian" [China Olympic tourism year], http://zhuanti.cnta.gov.cn/2008aoyun/more. asp?newsid=005050002 (accessed 16 July 2008).

Comer, J., and Harvey, S. (1991) "Mediating tradition and modernity: the heritage/enterprise couplet," in J. Comer and S. Harvey (eds) *Enterprise and Heritage: Crosscurrents of National Culture* (pp. 44–75). London and New York: Routledge.

Deccio, C., and Baloglu, S. (2002) "Nonhost community resident reactions to the 2002 winter Olympics: the spillover impacts," *Journal of Travel Research*, 41(1): 46–56.

ETOA (European Tour Operators Association) (2006) *Olympic Report*. London: ETOA.

ETOA (European Tour Operators Association) (2008) *Olympics & Tourism: Update on Olympic Report 2006*. London: ETOA.

Faulkner, B., and Tideswell, C. (1997) "A framework for monitoring community impacts of tourism," *Journal of Sustainable Tourism*, 5(1): 3–28.

French, S. P., and Disher, M. E. (1997) "Atlanta and the Olympics: a one-year retrospective," *Journal of the American Planning Association*, 63(3): 379–92.

Hall, C. M. (1987) "The effects of hallmark events on cities," *Journal of Travel Research*, 26(2): 44–5.

Hargreaves, J., and Ferrando, M. G. (1997) "Public opinion, national integration and national identity in Spain: the case of the Barcelona Olympic Games," *Nations and Nationalism*, 3(1): 65–87.

Hiller, H. H. (1998) "Assessing the impact of mega-events: a linkage model," *Current Issues in Tourism*, 1(1): 47–57.

Hofstede, G. (1980) *Culture's Consequences: International Differences in Work-Related Values*. Beverly Hills, CA: Sage.

Hofstede, G. (2001) *Culture's Consequences: Comparing Values, Behaviors, Institutions, and Organizations across Nations*. 2nd edn, Thousand Oaks, CA: Sage.

Hogan, J. (2003) "Staging the nation," *Journal of Sport & Social Issues*, 27(2): 100–23.

Jeong, G., and Faulkner, B. (1996) "Resident perceptions of mega event impacts: the Taejon international exposition case," *Festival Management and Event Tourism*, 4: 3–14.

Jurowski, C., Uysal, M., and Williams, D. R. (1997) "A study of visitor preferences in relation to environmental attributes," *24th TTRA Conference Proceedings* (pp. 242–52). Whistler, BC: Travel and Tourism Research Association.

Kang, Y. S., and Perdue, R. (1994) "Long-term impact of a mega-event on international tourism to the host country: a conceptual model and the case of the 1988 Seoul Olympics," *Journal of International Consumer Marketing*, 6(3–4): 205–27.

Kasimati, E. (2003) "Economic aspects and the summer Olympics: a review of related research," *International Journal of Tourism Research*, 5: 433–44.

King, A. (2000) "Football fandom and post-national identity in the New Europe," *British Journal of Sociology*, 51(3): 419–42.

Kirkup, N., and Major, B. (2006) "The reliability of economic impact studies of the Olympic Games: a post-games study of Sydney 2000 and considerations for London 2012," *Journal of Sport & Tourism*, 11(3–4): 275–96.

Long, X., and Ma, L. (2004) "2008 nian ao yun lv you xiao ying yu zhong guo ao yun lv you quan gou xiang" [The tourism effect of the 2008 Olympics and conceiving the Olympic Games tourism circle of China], *Renwen Dili* [*Human Geography*], 19(2): 47–51.

Madden, J. R. (2002) "The economic consequences of the Sydney Olympics: the CREA/ Arthur Andersen study," *Current Issues in Tourism*, 5(1): 7–21.

Martin, M. F. (2008) *China's economy and the Beijing Olympics*. Washington, DC: Library of Congress; http://digital.library.unt.edu/govdocs/crs/permalink/meta-crs-10782:1 (accessed 30 September 2009).

May, V. (1995) "Environmental implications of the 1992 winter Olympic Games," *Tourism Management*, 16(4): 269–75.

Mihalik, B. J,. and Simonetta, L. (1999) "A midterm assessment of the host population's perceptions of the 1996 summer Olympics: support, attendance, benefits, and liabilities," *Journal of Travel Research*, 37: 244–8.

Nielsen (2008) "Beijing Olympics draw largest ever global TV audience," 5 September, http://blog.nielsen.com/nielsenwire/media_entertainment/beijing-olympics-draw-largest-ever-global-tv-audience (accessed 29 December 2009).

Perdue, R. R., Long, P. T., and Allen, L. (1990) "Resident support for tourism development," *Annals of Tourism Research*, 17: 586–99.

Perdue, R. R., Long, P. T., and Kang, Y. S. (1999) "Boomtown tourism and resident quality of life: the marketing of gaming to host community residents," *Journal of Business Research*, 44(3): 165–77.

Quelch, J., and Jocz, K. (2005) "Positioning the nation-state," *Place Branding*, 1(3): 229–37.

Ritchard, K. (2004) "The hotel industry is pinning its hope on gold at Beijing in 2008 – but is it a sure winner?" *Hotel Asia Pacific*, December.

Ritchie, J. R. B. (1989) "Promoting Calgary through the Olympics: the mega-event as a strategy for community development," in S. H. Fine (ed.) *Social Marketing* (pp. 258–74). Boston: Allyn & Bacon.

Ritchie, J. R. B., and Aitken, C. E. (1984) "Assessing the impacts of the 1988 Olympic winter games: the research program and initial results," *Journal of Travel Research*, 22: 17–25.

Ritchie, J. R. B., and Aitken, C. E. (1985) "Olympulse II: evolving resident attitudes toward the 1988 Olympic winter games," *Journal of Travel Research*, 23: 28–33.

Ritchie, J. R. B., and Lyons, M. (1987) "Olympulse III/IV: a mid-term report on resident attitudes concerning the XV Olympic winter games," *Journal of Travel Research*, 26(1): 18–26.

Ritchie, J. R. B., and Lyons, M. (1990) "Olympulse VI: a post-event assessment of resident reaction to the XV Olympic winter games," *Journal of Travel Research*, 28(3): 14–24.

Ritchie, J. R. B., and Smith, B. H. (1991) "The impact of a mega-event on host region awareness: a longitudinal study," *Journal of Travel Research*, 30(1): 3–10.

Rogge, J. (2008) "Speech by Jacques Rogge at the closing ceremony," http://en.beijing2008. cn/ceremonies/headlines/n214584113.shtml (accessed 22 May 2010).

Searle, M. (1991) "Propositions for testing social exchange theory in the context of ceasing leisure participation," *Leisure Studies*, 13: 279–94.

Tang, Y. (2001) "Beijing creates history," *Beijing Review*, 2 August, pp. 12–16.

Teigland, J. (1999) "Mega-events and impacts on tourism: the predictions and realities of the Lillehammer Olympics," *Impact Assessment and Project Appraisal*, 17(4): 305–17.

Tervo, M. (2002) "Sports, 'race' and the Finnish national identity in Helsingin Sanomat in the early twentieth century," *Nations & Nationalism*, 8(3): 335–56.

Tomlinson, A., and Young, C. (eds) (2006) *National Identity and Global Sports Events: Culture, Politics, and Spectacle in the Olympics and the Football World Cup*. New York: State University of New York Press.

Waitt, G. (2001) "The Olympic spirit and civic boosterism: the Sydney 2000 Olympics," *Tourism Geographies*, 3(3): 249–78.

Waitt, G. (2003) "Social impacts of the Sydney Olympics," *Annals of Tourism Research*, 30(1): 194–215.

Wamsley, K. B., and Heine, M. K. (1996) "Tradition, modernity, and the construction of civic identity: the Calgary Olympics," *Olympika: International Journal of Olympic Studies*, 5: 81–90.

Weed, M. (2007) *Olympic Tourism*. Burlington, MA: Butterworth–Heinemann.

Wei, Y. H. D. and Yu, D. L. (2006) "State policy and the globalization of Beijing: emerging themes," *Habitat International*, 30: 377–95.

Xu, X. (2006) "Modernizing China in the Olympic spotlight: China's national identity and the 2008 Beijing Olympiad," *Sociological Review*, 54 (Supplement 2): 90–107.

9 Nation in transformation

Tourism and national identity in the Kyrgyz Republic

Peter Schofield and
Agata Maccarrone-Eaglen

Introduction

This chapter outlines the socio-cultural, economic and political factors in the transformation of the Kyrgyz Republic and examines the issue of Kyrgyz identity and its relationship with tourism within this framework. The discussion focuses on cultural heritage tourism and the development of a collective identity within the context of recent political events and the resurgence in Central Asia of both Kyrgyz nationalism and Turkic culture.

After gaining independence from the USSR in 1991, the Kyrgyz Republic (see Figure 9.1) instigated democratic and economic reforms and established a reputation as a pro-Western, liberal economy, which attracted both the support of Western states anxious to establish a showcase of neo-liberalism in Russia's backyard and a steady flow of soft loans from international organisations. Democratisation and the adoption of market principles differentiated the state from its Central Asian neighbours – China, Kazakhstan, Uzbekistan and Tajikistan – and, like many of the independent states that emerged from the fragmentation of the Soviet federal structure, Kyrgyzstan was eager to establish and articulate a national identity and statehood. One way in which, under similar circumstances, such an identity has often sought expression is through tourism (Hall 1999), and the new Kyrgyz government soon recognised tourism's potential to achieve this goal.

Tourism is not exclusively a postcolonial phenomenon in Kyrgyzstan; during the period of Soviet occupation, health and sports tourism flourished in connection with the sanatoria that developed at hot springs and lakes. There was some contraction over the 1990s because of the reduction in the size of the domestic market after independence, but significant remnants of Soviet-era tourism regenerated on account of demand from nearby states, Western Europe and the USA. Over the same period, other types of tourism, notably cultural tourism, grew as a result of this international interest. By 2001 the government had outlined its vision for the further development of tourism; "health and recreational tourism", "cultural tourism", "adventure tourism and mountaineering" and "ecological tourism" were identified as the country's four main product markets (KSATS 2001). However, the Republic's remote location, outdated political framework, complex economic legacy, social instability, poor infrastructure, and outdated

Figure 9.1 Kyrgyzstan in Central Asia.

amenities and service standards have proved to be significant constraints on development.

Tourism is nevertheless high on the political agenda, given Kyrgyzstan's natural assets and the industry's potential both to generate foreign exchange earnings and to facilitate the creation of a distinct image and identity for the state. The issue of Kyrgyz identity is complex; the country is torn between its traditional culture, Soviet patterns and Western influence, with deep divisions on the basis of ethnicity, religion and clan affiliation. Moreover, the economic disparity between the north and south of the country and between its rural and urban areas is fuelling social unrest, politico-religious extremism and an informal economy in which organised crime groups have formed a parallel authority structure.

Postcolonial reformation and the search for a Kyrgyz identity

The political and economic context

The disintegration of the Soviet Union, the emergence of five independent Central Asian republics – Kazakhstan, Tajikistan, Turkmenistan, Uzbekistan and Kyrgyzstan – and the formation of the Commonwealth of Independent States (CIS) attracted the world's attention because of the area's strategic importance from a geopolitical perspective. Subsequent political developments, particularly the wars in Afghanistan and Iraq and the al-Qaeda terrorist attack on the USA on 11 September 2001, served to focus that attention. While Kyrgyzstan faced similar political and socio-economic issues to the other emerging CIS states, its development path took a different path on account of President Askar Akayev's pro-Western democratic orientation (Starr 1996). The adoption of a market economy was supported by financial aid from a number of international organisations, – aid which was used to bolster a dysfunctional economy characterised by hyper-inflation, increasing shortages and widespread unemployment (Platt 1994). Social and economic indicators placed the new republic in the range of lower middle-income developing countries rather than that of the industrial reforming states, with over half of national output and employment coming from agriculture, despite the relatively small area of fertile land. Three-quarters of the state's food requirements were met by imports, and the country's problems were compounded by severe environmental pollution and poor infrastructural conditions (UNICEF/ WHO 1992).

Despite significant progress in respect of market-oriented reforms during the 1990s, Kyrgyzstan's economic growth was stymied by the lack of resources, the absence of processing infrastructure, inefficient state enterprises, and widespread corruption in both the public and the private sector. Gross Domestic Product (GDP) plummeted and reached its lowest level in 1995, at about 55 per cent of its 1991 level. However, by 1998 there had been a significant upturn in the economy, and by 2001 the International Money Fund was commending Kyrgyzstan's macroeconomic policy performance, although it also acknowledged that resolute implementation of the new economic programme was needed to enhance prospects for sustained growth and reduction in the state's $US1.5 billion external debt (Europe-East 2002). By 2004 the service sector's contribution to GDP was 32 per cent, a combination of buoyant foreign trade, increasing tourist arrivals and small business taxes (Asian Development Outlook 2005), but, with the exception of a few high-profile projects like the Kumtor gold-mining complex, the economy remained heavily dependent on its agrarian sector (World Bank 2006).

Theoretically, within the context of post-communist transition, the introduction of privatisation and the diversification of ownership in the industrial and agricultural sectors should have created new organisational and social networks that mitigated the worst effects of ethnic, tribal or religious identities (Anderson 2000). However, from the outset Kyrgyzstan experienced difficulties arising from the change in ideology, exacerbated by severe economic and social problems (Huskey 1995; Anderson 1999). The Democratic Party, Republican Party and National Rebirth Party attempted to fill the vacuum left by the demise of the Communist Party, but it was the two pre-eminent clans, Salto and Saribagish, that dominated state politics. While there was a tolerance of diversity that stems from the country's hospitable tradition, many interest groups, particularly in the south of the country, were not supportive of either democratisation or Akayev's policy of "selling out to the West", reflecting the close links between Islam and the state (Lipset 1994). Moreover, there were widespread misgivings about attempts to impose Western notions of a civil society, rooted in individual choice, on a country where group identities are more potent and there is a natural inclination to look for strong leadership within the community and the state (Schofield 2004a).

The "Tulip" Revolution in 2005 and the continuing crisis

Over the 1990s, President Akayev shifted to a more authoritarian position, and the government failed to develop the rule of law and address the deepening socio-economic crisis. After a controversial extension to Akayev's presidential term in 2000, the Aksy riots in 2002 and continuing political unrest, the fraudulent parliamentary elections in February 2005 were the tipping point for countrywide protests, fuelled by widespread poverty, increasing inequality and perceived corruption at local, regional and national levels. On 24 March 2005, an insurrection led by the People's Movement of Kyrgyzstan culminated in a crowd of demonstrators seizing the Kyrgyz White House in Bishkek, the emancipation of the opposition leader, Felix Kulov, who had been imprisoned in 2001, and Akayev reportedly fleeing to Moscow. The term "Tulip Revolution" is a reference to both the time of year and the previous "colour" revolutions, such as Georgia's "Rose Revolution" in 2003 and Ukraine's "Orange Revolution" in 2004.

Following two months of chaos and anarchy in Bishkek, an interim government consisting of an alliance between two veteran pro-Russian politicians, President Kermanbek Bakiyev and Prime Minisiter Felix Kulov (supported by the southern and northern political elites, respectively), was brokered by Moscow. It is interesting that, in their inaugural statements, both Bakiyev and Kulov depicted Russia as a history-ordained senior partner to Kyrgyzstan, but, while Bakiyev endorsed Moscow's calls for an end to the American military presence in the country, Kulov appeared to support the continuation of Akayev's policy of balancing among Russia, China and the USA (Socor 2005), reflecting the state's complex political identity.

Opinion among Kyrgyz citizens was divided on the events of 24 March 2005; some viewed it as a "coup d'état", arguing that it disrupted the political order established by Akayev, while others believed that Kyrgyzstan experienced a revolutionary shift towards democracy, an open society and a legitimate state (Marat 2006). However, one year later there was a general concern over the new government's unfulfilled promises and rising instability resulting from the rapid criminalisation of Kyrgyzstan, the pervasive corruption in the public sector, and the state's failure to introduce any visible economic reforms. There were open challenges to the government by criminal figures and widespread demonstrations and political skirmishes throughout 2006 and continuing political flux in 2007, with extensive criticism from both governmental and non-governmental sources (Marat 2007).

The Tulip Revolution resulted in significant changes to the political, economic and social landscape. Russia's hold on power, established during the Soviet era, was broken as politicians from the south of the country were given key government positions, and many Russians fled the country because of concerns, as a minority group, over security. The balance of power between state and non-state actors has also shifted since 2005; at least twenty-four organised crime groups are now operating and have formed a parallel authority structure. By comparison, many features remain unchanged. Widespread corruption still permeates all state structures and deep inter-ethnic cleavages persist. The government has failed to introduce economic reform, unemployment rates remain high, and an independent mass media has not been encouraged (Marat 2008).

One of the key priorities for the government is the introduction of viable economic policies to address unemployment and tackle poverty. This, in turn, will strengthen civil society, help to alleviate inter-ethnic tensions and curtail the activities of criminal groups. However, economic progress requires political stability, and recent events have militated against such developments. On 7 April 2010, violent clashes between rioters and state security forces in Bishkek over President Kurmanbek Bakiyev's repressive rule left seventy-five people dead and over 1,000 injured. The president was forced to flee the capital, and a provisional government headed by the opposition under an ex-foreign minister, Roza Otunbayeva, was put in place (BBC News 2010).

Regional, ethnic and clan identity

Central Asia's ethnically based republics were carved from Turkestan by the Soviets after the 1917 revolution, and there is no correspondence between their arbitrary borders, drawn up in the 1920s and 1930s, and the region's ethnic and linguistic situation. As a result, many border regions are the subject of international dispute. In southern Kyrgyzstan, the Osh and Batken regions comprise pockets of Uzbek and Tajik territory, the city of Osh has a large population of ethnic Uzbeks, and the border with Tajikistan is disputed. This conflict is paralleled by hostilities within Kyrgyzstan between religious, ethnic and clan groups at a number of different levels and geographic scales (Lipset 1994).

The religious affiliation of the Kyrgyz population is primarily Muslim (83 per cent) with 14 per cent Russian Orthodox (UNDP 1999), although, reflecting their nomadic heritage and the retention of many tribal traditions, they are generally less dogmatic in their beliefs than their Tajik and Uzbek neighbours. Nevertheless, the southern provinces, where 30 per cent of the population is Uzbek, are Islamic and were so even during the Soviet era. By comparison, the northern region, including Bishkek, is more Russified and liberal, with a significant concentration of Slavs, and this has tended to restrict ethnic Central Asian access to jobs, modern housing and social services (Huskey 1995). It has also increased interregional and inter-ethnic tensions, and these north–south contradictions are widely regarded as the main destabilising factor in society.

A further complexity is the social significance of family and clan ties. Kyrgyz identity is closely aligned with membership in one of three clan groups which also have a regional orientation. In the north and west of the country the "Sol", or left wing, consists of seven clans, while in the south there are two clan groups: the right wing, or "Ong", which consists of one clan (the "Adygine"), and a second group, the "Ichkilik", comprised of many clans, some of which are not of Kyrgyz origin (Anderson 2000). Clan loyalties dominate life on both sides of the north–south divide and rivalry among clans has proved to be a significant barrier to the unification of Kyrgyzstan (Schofield 2004a).

Table 9.1 International tourism arrivals and expenditure for Kyrgyzstan

Year	Arrivals	+/– (%)	Expenditure (KGS)[a]	+/– (%)
1996	48,601	–	152,737,200	–
1997	87,386	+79.8	258,198,600	+69.0
1998	59,363	–32.7	305,474,400	+18.3
1999	48,272	–18.7	512,760,600	+67.9
2000	58,756	+21.7	556,399,800	+8.5
2001	98,558	+67.7	1,163,712,000	+109.2
2002	139,589	+41.6	1,927,398,000	+65.6
2003	341,990	+144.9	2,363,790,000	+22.6
2004	737,500	+115.6	n/a	–
2005	601,100	–18.5	n/a	–
2006	1,500,000	+149.5	n/a	–
2007	1,600,000	+6.7	12,426262,200	–
2008	1,895,000	+18.4	n/a	–

Sources: National Statistical Committee of the Kyrgyz Republic (2005, 2009); UNWTO (2006); AKIpress (2008).

Note: [a]1 KGS = US$0.02.

Tourism development and national identity

Kyrgyzstan has received US$3 billion in foreign investments since 1993, but the Republic remains one of the poorest countries in the world, with 40 per cent of its 5.3 million population, approximately three-quarters of whom live in rural areas, below the poverty line (World Bank 2006). It is therefore not surprising that, given the country's physical terrain, the global growth in the tourism market and the willingness of external financial institutions to fund tourism projects, the state has recognised the strategic potential of tourism in political, economic and social terms. The Kyrgyz tourism industry has survived the cumulative effects of three poor seasons from 2001 to 2003 resulting from 9/11, the wars in Afghanistan and Iraq, and the outbreak of SARS (see Table 9.1). The number of arrivals has continued to grow, albeit erratically, with the exception of the years 1998, 1999 and 2005 – the unreliability of official statistics notwithstanding. Before the revolution, the forecast for 2005 was approximately 1 million. While its effect on inbound tourism flows from neighbouring CIS countries, particularly Kazakhstan, was minimal, the security concerns of Western tourists took their toll. Moreover, in the immediate aftermath of the revolution, many of the largest new tourism projects, driven by the funding agendas of international development actors and the dependency of the government on external technical assistance, were delayed pending the outcome of an election. The tourism arrivals figure for 2005 was therefore higher than expected under the circumstances (only 18.5 per cent down on the previous year) and reflects the success of marketing activities which targeted neighbouring countries in an effort to offset the decline in visitors from key markets in the USA, the UK, France, Austria and Japan. The available figures for 2006, 2007 and 2008, together with the 5 per cent increase on the last year reported by Euromonitor (2010), indicate that the sector has recovered and is continuing to grow. However, Kyrgyzstan has still not reached normalisation, and indications suggest that investors are hesitant and frustrated with the slow development of tourism over the past few years compared with its trajectory in the two years before the revolution. Moreover, the continuing political instability is likely to constrain development in the near future.

State policy-makers have two overriding priorities for tourism. The first is to increase its competitiveness in order to raise per capita levels of foreign exchange earnings and the second is to enhance regional development by creating economic opportunities in some of the most underdeveloped areas of the Republic. A key aspect of the first priority is to develop a brand image, because awareness of the destination in Western tourism markets is poor and the country is, to a large extent, indistinguishable from other Central Asian states (Schofield 2004a). This under-positioning is the result of a number of factors, including the lack of a strong political identity and the failure of the Kyrgyz State Agency for Tourism and Sports (KSATS) to promote the country's distinguishing features because of the emphasis on scenic beauty. In 1993, the Kyrgyz Constitution set out the government's intention to promote the Republic as "Asia's Switzerland", thus positioning it apart from neighbouring CIS states on the basis of its democratic society and free market economy (Thompson *et al.* 2006). The direct comparison with Switzerland created a distinctive external image both politically and in relation to its physical landscape, which proved to be beneficial from the perspective of international relations and foreign investment in the short term, but failed to address the issue of unification through a coherent Kyrgyz identity.

Culture, ethnicity, tourism and identity

The new global economic order has had a profound effect on post-communist Kyrgyzstan. While the mining of rare metals including gold makes a significant contribution to GDP, the country's transformation has been driven by post-industrial activities associated with the increasingly sophisticated cultures of consumption. Within this context, there has been a growing recognition of the role of culture in framing and shaping the country's economy and society, resulting in attempts to develop a cultural strategy for regeneration. A reaction to the imposition of national consciousness and collective culture during the Soviet era has encouraged the creation of a revised cultural identity linked to pre-communist heritage; this new identity has been expressed with a heavy emphasis upon ethnicity and reflects self-expression and self-assertion as much as historical evidence (Thompson *et al.*, 2006).

Much of Kyrgyzstan's tourism development has focused hitherto on the country's natural environment, although the Republic's cultural heritage is beginning to emerge as a significant feature. Silk Road heritage has traditionally been a key element in the tourism portfolio, but other facets of Kyrgyz history and culture are now being harnessed to satisfy a number of important objectives – not least the creation of national identity and brand equity. However, Kyrgyzstan's rich cultural heritage and ethnic diversity are both a blessing and a blight. On the one hand, it is an important feature of the tourism product which augments the country's natural attractions. On the other hand, the post-Soviet awakening of ethnic and clan identity, particularly marked in the south of the country, militates against the development of a coherent national identity, and, in an attempt to establish a common vision, particular emphasis has been placed on those aspects of Kyrgyz heritage which are common to, and recognised by, inhabitants of both southern and northern regions. These elements are the Manas *epos* and pastoral nomadism, both of which have emerged as core elements of the cultural tourism product, the latter as "*jailoo*" ("summer pasture") tourism, which describes the seasonal practice of Kyrgyz families moving with their livestock to mountain pastures in the month of May.

The Manas epos

Archaeological evidence of settlements in Kyrgyzstan can be traced back 300,000 years, although it was not until the sixteenth century that the Kyrgyz people migrated to the land which is now known as Kyrgyzstan and not until the October Revolution of 1917 that they acquired a written language. The prolonged reliance on the oral tradition of passing on information led to a series of epic poems known as "*epos*", which played a significant role in passing value systems from one generation to another. Among the thirty-four Kyrgyz *epos* which have been identified by the Turkish Language Institution, by far the longest (some 553,000 lines), best known and most enduring is the Manas *epos*. It tells of the life and death of Manas, the leader of the Kyrgyz tribes during the most successful period of their history, when the Kyrgyz conquered Chinese Turkestan and won a great victory over the Uyghurs (Auezov 1999). Not surprisingly, given his status in Kyrgyz cultural heritage, Manas became the central figure on which the Kyrgyz cultural identity was based. During the Soviet era, many of those responsible for research into the Manas *epos* were imprisoned, disappeared or were shot. The *epos* was suppressed because of fears relating to pan-Turkic and pan-Islamic undercurrents that were considered to be damaging to the common, supranational Soviet culture (Paksoy 1995).

Nationalism requires a shared sense of history, whether it is based on fact or myth, and much of the mythology behind modern forms of nationalism is militaristic. The Manas legend is typical in this respect, although it is atypical in the sense that Manas is an important cultural icon for all Turkic peoples in Central Asia, irrespective of their political or geographical affiliations (Musayev 1994). However, Manas promotes the collective consciousness of the Kyrgyz nation and is an integral part of national identity only in Kyrgyzstan (Thompson *et al.* 2006). Its strategic importance to the Republic's cultural and political identity is demonstrated by the fact that, less than a year after gaining independence, President Akayev declared plans for the celebration of the 1,000th anniversary of the

Manas *epos* in 1995, a largely extraneous date given the lack of clarity over its exact period of origin. A key objective of the millennium celebrations was the promotion of national identity following cultural repression, and their importance is reflected in the cost of the four-day event, which exceeded US$8 million (Mayhew *et al*. 2000). Manas embodies the spiritual unity of the Kyrgyz, their democratic principles and their independence (Guttman 1999), and is a potent symbol of the Republic, underpinning both Kyrgyz national identity and the country's cultural tourism product.

Emerging nations which are in the process of developing tourism require strong and differentiated brands to improve their identity and image in order to position themselves effectively in the minds of prospective visitors. To this end, tourism promotional literature often draws on indigenous markers and cultural symbols to facilitate particular ways of seeing and interpreting a destination, and, not surprisingly, given Manas's iconic status and contemporary relevance, Kyrgyzstan's official state promotional literature is no exception. This is an effective means of symbolising many of the Republic's post-Soviet Turkic and Kyrgyz values and characteristics while presenting a broader cultural tourism portfolio (over and above the Silk Road heritage) to the international marketplace (Thompson *et al*. 2006). It also represents a means of both positioning the brand away from its "Switzerland in Central Asia" image (Schofield 2004a) and differentiating the tourism offer from competitors with similar natural resources and nomadic heritage. The Akaev government's post-2001 development path followed the Swiss model because of its political, economic and social aspirations and its topographical similarities. Moreover, the state's official promotional literature actually featured the explicit comparison with Switzerland (see Schofield 2004b; Thompson *et al*. 2006). The Manas legend is rapidly becoming part of the Kyrgyz self-image; its use in promotion is therefore as relevant to rekindling deep-rooted Kyrgyz ethnic identities as it is to presenting a coherent image to external audiences and promoting the cultural tourism product.

Pastoral nomadism, jailoo *and community-based tourism*

Before Soviet collectivisation the Kyrgyz people were pastoral nomads, and this tradition has been developed into "*jailoo*" tourism, which is popular with international visitors who want to experience the traditional Kyrgyz way of life and its customs. Visitors are able to stay with families in "*bozu*" (yurts) and enjoy authentic Kyrgyz hospitality. This "Shepherd's Life" product was developed through a joint venture between the Kyrgyz government and Helvetas, the Swiss Association for International Cooperation. The initiative provided training to residents in rural locations and has helped to spread economic and social benefits into some of the more remote and poorest areas of the country, thereby addressing one of the government's key priorities for tourism development.

Following this successful model, Helvetas has supported the development of other community-based tourism (CBT) projects in poor rural areas. CBT is a form of "for-profit" ecotourism based on participatory stakeholder decision-making, local economic development, the provision of investment opportunities for local inhabitants, and sustainable environmental practices. This type of tourism is particularly important for Kyrgyzstan given the acute social problems and the sector's heavy dependence on the physical environment. There are seventeen CBT groups, together with a five-group association of shepherd families, offering yurt-based *jailoo* tourism throughout Kyrgyzstan. In January 2003, the CBT groups amalgamated and established their own Kyrgyz Community-Based Tourism Association (KCBTA) and the "Hospitality Kyrgyzstan" brand.

The objective of KCBTA is to improve living standards in remote rural areas by developing a sustainable ecotourism model that utilises local resources (KCBTA 2007). It is trying to achieve this through a pro-poor strategy that includes the development of CBT as a niche and its integration into the mainstream tourism industry (Raeva 2005). Overall, the concept appears to be working well in rural areas where there are very few alternative sources of income, although progress is slow because of the lack of market orientation and entrepreneurial skills among local communities. Revenues from this source typically represent between 30 and 40 per cent of total family income and are a viable means of redistributing tourism wealth from the dominant Bishkek-based tour operators to Kyrgyzstan's poor communities.

The development of CBT in Kyrgyzstan is illustrated in Table 9.2. There has been a steady increase since 2000. Although there was some decline in individual CBT group membership in 2005 after the revolution, this was offset by growth in other areas, and three new CBT groups emerged. The net result was a 19 per cent increase in membership. Compared with the 100 per cent increase between 2003 and 2004, this suggests that the immediate effect of the political upheaval was to reduce the rate of development rather than curtailing or reversing the upward trend. The figures for 2006 show that, overall, there was a 17 per cent rise in membership. Some individual groups increased their membership, five new area groups were established and a few retained their 2005 figures, while a number of areas declined. By comparison, in 2007 membership decreased by 9 per cent. It is interesting to note that, while many groups increased their membership and a few remained stable, others declined. Clearly, the political situation has affected CBT development, but its impact has been smaller than expected. The remoteness of many group locations may have insulated them from the worst effects of the political events, although some southern groups, such as CBT Talas and Osh, have experienced difficulty in recovering their pre-revolution trajectory, and CBT Bokonbaevo appears to be in slow decline. This may reflect local politics and/or Western market perceptions of risk associated with visiting southern regions, despite the relative stability in the country overall.

Clearly CBT development is important from an economic standpoint in terms of creating jobs in poor rural areas with limited alternative opportunities for wealth creation, but it is also significant from a social and cultural perspective. It provides an opportunity to conserve, develop and promote local and regional aspects of cultural heritage, particularly those aspects relating to the nomadic tradition. As

Table 9.2 Community-based tourism membership

CBT Groups	2000	2001	2002	2003	2004	2005	2006	2007
CBT Kochkor	14	41	38	30	32	32	32	32
CBT Naryn	15	21	22	12	15	13	15	15
CBT Jalalabat	9	18	20	20	11	13	20	25
CBT Arsalanbob	–	20	12	20	22	27	29	32
CBT Karasuu	–	25	20	11	20	23	23	23
CBT Karakol	–	24	15	18	17	20	17	18
CBT Kazarman	–	–	9	11	15	9	8	10
CBT Talas	–	–	–	14	43	17	16	13
CBT Osh	–	–	–	16	28	18	14	10
Shepherd's Life	–	–	–	–	101	101	91	93
CBT Tamchy	–	–	–	–	–	12	12	13
CBT Bokonbaevo	–	–	–	–	–	20	18	14
CBT Kyzyl–Oi	–	–	–	–	–	12	13	15
CBT Chong–Kemin	–	–	–	–	–	–	9	9
CBT Alay (Gulcho)	–	–	–	–	–	–	15	13
CBT Sary–Mogul	–	–	–	–	–	–	14	15
CBT Batken	–	–	–	–	–	–	15	15
CBT Kerben	–	–	–	–	–	–	13	16
Excluded groups								
CBT Kopuro–Bazar	–	–	–	–	–	–	20	–
CBT Aral	–	–	–	–	–	–	25	–
Total	38	149	140	152	304	362	419	381

Source: KCBTA (2007, 2008).

such, it reinforces Kyrgyz identity and community self-image at the grassroots level and provides an authentic experience for visitors who, in turn, present a coherent image of Kyrgyz cultural heritage via word of mouth communication.

Table 9.3 shows that the number of tourists who visit CBT groups in Kyrgyzstan has grown significantly since 2000, and it is interesting that 5,122 tourists were received during 2005, an increase of 5 per cent over 2004. However, reflecting the membership statistics, southern groups – notably Jalalabad and Kazarman – experienced a decrease in the number of tourists compared with groups in the north and central areas – for example, Karakol and Naryn. In 2006, CBT visitor numbers increased by just under 14 per cent. Kochkor and especially Naryn continued to grow; Jalalabad, Karasuu, Arsalanbob and Osh significantly expanded their visitor numbers and reversed the contraction experienced in 2005; and CBT Chong-Kemin and Alay were added to the portfolio. By comparison, visitor numbers fell at CBT Karakol and Shepherd's Life after increasing over 2005, and visitor numbers continued to decline at CBT Tamchy, Kazarman and Talas. Interest in Kazarman and Talas was constrained because of the corresponding lack in these

Table 9.3 Community-based tourism visitor numbers

CBT Groups	2004	2005	+/− (%)	2006	+/− (%)	2007	+/− (%)
CBT Kochkor	1,164	1,588	+36.4	1,675	+5.48	1,837	+9.7
CBT Naryn	205	360	+75.6	807	+124.17	1,146	+42.0
CBT Karakol	264	473	+79.2	373	−21.14	779	+108.8
CBT Tamchy	314	231	−36.4	312	−35.06	393	+25.9
CBT Kazarman	134	75	−44.0	69	−8.00	134	+94.2
CBT Jalalabad	864	269	−68.9	346	+28.62	426	+28.6
CBT Karasuu	77	72	−6.5	105	+45.83	55	−47.6
CBT Arsalanbob	687	545	−20.7	830	+52.29	998	+20.2
CBT Talas	135	143	−8.3	95	−33.57	105	+10.5
CBT Osh	232	217	−6.5	365	+68.20	584	+60.0
Shepherd's Life	763	888	+16.4	599	−32.55	651	+8.7
CBT Bokonbaevo	–	133	–	154	+15.79	223	+44.8
CBT Kyzyl-Oi	–	128	–	75	−41.41	151	+101.3
CBT Chong-Kemin	–	–	–	5	–	57	+1040.0
CBT Alay (Gulcho)	–	–	–	1	–	52	+5100.0
CBT Sary-Mogul	–	–	–	–	–	77	–
CBT Batken	–	–	–	–	–	6	–
CBT Kerben	–	–	–	–	–	73	–
Total	4,860	5,122	+5.4%	5,812	+13.5%	7,747	+33.2%

Source: KCBTA (2005, 2006, 2008).

areas of available activities such as treks (KBTA 2007). In 2007 visitor numbers grew by 33 per cent, and only CBT Karasuu experienced difficulties. Visitor numbers at the two groups added in 2006 had increased exponentially and three further groups were in operation. The availability of organized tours and treks in the areas where CBT developments are situated is a significant influence on tourist arrivals.

CBT is a sustainable tourism strategy for Kyrgyzstan because it provides an economic solution that promotes community buy-in while preserving the traditional Kyrgyz way of life and customs. The government's commitment to this model, its growing popularity among tourists and its expansion throughout the country suggest that CBT is likely to make an increasing contribution to the development of tourism in Kyrgyzstan. Perhaps more importantly, however, its core values and widespread adoption mean that CBT has significant potential to consolidate Kyrgyz ethnic identity and facilitate cultural unification.

The negative impacts of political and economic change in transitional countries are often most significant in rural areas. In the case of Kyrgyzstan, the results suggest that the CBT programme has helped to offset the worst effects of the political upheaval, particularly in relation to the 2005 revolution and its aftermath, notwithstanding the significant levels of poverty in rural areas and the resulting outmigration. Nevertheless, there are regional variations, and the negative image of the south, in terms of its political instability (particularly in and around Osh) and the attendant risks for visitors, may have been exacerbated at least in the short term by the events of 2005. However, the KCBTA report for 2008 records that interest in visiting southern regions is now growing, as is the overall number of international visitors to the Republic since 2005, including visitors to CBT groups. This may reflect the greater awareness of Kyrgyzstan in global markets through media coverage of the revolution. More locally, the CBT initiative and the "Hospitality Kyrgyzstan" brand in particular have been effective vehicles for the development of a distinctive rural identity which links directly with the cultural heritage of the Kyrgyz nomadic tradition.

Restructuring processes resulting from political and economic transformation often affect the role and identity of women (Weiner 1997), who are often less well positioned to take advantage of new economic opportunities (Hall 2004). Community involvement and ownership of tourism development for women has often been inhibited by the legacy of minimal experience of bottom-up initiatives and lack of opportunity to participate in local decision-making on account of the tradition of male dominance. The CBT initiative has also addressed this issue and provided Kyrgyz women with employment opportunities and support for self-determination. They have therefore been able to ameliorate their conditions and express their own identity (KCBTA 2007).

Conclusion

The development of national identity can raise contradictions and tensions between the generation of a collective identity for a country's citizens (to inculcate a sense of pride and to forge domestic unity and common aspirations) and an acceptable image for the consumption of international tourists and investors (Hall 2004). Kyrgyz identity is a complex issue which is underpinned by a range of factors at individual, local, regional and national levels. Kyrgyzstan is now beginning to emerge as a distinct socio-political entity, despite the heritage it shares with other newly independent Central Asian states: Islamic faith, Turkic language and culture, deep-rooted clan loyalties, a pre-Soviet nomadic lifestyle and Marxist–Leninist rule. However, recent events have destabilised the basis of the Republic's distinctiveness vis-à-vis its neighbours: its commitment to democracy and free market economics and its stand against Islamic fundamentalism. The challenge for the country is to construct a national identity that is both socially and politically acceptable and to ensure that interregional enmity does not deteriorate into hostilities fuelled by religious, ethnic or clan affiliations.

The government recognises tourism's potential to integrate Kyrgyzstan into the global economy, and this sector is beginning to make a useful contribution to foreign exchange earnings and the creation of employment opportunities, not least through the development of CBT in rural areas. Furthermore, the development of the Kyrgyz state tourism product is providing an opportunity to forge a national identity and secure political reimaging objectives to support the country's economic and social development goals. Within the context of tourism branding, cultural heritage is value laden; economic and political power have significantly influenced the selection and interpretation of the nation's history. The communist legacy clashes with Kyrgyzstan's contemporary aspirations, and this is reflected in the lack of emphasis on the country's communist past and the selection of pre-Soviet historical icons such as Manas both to differentiate the brand and to establish a distinct identity for the nation. This is helping the government to develop a clear, credible and sustainable position for the Republic in a tourism market characterised by increasing regional and international competition, product parity and substitutability.

There is no question that the Tulip Revolution in 2005 liberated the nation from a corrupt, autocratic regime and restated Kyrgyzstan's political identity. However, the subsequent instability, particularly events since April 2010, indicates that the country's problems will not be solved in the short term. A key question is whether or not Kyrgyzstan is ready for democratisation; its multi-ethnic identity and recent history have combined to demonstrate that it is still torn between its traditional culture, its Soviet legacy and Western influence. Clearly, the development of a modern civil society and a viable economy are important factors on the country's road to democracy. What is less clear is whether domestic interests or those of its Central Asian neighbours will permit it to consolidate its identity, without which it will struggle to attract international attention and achieve its integration into world markets. Without political and economic stability, a strong legal system and the eradication of corruption, the prospects for international assistance and tourism development remain in the balance. The weight of evidence suggests that, in terms of both politics and tourism, the identity of this former Soviet Asian republic is likely to remain in a transitional state for the foreseeable future.

References

AKIpress (2008) "Report by AKIpress News Agency", www.akipress.com/en_news.php?id=27162 (accessed 13 March 2008) [subscription].

Anderson, J. (1999) *Kyrgyzstan: Central Asia's Island of Democracy*. Amsterdam: Harwood Academic.

Anderson, J. (2000) "Creating a framework for civil society in Kyrgyzstan", *Europe–Asia Studies*, 52(1): 77–93.

Asian Development Outlook (2005) "Economic trends and prospects in developing Asia: Central Asia", www.adb.org/Documents/Books/ADO/2005/kgz.asp (accessed 15 April 2008).

Auezov, M. A. (1999) "Time of the *epos* 'Manas' origin", in M. T. Bayjiev (ed.) *The Great Kirghiz* Epos *"Manas"*, Book 1: *Manas* (pp. 213–61). Bishkek: State Directorate for the Promotion of Manas.

BBC News (2010) "Kyrgyzstan President Bakiyev refuses to resign", http://news.bbc.co.uk/1/hi/8609775.stm (accessed 13 April 2010).

Euromonitor International (2010) *Travel and Tourism – Kyrgyzstan*, www.marketresearch.com/product/print/default.asp?g=1&productid=2743616 (accessed 11 November 2010).

Europe–East (2002) "IMF concludes 2001 consultation with the Kyrgyz Republic", *Europe–East*, 23 January: 317–18.

Guttman, C. (1999) "Kyrgyzstan: breaking out of the old shell", *UNESCO Courier*, November: 21–2.

Hall, D. (ed.) (1999) *Tourism and Economic Development in Eastern Europe and the Soviet Union*. London: Belhaven Press.

Hall, D. (ed.) (2004) *Tourism and Transition: Governance, Transformation and Development*. Wallingford: CAB International.

Huskey, E. (1995) "The rise of contested politics in Central Asia: elections in Kyrgyzstan, 1989–90", *Europe–Asia Studies*, 47(5): 813–33.

KCBTA (Kyrgyz Community-Based Tourism Association) (2005) *"Hospitality Kyrgyztan" Yearly Report*. Bishkek: KCBTA.

KCBTA (Kyrgyz Community-Based Tourism Association) (2006) *"Hospitality Kyrgyztan" Yearly Report*. Bishkek: KCBTA.

KCBTA (Kyrgyz Community-Based Tourism Association) (2007) *"Hospitality Kyrgyztan" Yearly Report*. Bishkek: KCBTA.

KCBTA (Kyrgyz Community-Based Tourism Association) (2008) *"Hospitality Kyrgyztan" Yearly Report*. Bishkek: KCBTA.

KSATS (Kyrgyz State Agency of Tourism and Sport) (2001) *Development of the Tourism Sector of the Kyrgyz Republic until 2010*. Bishkek: KSATS.

Lipset, S. M. (1994) "The social requisites of democracy reviewed", *American Sociological Review*, 59: 1–22.

Marat, E. (2006) *The Tulip Revolution: Kyrgyzstan One Year After*. Washington, DC: Jamestown Foundation.

Marat, E. (2007) "Parliamentary reelections looming as another constitution adopted in Kyrgyzstan", *Eurasia Daily Monitor*, 4(3).

Marat, E. (2008) *National Ideology and State-Building in Kyrgyzstan and Tajikistan*, Silk Road Occasional Paper. Uppsala University, Silk Road Studies Program.

Mayhew, G., Plunkett, R., and Richmond, S. (2000) *Central Asia*. London: Lonely Planet.

Musayev, S. (1994) *The* Epos *"Manas"*. Bishkek: Kyrgyz Polygraph Kombinat.

National Statistical Committee of the Kyrgyz Republic (2005) *Kyrgyzstan Tourism Market Report*. Bishkek: State Agency for Tourism.

National Statistical Committee of the Kyrgyz Republic (2009) *Kyrgyzstan Tourism Market Report*. Bishkek: State Agency for Tourism.

Paksoy, H. B. (1995) "Nationality or religion", *Association for the Advancement of Central Asian Research (AACAR) Bulletin*, 8(2): 13–25.

Platt, G. (1994) "Development bank approves financing for Kyrgyzstan", *Journal of Commerce*, 401 (September): 3–4.

Raeva, D. (2005) "Development of rural regions of Kyrgyzstan through investments in community based tourism", paper given at the international workshop Strategies for Development and Food Security in Mountainous Areas of Central Asia, Dushanbe, Tajikistan, 6–10 June.

Schofield, P. (2004a) "Positioning the tourism product of an emerging industry: image, resources and politics in Kyrgyzstan", in D. Hall (ed.) *Tourism in Transition: Global Processes, Local Impacts* (pp. 105–18). London: CAB International.

Schofield, P. (2004b) "Health tourism in the Kyrgyz Republic: the Soviet salt mine experience", in T. V. Singh (ed.) (2004) *New Horizons in Tourism: Strange Experiences and Stranger Practices* (pp. 135–46). Wallingford: CAB International.

Socor, V. (2005) "Anticlimactic end to Kyrgyz revolution", *Eurasia Daily Monitor*, 2(162).

Starr, F. (1996) "Making Eurasia stable", *Foreign Affairs*, 74(1): 80–93.

Thompson, K., Schofield, P., Foster, N., and Bakieva, G. (2006) "Kyrgyzstan's Manas *epos* millennium celebrations: post-colonial resurgence of Turkic culture and the strategic marketing of cultural tourism", in D. Picard and M. Robinson (eds) *Festivals, Tourism and Social Change: Remaking Worlds* (pp. 172–90). Clevedon: Channel View.

UNDP (1999) *Kyrgyzstan: National Report on Human Development*. Bishkek: UNDP.

UNICEF/WHO (1992) *The Looming Crisis and Fresh Opportunity: Health in Kazakhstan, Kyrgyzstan, Tajikistan, Turkmenistan and Uzbekhistan*. New York: UNICEF/WHO.

UNWTO (2006) *Yearbook of Tourism Statistics*. Madrid: World Tourism Organization.

Weiner, E. (1997) "Assessing the implications of political and economic reform in the post-socialist era: the case of Czech and Slovak women", *East European Quarterly*, 31(3): 473–502.

World Bank (2006) *Brief Report: Kyrgyz Republic*, www.worldbank.org/kyrgyzstan (accessed 22 November 2006).

10 Where mega meets modest

Community events and the making of Canadian national identity

Chantal Laws and Rob Ferguson

Introduction

This chapter considers the nexus of tourism and events in the creation and promotion of national identity as expressed through the annual Canada Day celebrations within Parksville, a small coastal community in the western province of British Columbia. Parksville incorporated the theme of the Olympics for their 2009 celebration in acknowledgement of nearby Vancouver's hosting of the XXI Olympic and Paralympic Games the following winter. This choice offered a unique opportunity to consider juxtaposed expressions of national belonging and to examine whether Canada, as a modern postcolonial power with relatively low population density whose collective identity is still in the process of negotiation, could proffer a fresh perspective on the role of event tourism in the making of destinations.

For this study, a multidisciplinary and multiple methods case study approach has been implemented to map the community event experience and inform the proposition that a bottom-up way towards understanding national identity within a glocalised tourism destination marketing framework offers a richer, deeper and more holistic model of event tourism strategy.

Thematic contexts

There has been recent debate within tourism studies about the state of knowledge in the field (Tribe 2006), and this chapter seeks to adopt a post-disciplinary perspective (Coles *et al.* 2006) in moving beyond accepted boundaries of enquiry into the social phenomena of tourist activity. Drawing on recent research in the fields of cultural tourism and events management (Derrett 2003; Getz 2007, 2008; Crouch 2009; Quinn 2009), the means by which experience of an event contributes to notions of identity are explored and can be seen to be more complex and reflexive than previously suggested.

While the use of large-scale events as a tool for place marketing and related top-down socio-economic ambitions of regeneration and fostering of national pride are well established, discussions about the nature of the identity thus created are still fluid (Robinson *et al.* 2000; Meethan *et al.* 2006), and specific attention has turned only recently to the equally important role that smaller-scale events play in defining place and shaping identity (see, for example, Bell and Jayne

2006; Bradley and Hall 2006). The authors have argued elsewhere (Laws and Ferguson 2008) that a research focus on smaller-scale, niche and fringe events provides a better fit with established academic and professional definitions of events where emphasis is placed on the centrality of human interaction, rather than the logistics or impacts models that can be found in any standard text.

In outlining the human element, Bowdin *et al.* (2006: 4) recognise that, "Both in private and in public, people feel the need to mark the important happenings in their lives", and the ethical guidelines of the International Festivals and Events Association state that "festivals, events and civic celebrations are at the foundation of characteristics that distinguish human communities and interaction" (IFEA 2008: 1). There is considerable scope for further investigation into both the role of smaller-scale events in creating community and how the local to global intersections that are forged in this process might enrich our understanding of the relationship between tourism, events and national identity.

Defining the events/tourism relationship

There is a substantial and growing body of literature that considers the nature and extent of interaction between events and tourism: Getz (2008) and Quinn (2009) have provided recent reviews of the body of knowledge in this area, and these authors highlight not only the potential benefits of cross-disciplinary consideration but also the concerns that may result from viewing the utility of events purely through an exclusively tourism lens.

Increasingly, commentators from the fields of leisure and cultural studies (see, for example, Sharpe (2008) and Ravenscroft and Gilchrist (2006)) have revisited events as spaces and places of social change, where power discourses between dominant and resistant ideologies are at play and notions of festivalisation and the carnivalesque provide emancipation from hegemonic social structures.

Events management perspectives

Early contributions emphasised the public, celebratory and community characteristics of events, with Janiskee (1980: 97) proposing that festivals be conceived as formal constructs programmed around "some concept, happening or fact". Quinn (2009), however, notes that this early interest in events as an agent of cultural and social change did not have longevity, and that the theme which would come to dominate was the strategic and operational management of events.

Restrictions in the events management vocabulary are often justified by the fact that the field is still in its relative infancy, in terms of its recognition both as a stand-alone profession (Bowdin *et al.* 2006) and as a discrete area of academic enquiry (Getz 2007). Perhaps driven by the need to establish legitimacy, or possibly in response to the nature of the business environment, event professionals have often sought to couch their successes in quantitative terms and with a focus on the mega end of the scale, where such events are defined as "so large that they affect whole economies and reverberate in the global media" (Bowdin *et al.* 2006: 18).

Getz (2005) has identified that events on this scale generate extraordinarily high levels of tourism, while Hall (1997) states that mega-events are intentionally targeted at the international tourism market.

Brown and James have put forward a strong argument that such instrumental agendas, driven by sponsors, government and funding agencies, have led to the abandonment of "the meaningful and authentic, in favour of the successful" (2004: 55). They critique the proliferation of carbon-copy, risk-averse events that repeat proven success rather than engaging with community aspirations to develop new events, and make a call for alternative strategies that are truly reflective of sense of place and cultural authenticity. As these authors eloquently state, "Great events, whether major, minor or hallmark, need to be not safe" (ibid.: 62).

Getz (2007) has recently proposed a new paradigm of event studies which emphasises the social contexts for events as the discipline moves towards maturation. Event studies shift analysis from processual approaches towards the meanings attached to our experiences of events, and therefore demonstrate an academic progression of the body of knowledge. Despite this, the language of the events industry is still conditioned by applied discourse, as can be seen particularly where the use of events within destination branding and place-marketing initiatives is considered.

Destination management perspectives

Tourism initiatives, particularly events, have been identified as strategic means to increase civic pride, create a sense of cultural identity, increase community cohesion, and create opportunities for the exchange of ideas (Gursoy *et al.* 2004). Rao (2001) relates that festivals form a public good above and beyond their basic entertainment function, as they provide an opportunity for families to display their commitment to the community. Events can thus be seen as a noble endeavour for their promoters and trumpeted for the cultural worth they can bring to the community in addition to any economic benefits.

For larger-scale events, the need for integrated planning and the involvement of major stakeholders is clearly evident, and work on their impacts, such as that by Garcia (2005), demonstrates the benefits that systematic planning can reap, particularly in building long-term legacies. However, in focusing on hallmark, special and mega-events, such impact studies are necessarily limited, since events on this scale are "hardly typical of planned events or event tourism" (Getz 2008: 412).

Events utilised for tourism gain can be conceived as planned spatial-temporal phenomena, where the interaction of people, settings and management systems creates a unique experience for all participants (Getz 2008). Planned events are conceived historically as community initiatives, whereas oversight is now increasingly in the hands of professionals and entrepreneurs, indicating that such forms of celebration may have become marginalised within destination management frameworks. Their value (in itself a contested expression) to tourism industry stakeholders is considered minimal in terms of demand and return on investment; Getz identifies that local and regional events are "problematic from a tourism perspective" (ibid.: 407). Thus, the limitations of hierarchical planning models are revealed and the need for more collaborative approaches that promulgate local involvement and support are made apparent (Gursoy and Kendall 2006).

Events and the making of identities

In terms of the way in which commemoration of nationhood is affected by the staging of participatory celebratory events, there has been much debate regarding control of the identities being performed. In considering the development of national celebrations in the United States and Australia in the course of the nineteenth and twentieth centuries, Spillman (1997: 6) identifies that "organized public festivals have long been seen as important representations and affirmations of collective identity", but that the organisational constraints of the cultural production process will have a profound influence on the type of culture that is produced. She further notes that, in particular, the nature of the relationship between planning organisations and other interest groups will also have a determining effect, concluding that: "cultural events are the arena for claims about national identity made by elite groups for whom the concept itself is most important" (ibid.: 8).

Edensor (2001, 2002) expands upon this point, critiquing previous authors who have considered sanctioned spectacle as the only means by which national identity can be expressed. He calls for a less reified consideration which acknowledges that the "dynamic, contested, multiple and fluid" identities of nationhood are very much grounded in the mundane and that exploring this "dense and murky cultural realm" requires a new set of theoretical tools (2002: vi). Edensor's argument strongly mirrors the call for post-disciplinary research in tourism (Coles *et al.* 2006) and is critical of the limitations of top-down research perspectives. Reflecting on the particular qualities that the Canadian context presents, Dittmer and Larsen (2007: 736) also recognise that the country's complex, diffuse and contested national identity is located in the "interplay of popular culture production and consumption", that socially constructed populist research projects are a rich vein to develop new or alternative perspectives, and that such investigations represent a constantly evolving body of work.

Constructing Canada's national identity

National identity is a social construct and as such is fluid and continually being (re)negotiated, particularly in response to an increasingly globalised world (Giddens 2006). There are multiple contemporary perspectives on how Canadian national identity can be understood which recognise the contested and emergent nature of the country as a modern postcolonial power. As both Canada Day and the Olympics are national events, the community of Parksville's celebrations present an opportunity to examine the intersections of identity formation at both the community and the national level.

Canada has a unique geopolitical position within the international community. Whitson (2004) rightly recognises that, although the country is affluent, rich with natural resources and a member of the G8, it can be considered peripheral in the sense that it has a relatively small population and economy, resulting in the need to exercise political influence through multilateral institutions rather than independently. Winter (2007) comments that boundaries relating to national identity are produced in confrontation and reaction to some external other: in the Canadian context, that other refers to "an external dominant player, the United States" (ibid.: 499). The legacy of the real or perceived dominance of the United States has resulted in a situation where "Canada has been seen – by others and even by many Canadians themselves – as culturally derivative" (Whitson 2004: 1217). There is no question that the two nations are meaningfully connected through strong economic and cultural ties that reflect their shared new world history; however, "being" Canadian requires a recognition of the fundamental differences in how the two societies are perceived both internally and externally.

Canada is portrayed as the kinder, gentler nation by virtue of its aspirational "civic ideology" (Francis 1997: 10), which encompasses such notions as universal social and health programmes and a multicultural vision of a diverse society (Dib *et al.* 2008). This is contrasted, at least within Canada, with the United States, which is perceived to value individualism, capitalism and a melting-pot approach to the cultural assimilation of visible minorities (Winter 2007).

The notion that this kinder, gentler identity is universally shared and reflects the lived experience of all Canadians is, of course, contestable. Tensions between the English-speaking majority and French-speaking minority are well documented (Winter 2007), as are tensions surrounding aboriginal aspirations for self-government and autonomy (Russell 2000; Francis 1992). Arat-Koc (2005) additionally argues that the Canadian–American dichotomy is far less ambiguous in the post-September 11 world. The assertion by a variety of actors within Canada – and further understood within the context of the "global war on terror" – that the country is integrally part of the West and an ally of the United States has implied what Arat-Koc describes as the "re-whitening of Canadian identity" (ibid.: 34) and has exasperated tensions along ethnic lines.

The hallmark of Canadian nationalism has been the perceived quiet manner in which Canadians express their collective identity. Dittmer and Larsen (2007: 740) describe this as "quiet passion", while Millard *et al.* (2002: 11) characterise it as the "myth of diffidence", observing that representations of Canadian versus American national identity appear throughout Canada's popular culture and actually present a form of nationalism that is "noisy, assertive and even bellicose". They further argue that the internal perception of a tepid commitment to nationalism allow Canadians "to deploy a 'suspiciously' American style of patriotism" (ibid.). Francis implies the importance of myths in informing the Canadian identity through the (re)telling of Canada's cultural "stories", and that these form a "consensual hallucination" in which the meaning of Canadianness can be envisioned and fully understood (1997: 10).

Canada's national identity is not easily fixed, particularly in light of the dynamic socio-political and economic relationship with the United States, which, as illustrated, serves as the primary force against which Canadian identity is constructed. It is also interesting to note that the American celebrations of independence have a longer tradition than Canada's; however, the forms the two celebrations take are nearly indistinguishable, further demonstrating the close cultural proximity between the two nations.

Establishing to what extent Canadian and American identities are intertwined is beyond the scope of this chapter, but it is evident that national celebratory events, such as Canada Day, serve as meaningful platforms for nationalistic expression. The manner in which these events are manifested and experienced locally can therefore be seen both as a powerful arena for the expression of community identity and as a mechanism to reinforce or contest the hegemonic narrative of national identity.

What is Canada Day?

In 1879 royal assent was given to create Dominion Day as a public holiday to celebrate the anniversary of the British North America Act of 1 July 1867, which had unified Canada as a single country within the dominion of the United Kingdom. Complete independence from the UK occurred some 115 years later, when royal assent was given to the Canada Act of 1982, recognising the patriation of Canada's constitution. That year also saw a change in Canada's national public holiday in name and form, from "Dominion Day" to "Canada Day", and from a celebration focused on the nation's capital city, Ottawa, towards much wider participation across the country. According to the Department of Canadian Heritage (2008), "Canada Day is an opportunity to gather in our communities, from [Pacific] coast to [Arctic] coast to [Atlantic] coast, and to proudly celebrate all we have in common." Canada Day is celebrated differently across the country in ways that reflect the diverse cultural backgrounds of its citizens; however, it is usually associated with parades, festivals, sporting events, fireworks and the like.

Case study: Parksville's 2009 Canada Day celebration

The city of Parksville is one of twelve small coastal communities located on Vancouver Island which are collectively referred to in the tourism media as Vancouver Island's Oceanside Region. The region has a combined population of approximately 40,000, the majority of whom live in the municipalities of Parksville and Qualicum Beach (with approximately 12,000 and 9,000 residents respectively). The communities within the region utilise a collective branding strategy through the establishment of a non-profit, tourism industry-led destination marketing organization known as the Oceanside Tourism Association (Regional District of Nanaimo 2009).

Oceanside's tourism strategy leans heavily upon the nature of its small and friendly communities, the variety of opportunities for outdoor recreation, its boutique shopping and its accessible natural beauty, including numerous protected natural areas of regional, national and international importance (OTA 2009).

Local festivals and events are also seen to be a central element of the tourism offer, with the Oceanside area boasting over 140 annual community events. Parksville's 2009 Canada Day celebrations, themed "The Spirit of Community", were tagged as the largest on Vancouver Island. A variety of activities were scheduled, among them one of the nation's largest parades, which gave a subtle nod to the Olympic and Paralympic Games by encouraging an Olympic theme. This event is widely recognised to be of regional significance and draws approximately 25,000 spectators annually, effectively doubling Parksville's population for the celebration (OTA 2009; Parksville Canada Day Committee 2009).

Parksville's position on the east coast of Vancouver Island and its reputation as a retirement destination for active seniors stands in juxtaposition to Vancouver's multicultural population and reputation for youthful vibrancy: it is the "modest"-to Vancouver's urban "mega"-event environment. While the two districts are in relatively close proximity (at around 70 km distance), travel between them necessitates a planned journey involving either ferry or air transport, and their divergent characters provide a novel case for considering the scale and impact of community-led events.

In response to the call for a more holistic methodology (Tribe 2006), a reflexive approach utilising multiple interpretive methods has been adopted in acknowledgment of the complexity of staging events within small and closely bonded communities. The range of methods selected allowed the authors to access key informants across the range of production and consumption perspectives. Those considered most appropriate were autoethnography, participatory action research, semi-structured interviews and semiotic analysis of promotional materials and media coverage.

Autoethnography allows researchers to connect the personal and the cultural by placing themselves within the social context of the research (Alsop 2002). Furthermore, it facilitates the means to "challenge the canonized genre of 'objective' depictions of social reality" (Motzafi-Haller 1997: 219) by relinquishing their expert outsider status in favour of a reflexive position as an in-group researcher. Related to this, many studies of events emphasise the measureable outputs and impacts, at a potential loss of the human experiential elements. Participatory action research also enables subjects to account for their own agency within the construction of the event experience (Reason and Bradbury 2007), which encompasses more than consideration, typical of many empirical studies, of the motivations to attend an event (Moscardo 2008; Angrosino 2009). Attendees were encouraged to record and reflect on their experiences throughout the duration of the Canada Day celebrations, and follow-up interviews were conducted to discuss these after the event. Community and industry leaders were consulted via semi-structured interviews in order better to understand the role of events in the community with regard to their tourism and leisure values.

Contrasting the linear, processual view, that event organisers precisely orchestrate experiences which are then passively consumed by participants, the dynamics of Parksville's Canada Day celebrations reflect a much more dialectical relationship.

This is perhaps most evident in how those people engaged in the event find themselves shifting roles throughout the celebration. To illustrate, an individual could easily, in succession and/or simultaneously, be acting as a local resident assisting a visitor to find their way to the best spot to view the parade; as a volunteer marshalling the parade route, or as a spectator enjoying the sights and sounds of the parade. The ease with which people shift between roles demonstrates how the distinction between consumer and producer can be blurred beyond any meaningful distinction; a more dynamic concept of event management then emerges in which events are, to some extent, recognised to be co-produced and co-consumed by all. Parksville's Canada Day therefore offers an opportunity to explore how notions of performance, embodied practice and performativity can be understood within the event experience context, and subsequently adds to the discourse on identity formation at the individual, community and national levels.

Pancakes' performative powers

In a rallying call for a more holistic understanding of the nature of tourism and, by extension, event experiences, Crouch (2009: 90) reminds us that "people matter" and recognises the centrality of bodily actions, sensory inputs and mental reflexivity within a notion of feeling of doing (Crouch 2001). The manner in which we act out the routine mundane bodily rituals of everyday life forms the means by which we communicate to others our being. Thrift alludes to this within the discourse of non-representational theory, in that it is concerned with "mundane everyday practices that shape the conduct of human beings towards others and themselves in particular sites" (Thrift 1997, cited in Nash 2000: 655). It is the uncontested, unquestioned and routine aspect of these actions that masks their complex transformative power on how the world is understood and negotiated.

To illustrate, Canadian national celebrations tend to have familiar forms to the manner in which they are enacted. For Canadians, one such form appears to be consistently present within small-scale local celebrations, namely the pancake breakfast. The humble pancake and maple syrup combination has a special place within the Canadian psyche; like the Royal Canadian Mounted Police and other representations of Canadianness, pancakes take on additional meaning within this celebratory context. A community event in Parksville would simply not be complete without the requisite pancake breakfast. The relatively simple act of sitting opposite one's neighbour while sampling a steaming stack of pancakes, prepared by a local service group and smothered in maple syrup, exemplifies how the sights, sounds, tastes, smells and tactile inputs inform an embodied experience that can provide an opportunity for the "(re)making of the self, identities and relationship with the world" (Crouch 2001: 62) and a means of reinforcing communally held values. The concept of performance in this context can be understood to be manifested in the normative embodied experience and typified within Parksville Canada Day celebrations by the pancake breakfast, community parade, market stalls, live music and evening fireworks display. It is only by the inclusion of these essential elements that participants can successfully understand what the

Figure 10.1 Spectators await the start of Parksville's Canada Day parade, reported to be one of the largest in the nation.

event is about and negotiate their role within it by unconsciously, instinctively deciphering the culturally coded meanings attached.

The "glowing heart" of Canadian communities

As Canada's national anthem and the theme of the XXI Olympic Games suggests, Canadians approach nationalism and identity with "glowing hearts". National events like the XXI Olympics communicate Canadianness not only to the world but also to Canadians themselves. In this sense mega-events are about "putting the global on show for the locals and inviting them to take on new identities as citizens of the world" (Whitson 2004: 1223). This self-representation of national identity provides prompts for how Canadianness should be enacted, and it is the performative nature of these embodied actions that further strengthens cultural norms and leads to the self-fulfilment of community and national identity. Figure 10.1 exemplifies how donning national emblems, colours and symbols to await the parade alongside one's neighbour and fellow Canadian illustrates how these normative ideals lead to self-fulfilment of home and identity.

As highlighted earlier, the Oceanside area is marketed as small and friendly, with ample opportunities for recreation, and it is one of British Columbia's fastest growing regions (OTA 2009). What is also interesting to note is that, of the twenty-five oldest municipalities in Canada of more than 5,000 inhabitants, Qualicum Beach ranked first, with an average age of fifty-eight, while Parksville

Figure 10.2 Local residents entertain the parade crowd with traditional clog dancing.

ranked fifth, with an average of forty-nine (Statistics Canada 2002). The growth and unique demographic profile was no doubt fuelled by its attractiveness to affluent, active baby-boomers seeking a comfortable lifestyle in retirement. One supposition is that these new residents, who were attracted by the perceived friendly small-town values, could be eager to demonstrate their place within it by seeking opportunities to support local endeavours.

This is certainly the case in Parksville, as the 2009 Canada Day celebration was organized through a local volunteer group whose membership is active across a variety of community organizations and businesses. Figure 10.2 clearly illustrates the central role that senior members of the community perform through their active participation in Parksville's community events. This is noteworthy because, despite being a celebration of nationhood, Canada Day was organised separately from the conventional political apparatus of the state. The ownership of local people in this event not only illustrates the leisure value in event volunteerism but also illuminates notions of performativity in how community values are enacted, constituted and communicated to both locals and visitors. Indeed, local, small-scale community events appear to contradict the notion that event management is becoming more professionalised, as their success relies predominantly on local volunteer groups rather than on a cadre of event professionals.

Figure 10.3 An example of the many children and youth who actively participate in Parksville's Canada Day parade.

This challenge of framing community events within an industry context has been illustrated by Getz (2008: 413), who states that "Attending an event in one's own home community is experientially different from travelling to an event", and by Van der Wagen (2001, cited by Brown and James 2004), who argues that most events are in fact community related. Figure 10.3 shows how the attendance and participation of locals in Parksville's Canada Day parade is experientially and markedly different to the more passive consumption perspective of a visitor. The inclusion of children in the activities, primarily the parade, has for many launched a trajectory of participation from observer to participant to facilitator, thus reinforcing local cultural identity and the longevity of distinct community celebrations. As identified by Page and Connell (2009), such a high degree of participation provides a strong contrast with early events tourism literature, which emphasised the potential for negative impacts through host–visitor interactions during events (see, for example, Boorstin ([1961] 1992); Greenwood (1972); MacCannell (1973)), where communities were often framed as victims of the touristic process rather than as agents of their own experience.

Tourism, and particularly the act of being a tourist, is often defined as time and space apart from everyday life, and such a distinction privileges special locations and destinations as stages for these bodily enactments of difference. Events are necessarily rooted in place, space and time; yet the notion of locale becomes problematic with regard to community events, as the boundaries between self and other, or between here and there, are blurred to the point of irrelevance. The "multiplicity of spatial, sociocultural, political and environmental contexts", which Quinn (2009: 490) recognises are prevalent in events, has shifted debate away from criticisms of the commodification of place for tourist consumption towards a reflection on the processes by which authenticity is decided. Quinn outlines that such reflections differ from earlier theories, such as those of MacCannell (1973), which conceived of the authentic as a pristine and objective state destroyed through touristic appropriation, and considers instead that community is a negotiable cultural value reiterated through social processes, such as the retelling of Canada's story in Parksville's annual event.

Dib *et al.* (2008: 2) recognise the multiple and concurrent meanings for those involved in the production of commemorative events and explore how this works in a Canadian context, identifying common spaces where people can meet and interact – such spaces act as "the foundation for creating and enhancing a Canadian identity. They are the vehicle through which a multicultural, multi-racial, multi-religious population develops synergies that are strong enough to lead to a collective national identity." Belonging to a community entails participation and active involvement in a geographic space without artificial barriers, where local residents perform as both producers and consumers of events, and it is entirely possible for such activity to address the needs of the community and of visitors at the same time.

Conclusion

Populist and postmodern examinations of the cultural tourism experience (Smith 2004) have actively adopted multiple lenses to consider the development of events within a tourism context, and through this have engendered a more reflexive perspective on the notion of identity within events tourism. Underlying much of this shifting debate are the notions of performance, embodied practice and performativity (Crouch 2009), indicating the need for a more organic model of growth for community-led events. Despite this, consideration of events at the pre-hallmark stage remains marginal to the mainstream literature, and therefore the development of new approaches remains largely unexplored.

This chapter has outlined the ways in which events generated within, by and for the communities which host them might be benignly appropriated for tourism gain. In contrast to the established position that the success of local events is contingent upon their performance against a hierarchical scale, smaller-scale community events are demonstrated to be of far more import, meaning and value than previously thought: though relatively modest in scale, they speak of larger concerns in the community and as such reveal their more mega-scale influences.

Rather than being conceived as passive recipients of an external destination marketing strategy, communities engaged in event management are in this way seen to be instrumental in the construction of a destination's image. Participants, residents, organizers and spectators at such events actively, explicitly and deliberately construct the meaning of "home" through embodied actions in which a multiplicity of meanings is apparent.

In this way the making of national identity can be perceived as built upon a variety of local events celebrated in such a way that reflects the community's own perceptions and priorities while also being expressive of a shared national ethos. This combination of global awareness coupled with local priorities can be construed as an articulation of a globalised society in which events act as grounded transformative agents irrespective of category or scale of operation. Indeed, if, as many of the definitions purport, events are ultimately about the centrality of lived experience, then our ways of talking about their function within tourism, and our thinking about their meaning in society, must also be rehumanised.

References

Alsop, C. (2002) "Home and away: self-reflexive auto-/ethnography", *Forum: Qualitative Social Research*, 3(3); www.qualitative-research.net/index.php/fqs/article/view/823/1789 (accessed 11 January 2010).

Angrosino, M. (2009) *Doing Ethnographic and Observational Research*. London: Sage.

Arat-Koc, S. (2005) "The disciplinary boundaries of Canadian identity after September 11: civilizational identity, multiculturalism, and the challenge of anti-imperialist feminism", *Social Justice*, 32(4): 32–49.

Bell, D., and Jayne, M. (2006) "Conceptualising small cities", in D. Bell and M. Jayne (eds) *Small Cities: Urban Experience beyond the Metropolis*. Abingdon: Routledge.

Boorstin, D. J. ([1961] 1992) *The Image: A Guide to Pseudo-Events in America*. New York: Vintage.

Bowdin, G., Allen, J., O'Toole, W., Harris, R., and McDonnell, I. (eds) (2006) *Events Management*. 2nd edn, Oxford: Elsevier Butterworth–Heinemann.

Bradley, A., and Hall, T. (2006) "The festival phenomenon: festivals, events and the promotion of small urban areas", in D. Bell and M. Jayne (eds) *Small Cities: Urban Experience Beyond the Metropolis*. Abingdon: Routledge.

Brown, S., and James, J. (2004) "Event design and management: ritual sacrifice", in I. Yeoman, J. Ali-Knight, S. Drummond and U. McMahon-Beattie (eds) *Festival and Events Management: An International Arts and Culture Perspective*. Oxford: Butterworth–Heinemann.

Coles, T., Hall, C. M., and Duval, D. T. (2006) "Tourism and post-disciplinary enquiry", *Current Issues in Tourism*, 9(4/5): 293–319.

Crouch, D. (2001) "Spatialities and the feeling of doing", *Social and Cultural Geography*, 2(1): 61–75.

Crouch, D. (2009) "The diverse dynamics of cultural studies and tourism", in M. Robinson and T. Jamal (eds) *The Sage Handbook of Tourism Studies*. London: Sage.

Department of Canadian Heritage (2008) "Canada Day", www.pch.gc.ca/special/canada/11/canada-eng.cfm (accessed 11 January 2010).

Derrett, R. (2003) "Making sense of how festivals demonstrate a community's sense of place", *Event Management*, 8(1): 49–58.

Dib, K., Donaldson, I., and Turcotte, B. (2008) "Integration and identity in Canada: the importance of multicultural common spaces", *Canadian Ethnic Studies*, 40(1): 161–87.

Dittmer, J., and Larsen, S. (2007) "Captain Canuck, audience response, and the project of Canadian nationalism", *Social & Cultural Geography*, 8(5): 735–53.

Edensor, T. (2001) "Performing tourism, staging tourism: (re)producing tourist space and practice", *Tourist Studies*, 1(1): 59–81.

Edensor, T. (2002) *National Identity, Popular Culture and Everyday Life*. Oxford: Berg.

Francis, D. (1992) *The Imaginary Indian: The Image of the Indian in Canadian Culture*. Vancouver: Arsenal Pulp Press.

Francis, D. (1997) *National Dreams: Myth, Memory and Canadian History*. Vancouver: Arsenal Pulp Press.

Garcia, B. (2005) "De-constructing the city of culture: the long term cultural legacies of Glasgow 1990", *Urban Studies*, 42(5/6): 1–28.

Getz, D. (2005) *Event Management and Event Tourism*. 2nd edn, New York: Cognizant Communication.

Getz, D. (2007) *Event Studies: Theory, Research and Policy for Planned Events*. Oxford: Elsevier Butterworth–Heinemann.

Getz, D. (2008) "Event tourism: definition, evolution, and research", *Tourism Management*, 29(3): 403–28.

Giddens, A. (2006) *Sociology*. 5th edn, Cambridge: Polity.

Greenwood, D. J. (1972) "Tourism as an agent of change: a Spanish Basque case", *Ethnology*, 11(1): 80–91.

Gursoy, D., and Kendall, K. W. (2006) "Hosting mega events: modelling locals' support", *Annals of Tourism Research*, 33(3) 603–23.

Gursoy, D., Kim, K., and Uysal, M. (2004) "Perceived impacts of festivals and special events organizers: an extension and validation", *Tourism Management*, 25(2): 171–81.

Hall, C. M. (1997) *Hallmark Tourist Events: Impacts, Management and Planning*. Chichester: Wiley.

IFEA (International Festivals and Events Association) (2008) *IFEA Industry Code of Professional Conduct and Ethics*, www.ifea.com/pdf/IFEA%20Industry%20Code%20of%20Professional%20Conduct%20and%20Ethics.pdf (accessed 11 June 2008).

Janiskee, R. (1980) "South Carolina's harvest festivals: rural delights for day tripping urbanites", *Journal of Cultural Geography*, 1(1): 96–104.

Laws, C., and Ferguson, R. (2008) "From mega to modest: new perspectives on the contribution of events to identity and place-making activity", paper presented at the Leisure Studies Association conference Community, Capital and Cultures: Leisure and Regeneration as Cultural Practice, Liverpool, July.

MacCannell, D. (1973) "Staged authenticity: arrangements of social space in tourist settings", *American Journal of Sociology*, 79(3): 589–603.

Meethan, K., Anderson, A., and Miles, S. (eds) (2006) *Tourism, Consumption and Representation*. Wallingford: CAB International.

Millard, G., Riegel, S., and Wright, J. (2002) "Here's where we get Canadian: English-Canadian nationalism and popular culture", *American Review of Canadian Studies*, 32(1): 11–34.

Moscardo, G. (2008) "Analyzing the role of festivals and events in regional development", *Event Management*, 11(1/2): 23–32.

Motzafi-Haller, P. (1997) "Writing birthright: on native anthropologists and the politics of representation", in D. Reed-Danahay (ed.) *Auto/ethnography: Rewriting the Self and the Social*. Oxford: Berg.

Nash, C. (2000) "Performativity in practice: some recent work in cultural geography", *Progress in Human Geography*, 24(4): 653–64.

OTA (Oceanside Tourism Association) (2009) *Parksville and Qualicum Beach: Vancouver Island's Oceanside Region*. Parksville: OTA; www.visitparksvillequalicumbeach.com/cms.asp?wpID=223 (accessed 15 January 2010).

Page, S. J., and Connell, J. (2009) *Tourism: A Modern Synthesis*. 3rd edn, London: Cengage Learning.

Parksville Canada Day Committee (2009) *City of Parksville Canada Day Celebrations Official Sponsor Package*. Parksville: Parksville Canada Day Committee.

Quinn, B. (2009) "Festivals, events, and tourism", in M. Robinson and T. Jamal (eds) *The Sage Handbook of Tourism Studies*. London: Sage.

Rao, V. (2001) "Celebrations as social investments: festival expenditures, unit price variation and social status in rural India", *Journal of Development Studies*, 38(1): 71–97.

Ravenscroft, N., and Gilchrist, P. (2006) "Festivals of transgression: governance, discipline and reworking the carnivalesque", in S. Fleming and F. Jordan (eds) *Events and Festivals: Education, Impacts and Experiences*. Eastbourne: Leisure Studies Association.

Reason, P., and Bradbury, H. (2007) *The Sage Handbook of Action Research: Participative Inquiry and Practice*. 2nd edn, London: Sage.

Regional District of Nanaimo (2009) "Population statistics", www.rdn.bc.ca/cms.asp?wpID=440 (accessed 15 January 2010).

Robinson, M., Long, P., Evans, N., Sharpley, R., and Swarbrooke, J. (eds) (2000) *Expressions of Culture, Identity and Meaning in Tourism*. Sunderland: Centre for Travel and Tourism.

Russell, D. (2000) *A People's Dream: Aboriginal Self-Government in Canada*. Vancouver: UBC Press.

Sharpe, E. K. (2008) "Festivals and social change: intersections of pleasure and politics at a community music festival", *Leisure Science*, 30(3): 217–34.

Smith, M. K. (2004) *Issues in Cultural Tourism Studies*. London: Routledge.

Spillman, L. P. (1997) *Nation and Commemoration: Creating National Identities in the United States and Australia*. Cambridge: Cambridge University Press.

Statistics Canada (2002) *Profile of the Canadian Population by Age and Sex: Canada Ages*, http://dsp-psd.pwgsc.gc.ca/Collection/Statcan/96F0030X/96F0030XIE2001002.pdf (accessed 5 November 2010).

Tribe, J. (2006) "The truth about tourism", *Annals of Tourism Research*, 33(2): 360–81.

Whitson, D. (2004) "Bringing the world to Canada: 'the periphery of the centre'", *Third World Quarterly*, 25(7): 1215–32.

Winter, E. (2007) "Neither 'America' nor 'Quebec': constructing the Canadian multicultural nation", *Nations and Nationalism*, 13(3): 481–503.

11 Location and landscape

Small-scale sporting events and national identity

Elspeth Frew

Introduction

Events such as world championship basketball reflect mainstream sports. However, there are hundreds of smaller-scale sporting events, also called world championships, which showcase very specialised, off-beat or alternative forms of sports or games – for example, the World Flounder Tramping Championships and the World Bog Snorkelling Championships. Such small-scale events offer the opportunity for competitors to become a "world champion" in a unique sport or game and often reflect aspects of the culture and identity of the host region. This chapter examines some of these unusual world championships and considers their significance in relation to national identity.

Sports and national identity have been inextricably woven together since international competitions were introduced in the late 1800s (Crolley and Hand 2006). As such, there has been much debate about the relationship between sport, nationalism and national identities (see, for example, Allison 2002; Bairner 2001; Cronin 1999; Jarvie 2003; Smith and Porter 2004). Jarvie (2003: 540) has suggested that sport and sporting achievements contribute to a country's greatness and national identity and at times help to "transcend internal strife and social deference". For example, the involvement of the Dutch football team in global competition aided the construction of a myth of national football distinction, and the media coverage and discourse turned this myth into a key element of a reimagined national community (Lechner 2007).

Researchers have also considered the relationship between sport, the cultural landscape and the character of sports places (see, for example, Bale 2003; Kotnik 2007; Raitz 1987). Bale (1988) believes that place and locality lie at the heart of sport and suggests that sports events, whether at local, regional or national level, produce a communal spirit. He explains that sport meshes with place in at least three ways. First, place appears to affect sporting performance and outcomes; second, sports provide a means of satisfying a cultural voyeurism; and, third, aspects of sports relate to ideas of place attachment, place pride and "boosterism", with place attachment reflecting sport-induced localism, regionalism and nationalism. A recent example of place attachment was demonstrated in Slovenia, when the national television station constructed skiing as a national activity by presenting it through the country's natural scenery. In so doing, it established and reproduced an idealised vision of nationhood and national identity which was able to create a powerful collective identification (Kotnik 2007).

Sporting success has also often helped to foster a close symbolic link between specific sports and places. To illustrate this idea, Jarvie (2003) uses the examples of athletics and Kenya, football and Brazil, ice hockey and Canada/Sweden, golf and Scotland, sumo wrestling and Japan, cycling and France, baseball and Cuba, and hurling and Ireland. While it is increasingly difficult to sustain the argument that a single sport represents any one nation, he suggests that, nonetheless, certain "nation-specific" games survive – among them Gaelic games, American football, shinty (a game resembling hockey played predominantly in Scotland), Australian rules football and pelota (a ball game played against a speciality marked wall, popular among the Spanish and Spanish Americans) – and that these games "continue to play a central part within various national cultures" (ibid.: 541). Similarly, Ritchie (2005) notes that the hosts of sporting events such as marathons and endurance races often make use of the landscape and physical resources of a region.

Spectators and participants

Sport has been described as an "institutionalized game demanding the demonstration of physical prowess" (Loy 1979: 41) where the participants are motivated by personal enjoyment and external rewards (Coakley 2001). Games can also be physically demanding, but they can be sedentary and can include "non-physical pastimes such as board games and gambling" (Veal and Lynch 2001: 21).

Sports tourism is experienced when an individual is actively or passively involved in a sporting activity that is "participated in casually or in an organised way for non-commercial or business/commercial reasons" (Standeven and De Knop 1999: 7). It has recently received attention in the literature (see, for example, Gibson 2006; Higham 2005; Ritchie and Adair 2004; Weed and Bull 2004), with most research focusing on large-scale sporting events. Ritchie (2005) notes that, despite the popularity and number of small-scale events, little research has been published concerning their nature or tourism potential. He comments that this is particularly surprising given the potential that such events have for marketing and attracting economic development in an era when cities are competing against each other to attract investment and tourism.

There are two types of passive spectators at a sporting event, termed "connoisseur" and "casual" observers (Standeven and De Knop 1999). Connoisseur observers are those "who have extensive passive involvement and are discriminating in the sports activity they watch as spectators or officiators" (ibid.: 13). Casual observers are those who "simply enjoy watching an event and who usually happen across it rather than plan their visit" (ibid.: 14). Passive spectators can range from "connoisseur" or "avid" spectators at one end of a continuum to "casual" spectators at the other. Studies of special interest tourists (see, for example, Brotherton and Himmetoglu 1997) suggest there is potential for a middle group between avid and casual spectators/fans who may have mixed motivations between sport and tourism, and this may impact upon their travel behaviour. Spectators at sporting events may require a range of specialist knowledge or expertise built up over many years to appreciate fully the core activity of the event (such as the technical and artistic knowledge necessary to recognise the athleticism of certain sport-speople). However, at small-scale events the spectators may be able to appreciate the activities they are witnessing without necessarily having any specialist knowledge.

Novelli (2005: 143) defines attendance at an event where a tourist can become physically engaged as "activity based tourism", their holiday choice being "inspired by the desire to pursue an activity". Alternatively, such a tourist's choice of destination may be determined primarily by a particular interest (Hall 2007). With special interest tourism, Trauer and Ryan (2005: 486) note that "the tourist is involved in a personal project, that of a holiday or perhaps a business trip, pursuing his/her special interest away from home in a special place, chosen for special qualities and on the promise of a satisfying personal experience". Small-scale sports events may therefore have the potential to provide such experiences because of their strong use of novel and unique themes and activities – some with an emphasis on culture and history, some with an integration of elements such as participation and education (Hall 2007). An attendee who becomes physically involved in an event during their holiday is described by Standeven and De Knop (1999) as an active sport tourist. Such participation through competition may allow tourists to identify with the culture and identity of a region.

Light-hearted and fun small-scale sporting activities overlap with populist forms of entertainment. For tourism entertainment to exist, Pearce suggests that there must be managers and producers, performers or a performance, and an audience comprised largely of tourists who have usually paid for the privilege of being the spectators. Some small-scale sporting events fulfil these aspects, particularly where the passive passing of time through entertainment is a sufficient and valid reason to travel and where the entertainment can generate "deep feelings of group identity, offer challenges to the mentally alert, and help brand and define destinations" (Pearce 2008: 129). Indeed, Getz (2005: 191) notes that some not-for-profit organisations run events in order to "raise money for its owners, to promote a cause, or simply to give the community entertainment".

Fun is defined by Podilchak as a hedonistic, self-gratifying activity, perhaps inappropriate and childish. However, he suggests that "you cannot have fun by yourself" (Podilchak 1991: 124). When an individual is having fun, they are both "outside" themselves and, at the same time, interactively connected with others, and such feelings only emerge in this social bond when there is an equality condition among members. From a tourism perspective, this aspect of fun is important, as it suggests that tourists may want to engage with like-minded spectators and participants. Although sport is still pursued for traditional motives of fitness, health, competition and achievement, nowadays individuals often participate "simply for fun and pleasure" (Weed 2006: 306). Similarly, attendees tend to seek more immediate gratification, suggesting that, "from a value perspective, many are driven by a sense of 'fun and excitement' or other hedonistic values" (Hede *et al.* 2003: 8). The provision of fun and lighthearted small-scale sporting events may thus have numerous tourism-related benefits. For example, the generation of pleasant emotions among those attending such an event may result in high satisfaction levels and positive word of mouth recommendation about the experience and/or the destination (Frew 2006a).

Novelty world championships

A novelty world championship (NWC) is a small-scale sports event where locals and tourists either compete or are spectators during an off-beat, alternative or unusual sport or game – the term novelty reflecting the "new or unusual experience". The following definition is provided for this type of sport tourism event:

> A Novelty World Championship is an annual or biennial special event featuring an alternative or unusual sport or game. The event may be run by a local council, a voluntary non-profit organisation, a combination of local council and voluntary organisation or, by a private company as a trademarked event.
>
> (Frew 2006b: 99)

According to Higham (1999: 87), small-scale sports events include "regular season sporting competitions (ice hockey, basketball, soccer, rugby leagues), international sporting fixtures, domestic competitions, Masters or disabled sports, and the like". NWC events fall into the "*and the like*" part of Higham's definition. Compared with large hallmark events, they are beneficial to small communities, as they may use existing infrastructure, do not require much investment and are not necessarily dependent on the tourist season. In addition, the greater domestic, regional and international travel flows generated by such events and increased traveller awareness of destinations involved are "well in excess of the administrative costs of hosting such events" (ibid.). Such events may be particularly beneficial to the host region in which they are staged, as they "do not tax the resources of the host city in the same manner as hosting a mega event" (Gibson *et al.* 2003: 182) and have the added advantage of providing interesting opportunities for tourists to participate (Weed and Bull 2004).

Table 11.1 lists twelve NWC events. To create this sample, reference was made to various online sources such as travel sites (see, for example, 2camels 2010) and travel guides. Using the internet search engine Google, the term "World Championship" was typed in inverted commas, with the addition in turn of the terms "quirky", "unusual" and "alternative". These searches resulted in links to hundreds of webpages related in some way to aspects of novelty world championships. The events selected for detailed examination were those which appeared to be well established, attracted national and international visitors and/or had some support from local tourism authorities. In Table 11.1, the first nine events are described as "location specific", as their venue reflects some aspect of the history and culture of the region. The final three are described as "itinerant", as their

Table 11.1 A sample of novelty world championships

	Type	Location	National heats held prior to event	Time of year held	When established	Duration	Organiser
Location-specific events							
World Wife Carrying Championships	Sport	Sonkajaru, Finland	Yes, but also open entry	July	1992	2 days	Finland Tourist Board + limited company
World Bog Snorkelling Championships	Sport	Llanwrtyd Wells, Powys, Wales	No	August	1985	1 day	Local tourist information centre and volunteers
The Grande Internationale World Flounder Tramping Championships	Sport	Palnackie, Dumfries and Galloway, Scotland	No	July/ August	1973	1 day	Local volunteers to raise money for Royal National Lifeboat Institution (RNLI)
World Black Pudding Throwing Championships	Sport	Ramsbottom, Lancashire, England	No	September	c. 1850s	1 day	Local community trust
World Gurning Championships	Game	Egremont, Cumbria, England	No	September	1267	1 day	Local voluntary management committee
World Championship Cow Chip Throwing Contest	Sport	Beaver, Oklahoma	No	April	1970	1 day	Local county chamber of commerce
Mobile Phone Throwing World Championships	Sport	Savonlinna, Finland	Yes, but also open entry	August	2000	1 day	A Finnish translation and interpretation service

Table 11.1 (Continued)

	Type	Location	National heats held prior to event	Time of year held	When established	Duration	Organiser
Rock Paper Scissors International World Championships	Game (trademarked)	Toronto, Canada	Yes	October/ November	2002	1 day	World Rock Paper Scissors Society
Air Guitar World Championships	Music (trademarked)	Oulu, Finland	Yes, but also open entry	September	1995	3 days	Oulu Music Video Festival – a not-for-profit organisation
Itinerant events							
World Rubik's Cube Championships	Game (trademarked)	Held in a different city each time	Yes	October	1982	3 days	World Cube Association
World Scrabble Championships	Game (trademarked)	Held in a different city each time	Yes	November	1991 (biennial event)	4 days	Mattel Inc. (toy manufacturer)
World Beard and Moustache Championships	Personal grooming	Held in a different city each time	Yes	Various	1990 (biennial event)	1 day	World Beard and Moustache Association

Sources: Sonkarjarvi (2010); Llanwrtyd Wells (2010); Visit Southern Scotland (2008); Gail Corner Pin Public House (2006); Beaver County Chamber of Commerce (2010); Savolinna Festivals (2010); World RPS Society (2010); Egremont Crab Fair and Sports (2010); Air Guitar World Championships (2010); World Rubik's Cube Championship (2008); World Scrabble Championship (2009); World Beard and Moustache Championships (2010).

location moves from country to country each year, reflecting its commercial nature. However, all represent off-beat or unusual sports or games.

Itinerant and location-specific events

Six of the nine location-specific NWC events have a strong association with the places in which they are held, reflecting the culture and identity of the area. For example, the World Flounder Tramping Championships involve the natural environment, as visitors are encouraged to wade out onto the mud flats of the Urr estuary in the Solway Firth and use only their feet to catch the small flat fish (Visit Southern Scotland 2008). Similarly, in the World Bog Snorkelling Championships, held in Llanwrtyd Wells, Wales, competitors must swim two lengths of a specially excavated peat bog filled with muddy water while wearing a snorkel and flippers. The region recently introduced additional related events, such as the Bog Snorkelling Triathlon, involving a run, a cycle and the bog snorkelling, and the World Mountain Bike Bog Snorkelling Championships, where competitors cycle along the bottom of the peat bog, which is 6 feet deep, using specially prepared bikes (Green Events 2010).

The World Black Pudding Throwing Championships reflect the ancient rivalry between the neighbouring English counties of Lancashire and Yorkshire (BBC Manchester 2004). According to one local councillor, it is "a uniquely Lancastrian event, a unique feature of the area's events calendar, a boost for tourism and a great showcase for one of Bury's most famous products" (BBC Manchester 2003). The event is organised by a local community trust to raise funds for various local charities. In 2009 the trust set up a website on the social networking forum Facebook as a tongue-in-cheek attempt to seek support for black pudding throwing to be made an Olympic event for the 2012 London games. A member of the community trust said: "We are trying to raise the profile of black pudding throwing and have it recognised, if not as an official event, at the least as part of the opening ceremonies to celebrate the diversity of the British" (Lancashire Telegraph 2009).

The World Gurning Championships, which date back to 1267, are held in the town of Egremont, in England's Lake District. Contestants have to stick their head through a horse's collar and pull an ugly face. The event, which is part of a local celebration during the crab apple harvest, which includes an applecart parade where children vie for apples thrown from a cart (Le Vay 2005), is believed to have originated when the local labourers made disgusted faces after tasting bitter crab apples thrown to them by their landlords (Short 2001). The winner of the competition is determined by the amount of audience applause and is the person who is considered to have contorted their face the best (Egremont Crab Fair and Sports 2010). The World Championship Cow Chip Throwing Contest (whereby cattle faeces is dried and then thrown like a discus) is part of the annual Cimarron Territory celebration in Beaver, Oklahoma, held in remembrance of the area's early settlers, who used dry cow chips for cooking and heating.

The sport developed because families threw the cow chips into wagons before taking them into town to trade for food and other essentials. The event thus reflects the heritage of the area "based on one of nature's most fundamental elements" (Beaver County Chamber of Commerce 2010). The World Wife Carrying Championships in Sonkajaru, Finland evolved as a test of physical strength for local men, dating back to a time when it was common practice to steal women from neighbouring villages (Stewart 2009).

These six location-specific events reflect deep-rooted history and ancient customs –inspired by superstition, commemorating a historical event, or with origins so far back as to have been forgotten (Short 2001). More recent NWC events may have been developed for more pragmatic reasons – for example, with the intention of raising a town's profile. However, Short believes that the reasons for viewing or participating in the events are similar for both competitors and spectators, as they are seeking fun and escapism by engaging in a quirky and eccentric activity.

The remaining three location-specific events have no obvious link to the places in which they are run. However, each of these competitions holds national heats, with only the winning competitors competing in the world championship. For instance, there are national championships licensed by the Air Guitar World Championships held in twenty-four countries, and the winners have the honour of travelling to the Oulu Music Video Festival, Finland to compete in the world championship (Air Guitar World Championships 2010). So the staging of the championship finals at one specific location may increase the awareness of that town or city among competitors, who may associate the location with the event.

For an event to call itself a "world" championship it would be reasonable to expect that it would receive international competitors representing a range of countries. Indeed, the 2009 World Scrabble Championships involved competitors from thirty-eight different nations (World Scrabble Championships 2009), while thirty-three nations were represented at the 2007 World Rubik's Cube Championships (BBC News 2007) and thirteen at the 2009 World Beard and Moustache Championships (World Beard & Moustache Championships 2010). The change of city and country for these three itinerant events may create a higher profile for the championships and encourage more international competitors to participate. For example, the World Beard and Moustache Championships are held biannually and allow individuals to compete in various categories, such as Best Moustache, Best Partial Beard, Best Full Beard, and Freestyle (in which the most creative beard is judged the best). In 2007 the event was staged in London, hosted by the Handlebar Club of London, and the 2009 championships were held in Anchorage, Alaska, "the successful bidder in the recent selection process conducted by the World Beard and Moustache Association" (ibid.), suggesting that there is competition among national clubs and societies to act as host.

The participants in the location-specific NWC events originate from the host country or from a relatively small number of countries. It may therefore be relatively easy to become a world champion in an event which has only a handful of domestic and international competitors. The opportunity to gain such a title in a particular sport or game may appeal to the tourist ego, may be an attractive drawcard for some competitors and may be an important factor in the success of such events (MacCannell 2002). Indeed, the organisers often use this concept to promote events. For example, the website for the Air Guitar World Championships notes that "Anyone can taste rock stardom by playing the Air Guitar" (Air Guitar World Championships 2010) and that, "besides worldwide fame and glory", the winner in 2006 received a handmade guitar and an amplifier designed and donated by Queen guitarist Brian May. The opportunity for a country to claim a world champion may be important. For example, much of Cathy Freeman's claim to fame is her status as a world champion athlete in a country where sport plays a vital role in the construction of national identity (Bruce and Hallinan 2001: 261).

The NWC events provide an opportunity for participants and spectators to have fun and enjoyment. For example, one of the official rules of the World Wife Carrying Championships in Finland is that "All the participants must have fun" (Sonkarjarvi 2008) and one of the objectives of the World Beard and Moustache Championships is "to foster networks in the interests of friendship, conviviality and fun" (Handlebar Club 2008). As an illustration of this aspect, the winner of the 2004 World Black Pudding Throwing Championships said:

> We thought we'd go down and have a laugh. It was a pound to enter, so I thought I'd have a go – and I won! It feels a bit ridiculous to be honest. I'm getting a lot of stick at work – they all think it's hilarious. I keep saying it's not going to change me, though!
>
> (BBC Manchester 2004)

There are varying fees to enter an NWC event. It costs CAD$42 to enter the Rock Paper Scissors International World Championship (World RPS Society 2010) and €50 for the World Wife Carrying World Championships (Sonkarjarvi 2008). The prize money offered at the itinerant events ranges from US$15,000 in the World Scrabble Championship (World Scrabble Championships 2009) to CAD$10,000 in the Rock Paper Scissors World Championships (World RPS Society 2010). However, at the location-specific events the prizes are more modest. For example, the World Bog Snorkelling Champion wins £50, the winner of the World Gurning Championship receives a trophy cup, a rosette and the title "World Gurning Champion" (Egremont Crab Fair 2010), and the winner of the World Wife Carrying Championships in Finland gains the wife's weight in beer.

Thus, location-specific NWC events appear to reflect the flavour, culture and identity of the region in which they are staged, particularly as regards the local landscape, rural themes, agriculture and history. A sports event which symbolises a feature of its locality may help to define a town or a region's identity and embody its spirit, create a link with its past, develop a sense of pride among locals, and reflect the character of the area.

Conclusion

Sport is a dynamic phenomenon that evolves in numerous ways, including the development of new sports (Higham and Hinch 2002). The fairly recent introduction of some novelty world championship events may reflect a general trend towards developing new types of sports for an ever hungry audience of spectators and participants (Weed and Bull 2004). In addition, the spread of such events enhances social capital that goes beyond tourism and economic development (Misener and Mason 2006).

This chapter has considered off-beat and alternative sporting events and their significance for tourism from a national identity perspective. The two main issues identified are that location-specific events have the potential to reflect the culture and identity of the area and can provide locals and visitors with a memorable and culturally significant experience. Rather than conforming to mass consumer culture, these events reflect various eccentricities of the local culture and the idiosyncracies of the nation in which they were established. Novelty world championships are only the tip of the iceberg, since hundreds of off-beat and unusual events exist around the world (see, for example, Le Vay 2005), revealing a wealth of bizarre traditions and interesting customs that display the identity of the local area and are useful in attracting tourists to the region. Local tourist authorities could develop such events to enhance their localities, perhaps in partnership with private providers, particularly if location-specific events have the potential to become markers for the area, reflecting its history, culture and identity.

References

2camels (2010) "Bizarre festivals", www.2camels.com/festivals/bizarre-festivals.php (accessed 9 November 2010).

Air Guitar World Championships (2010) www.airguitarworldchampionships.com (accessed 1 November 2010).

Allison, L. (2002) "Sport and nationalism", in J. Coakley and E. Dunning (eds) *Handbook of Sports Studies* (pp. 344–55). London: Sage.

Bairner, A. (2001) *Sport, Nationalism and Globalization*. Albany: State University of New York Press.

Bale, J. R. (1988) "The place of 'place' in cultural studies of sports", *Progress in Human Geography*, 12: 507–24.

Bale, J. R. (2003) *Sports Geography*. 2nd edn, London: Routledge.

BBC Manchester (2003) "Rivalry revived by pudding throwers", http://news.bbc.co.uk/2/hi/uk_news/england/manchester/3146468.stm (accessed 1 November 2010).

BBC Manchester (2004) "The prince of puddings", www.bbc.co.uk/manchester/content/articles/2004/09/13/black_pudding_throwing_feature.shtml (accessed 1 November 2010).

BBC News (2007) "Japan teen in historic Rubik win", http://news.bbc.co.uk/2/hi/europe/7033519.stm (accessed 1 November 2010).

Beaver County Chamber of Commerce (2010) www.beaverchamber.com (accessed 9 November 2010).

Brotherton, B., and Himmetoglu, B. (1997) "Beyond destinations: special interest tourism", *Anatolia: An International Journal of Tourism and Hospitality Research*, 8(3): 11–30.

Bruce, T., and Hallinan, C. (2001) "Cathy Freeman: the quest for Australian identity", in D. L. Andrews and S. J. Jackson (eds) *Sport Stars: The Cultural Politics of Sporting Celebrity* (pp. 257–76). Abingdon: Routledge.

Coakley, J. (2001) *Sport in Society: Issues and Controversies*. 7th edn, Boston: McGraw-Hill.

Crolley, L., and Hand, D. (2006) *Football and European Identity: Historical Narratives through the Press*. London: Routledge.

Cronin, M. (1999) *Sport and Nationalism in Ireland: Gaelic Games, Soccer and Irish Identity since 1884*. Dublin: Four Courts Press.

Egremont Crab Fair and Sports (2010) www.egremontcrabfair.org.uk (accessed 17 July 2010)

Frew, E. A. (2006a) "The humour tourist: a conceptualisation", *Journal of Business Research*, 59(5): 643–6.

Frew, E. A. (2006b) "Novelty world championship events: an exploration", in C. Arcodia, M. Whitford and C. Dickson (eds) *Proceedings of the Global Events Congress and Event Educators' Forum* (pp. 98–108). Brisbane: University of Queensland Press.

Gail Corner Pin Public House (2006) http://members.lycos.co.uk/gailcornerpin (accessed August 2008).

Getz, D. (2005) *Event Management and Event Tourism*. 2nd edn, New York: Cognizant Communication Corporation.

Gibson, H. (ed.) (2006) *Sport Tourism: Concepts and Theories*. London: Routledge.

Gibson, H., Willming, C., and Holdnak, A. (2003) "Small-scale event sport tourism: fans as tourists", *Tourism Management*, 24: 181–90.

Green Events (2010) www.green-events.co.uk (accessed 17 July 2010).

Hall, C. M. (2007) *Introduction to Tourism in Australia: Development, Issues and Change*. Frenchs Forest, NSW: Pearson Education.

Handle Bar Club (2008) www.handlebarclub.co.uk/wbmchomef.html#objectives (accessed 10 August 2008).

Hede, A., Jago, L., and Deery, M. (2003) "An agenda for special events research: lessons from the past and directions for the future", *Journal of Hospitality and Tourism Management*, 10 (supplement): 1–14.

Highham, J. E. S. (1999) "Sport as an avenue of tourism development: an analysis of the positive and negative impacts of sport tourism", *Current Issues in Tourism*, 2(1): 82–90.

Higham, J. E. S. (ed.) (2005) *Sport Tourism Destinations: Issues, Opportunities and Analysis*. Oxford: Elsevier.

Higham, J., and Hinch, T. (2002) "Tourism, sport and the seasons: the challenges and potential of overcoming seasonality in the sport and tourism sectors", *Tourism Management*, 23: 175–85.

Jarvie, G. (2003) "Internationalism and sport in the making of nations", *Identities*, 10(4): 537–51.

Kotnik, V. (2007) "Sport, landscape, and the national identity: representations of an idealized vision of nationhood in Slovenian skiing telecasts", *Journal of the Society for the Anthropology of Europe*, 7(2): 19–35.

Lancashire Telegraph (2009) "TV stars join the black pudding throwers at Ramsbottom fiesta", *Lancashire Telegraph*, 14 September; www.lancashiretelegraph.co.uk/news/4627269.TV_stars_join_the_black_pudding_throwers_at_Ramsbottom_fiesta/?ref=rss (accessed 1 November 2010).

Le Vay, B. (2005) *Eccentric Britain: The Bradt Guide to Britain's Follies and Foibles*. 2nd edn, Chalfont St Peter: Bradt.

Lechner, F. (2007) "Imagined communities in the global game: soccer and the development of Dutch national identity", *Global Networks*, 7(2): 193–229.

Llanwrtyd Wells (2008) www.llanwrtyd.com (accessed 1 November 2010).

Loy, J. (1979) "The nature of sport: a definitional effort", in E. Gerber and W. Morgan (eds) *Sport and the Body: A Philosophical Symposium* (pp. 38–47). Philadelphia: Lea & Febiger.

MacCannell, D. (2002) "The ego factor in tourism", *Journal of Consumer Research*, 29: 146–51.

Misener, L., and Mason, D. (2006) "Creating community networks: can sporting events offer meaningful sources of social capital?", *Managing Leisure*, 11(1): 39–56.

Novelli, M. (ed.) (2005) *Niche Tourism: Contemporary Issues, Trends and Cases*. Oxford: Elsevier Butterworth–Heinemann.

Pearce, P. (2008) "Tourism and entertainment: boundaries and connections", *Tourism Recreation Research*, 33(3): 125–30.

Podilchak, W. (1991) "Establishing the fun in leisure", *Leisure Sciences*, 13 : 123–36.

Raitz, K. B. (1987) "Perception of sports landscapes and gratification in the sport experience", *Sport Place*, 1(1): 5–19.

Ritchie, B. W. (2005) "Sport tourism: small-scale event tourism: the changing dynamics of the New Zealand Masters games", in M. Novelli (ed.) *Niche Tourism: Contemporary Issues, Trends and Cases* (pp. 157–70). Oxford: Elsevier Butterworth–Heinemann.

Ritchie, B. W., and Adair, D. (2004) *Sport Tourism: Interrelationships, Impacts and Issues*. Clevedon: Channel View.

Savolinna Festivals (2010) "Mobile phone throwing world championships", www.savonlinnafestivals.com/en_Stoori.pdf (accessed 9 November 2010).

Short, A. (2001) "Nowt so queer as folk (strange festivals in Great Britain)", *Geographical Magazine*, 73(4): 74.

Smith, A., and Porter, D. (eds) (2004) *Sport and National Identity in the Post-War World*. London: Routledge.

Sonkarjarvi (2010) www.sonkajarvi.fi (accessed 17 July 2010).

Standeven, J., and De Knop, P. (1999) *Sport Tourism*. Champaign, IL: Human Kinetics.

Stewart, L. (2009) "Don't forget to pick up the wife", *Belfast Telegraph*, 12 September, p. 2.

Trauer, B., and Ryan, C. (2005) "Destination image, romance and place experience: an application of intimacy theory in tourism", *Tourism Management*, 26: 481–91.

Veal, A. J., and Lynch, P. (2001) *Australian Leisure*. Frenchs Forest, NSW: Pearson Education.

Visit Southern Scotland (2008) www.visitsouthernscotland.com/area/attraction_detail.asp ?townid=&sectionid=0&attractionid=2816 (accessed 15 August, 2008).

Weed, M. (2006) "Sports tourism", in J. Beech and S. Chadwick (eds) *The Business of Tourism Management* (pp. 305–22). Harlow: Prentice Hall.

Weed, M., and Bull, C. (2004) *Sports Tourism: Participants, Policy and Providers*. Oxford: Elsevier Butterworth–Heinemann.

World Beard & Moustache Championships (2010) www.worldbeardchampionships.com (accessed 17 July 2010).

World RPS Society (2010) http://worldrps.com (accessed 1 November 2010).

World Rubik's Cube Championship (2008) www.speedcubing.com/events/wc2007 (accessed 1 November 2010).

World Scrabble Championship (2009) www.wscgames.com (accessed 1 November 2010).

Part III
Heritage and history

12 Outlaw nations

Tourism, the frontier and national identities

Fiona Wheeler, Jennifer Laing, Lionel Frost, Keir Reeves and Warwick Frost

Introduction

Most discussions about national identity turn to nation-building, the establishment of national sovereignty and the collective "imagining" of national ties (Anderson [1983] 2006). Tourist attractions, particularly museums and heritage centres, can help build that national identity through communicating a "national story" and promoting national emblems and icons (Pitchford 2008). However, in some cases, tourism emphasises outlaws, individuals whom the state has defined as outside the law and, accordingly, in opposition to law and order, government and settled society. Such individuals are seemingly the antithesis of the nation, but paradoxically become symbolic of national identity.

An identification with outlaws is particularly the case in countries such as the USA and Australia where national myths are built on a recent frontier. While they are now stable urban societies, they proudly look back on a heritage of lawlessness and violence. In many parts of these countries, the frontier outlaw has become the dominant destination image and the subject of a wide range of museums, heritage centres and interpretive trails (Beeton 2004; Caton and Almeida Santos 2007; Frost 2006; Seal 1996, 2009). This intriguing identification is a good example of a "co-construction" (Chronis 2005) between the host communities and visitors. Towns, regions and attractions emphasise outlaws to attract tourists and, in turn, the interest of tourists reinforces and validates outlaws as symbolic of local, regional and national identities. Though they lack flags and other national symbols, outlaws become valid and valued national identities.

Despite the importance of outlaws to cultural heritage and tourism, research to date has been limited. This has been partly because studies of national identity have tended to focus on ethnic groups struggling for independence and nationhood (Pitchford 2008). It may also be that outlaws do not seem to be a worthy subject of academic interest. Sociologist Paul Kooistra, for example, explained that he felt embarrassed researching outlaws and that colleagues "looked at me a bit suspiciously" (1989: 2). Accordingly, research on outlaws as tourist attractions has tended to be fragmented and sporadic. Robin Hood, the template for all outlaws, has merited only one study (Shackley 2001). Tourism research into Ned Kelly has been primarily through the lens of popular culture, either via film-induced tourism (Beeton 2004; Frost 2006) or as a marketing icon (Pearce *et al.* 2003). The outlaws of the Wild West have garnered even less attention. Indeed, they are surprisingly missing from histories of tourism in the American West (for examples of these absences, see Rothman 1998; Wrobel and Long 2001).

In this chapter, our aim is to redress this imbalance by examining how tourism packages and presents outlaws as a key aspect of national identity in the frontier or "settler" societies of the USA, Australia and New Zealand. We consider five case studies. The first three – Jesse James, Billy the Kid and Ned Kelly – are arguably the most well known and accordingly have the most developed and wide-ranging tourism "product". The fourth is James McKenzie from New Zealand, who, while less known, has become strongly linked with the destination branding of a popular tourism region. The final study, of Joaquin Murieta, is included as a contrasting example of an outlaw who has not attracted any significant attention as far as tourism is concerned. We conclude with a broad comparative discussion examining how and why outlaws are of interest to tourists. Our chapter also considers that this interest is not universal and that outlaws as a tourism product may sit uncomfortably for many tourists and tourism operators.

Outlaws and national identities

Jesse James

Depending on which interpretation one accepts, Jesse James was either a noble robber who acted in response to unjust treatment and targeted only exploitative banks and railroad companies (Hobsbawm 1969) or a virulent psychopath who "hated as fiercely as anyone on the planet" (Stiles 2002: 394). He was a polarising figure because his criminal career was a result of the Civil War and the division of the nation into abolitionist and pro-slavery elements. His frontier was the violent border state of Missouri. As a teenager, James rode and killed with a band of Confederate guerrillas; after the war he and his gang robbed banks and trains that were seen as representing Yankee interests. Through his frequent letters and written statements to the press, and with the support of secessionist newspaper editors, an image developed of James as a Robin Hood figure who would fight to the death to preserve his own independence and that of the South. Armed with Colt revolvers – weapons that had not been widely available before the Civil War – James pursued a political agenda and planned his robberies with an eye to the effect they would have on the public (Kooistra 1989; Loy 2004; Stiles 2002). "In many respects, Jesse James was a forerunner of the modern terrorist" (Stiles 2002: 391). His sympathisers were nearly all former rebels, but a more silent majority of Americans disapproved both of James and of the causes that he championed – slavery, Southern separatism and racism. After Tyrone Power's sympathetic portrayal in the movie *Jesse James* (1939), the image of James as a noble robber was revived. As the newspaper editor in another western, John Ford's *The Man Who Shot Liberty Valance* (1962), remarked: "when the legend becomes fact, print the legend, not the fact".

James was aged sixteen in 1864 when he was part of a guerrilla group that murdered and mutilated over a hundred Union soldiers (twenty-two of them unarmed) and civilians – all fellow Missourians – at Centralia. There is no agreement about the number of murders he committed in his career. Kooistra (1989) records sixteen, but the figure may be much higher. Between 1866 and 1879, Jesse and his brother Frank led a gang that robbed banks, shot tellers and witnesses, and derailed trains to rob cash shipments throughout Missouri and Kentucky. In 1876, when the gang moved out of its familiar territory and attempted to rob a Union-supporting bank at Northfield, Minnesota, the townspeople killed or captured most of its members. On 2 April 1882, James was living under an assumed name in St Joseph and was at his home when he turned his back on two gang members, Bob and Charley Ford. They shot him in the back of the head and were later paid the reward for his capture.

The Jesse James tourist industry started almost immediately: the first entry in the visitors' registry book for the house where James was killed is dated 3 April 1883. Jesse's mother charged visitors to the family farm and sold pebbles from his grave site, and his brother Frank sold autographed pictures and appeared in a travelling theatre show. Bob Ford also appeared in a stage show, in which he re-enacted the shooting each night, to a mixture of boos and cheers from the audience (Stiles 2002).

In 1978 the derelict James farmhouse at Kearney was bought by Clay County and restored as the Jesse James Farm and Museum. It attracts 18,000 visitors each year. About 35 miles away in St Joseph, the Jesse James Home Museum attracts 25,000 tourists annually, its main attraction being a wall with "the legendary bullet hole", now over a foot wide as a result of years of people being allowed to touch the surrounding wood and surreptitiously break pieces from it as souvenirs. These and other local attractions cooperate in their marketing. For example, a brochure showing possible day trips from Kansas City lists nineteen separate museums, grave sites, jails, banks, train depots, courthouses and churches that have a link to James (SJCVB 2009).

The nature and content of these attractions is contested in several ways. On display at the Jesse James Farm is a feather duster which, it is claimed, James was using when he turned his back on the Fords. However, on display at the Jesse James Museum is a picture, as it is claimed that James turned to adjust its frame. At Stanton, Missouri, there is a Jesse James Museum established by a man who believed that the outlaw's death was a hoax (Roadside America 2009). It displays "evidence" that James lived until 1951 (similar disputes occur for Ned Kelly and Billy the Kid). The St Louis Iron Mountain and Southern Railway, a restored tourist steam railroad operating from Jackson, Missouri, hosts re-enactments of a robbery by the James gang in 1874. Kearney holds an annual Jesse James festival, as does Pineville, Missouri, to celebrate the filming in the area of *Jesse James*. Train robberies are re-created at events in Jamestown, California – not for any real connection, but because films were also made there. At Northfield, an annual festival called "The Defeat of Jesse James" features a very different type of re-enactment, stressing the Unionist townspeople's resistance to the gang.

Billy the Kid

Billy the Kid is "apparently the least deserving of individuals to be selected for heroisation, yet one who is persistently made an outlaw hero" (Seal 1996: 193). His story is one of pathos as well as pluck, of a flawed icon who is both revered and reviled and whose life and even death remain open to conjecture right up to the present day (Meyer 1980; Wallis 2007). Even during his life he was a symbol of resistance to the downtrodden (Wallis 2007), and this lends his name a glamour that persists amid the tawdry facts.

The nickname Billy the Kid suggests youth and insouciance, but "the Kid" was in fact a common moniker given to young delinquents or young men who knew how to handle a gun (Wallis 2007) and, as such, was given to Billy in the final year of his life. Billy was born around the time of the American Civil War. His birthplace is unknown, but he grew up in Wichita, Kansas, a town known for its crimes and mayhem. He was thus exposed from an early age to the lynch laws and "the frontier code placed on the remaining friends of a murder victim" (ibid.: 28) to seek vengeance through the gun. His mother died when he was fourteen years old, and thereafter he walked the tightrope "between the lawful and the lawless" (ibid.: 78). While more crimes were attributed to him than was probably the case (Tuska 1994; Wallis 2007) he did appear to court trouble, and this led to a career of horse-stealing and theft. He escaped from jail on a number of occasions and eventually went on the run as a man wanted for murder. His many aliases were a way of bypassing the law, and in 1877 he ended up in Lincoln County in New Mexico, which, like Wichita and other frontier towns, was known for attracting renegades and "desperadoes" and became "an especially fertile ground for spawning myth" (Wallis 2007: 159). The territory had a murder rate that was forty-seven times the national average, mainly on account of gunshot wounds.

As it turned out, the Kid met his end not in the crossfire of a gunfight, but betrayed, shot in the back by Sheriff Pat Garrett, which perhaps sowed the seeds for his enduring celebrity. His death received national attention (Mullin and Welch 1973) and novels and pulp fiction immediately began to be produced, telling the Billy the Kid story for an insatiable audience (Stevens 2001; Tuska 1994; Wallis 2007).

Tourism embraced the legend of Billy the Kid with a number of attractions and events. There is a Billy the Kid Museum in Fort Sumner, New Mexico, which exhibits such memorabilia as his rifle and the original "Wanted" poster. His headstone in Fort Sumner cemetery attracts visitors, although there are some who dispute that Billy died at the hands of Garrett and champion an alternative grave in Hico, Texas. There is also a Billy the Kid statue and Museum in Hico. Attempts have been made to exhume the grave in Fort Sumner for DNA testing, something that is still being resisted by both cemeteries. The motive for this exercise would appear to be linked at least in part to the consequences for tourism. As the governor of New Mexico remarked, "Getting to the truth is our goal. But if this increases interest and tourism to our state, I couldn't be happier" (Globe and Mail

2003). The Fort Sumner mayor, on the other hand, opposes exhumation on the grounds that "Billy the Kid tourism is all he has to keep people coming to his town" (Maier 2003). Others object to the disturbance of a legend. Trish Saunders of the Billy the Kid Historic Preservation Society notes that she receives emails from around the globe from people saying: "We want to see the mythic Old West as it is now – lonesome, undisturbed, preserved" (Boyle 2004).

The New Mexico Tourism Department has adopted the Billy the Kid legend in its destination marketing, using the brand "Billy the Kid Territory", which is a landscape "still so unfettered and free that if the Kid and Garrett were to return to its wide open spaces, they would feel, momentarily at least, as if nothing had changed" (NMTD 2009). Places to visit include the site of the Kid's early home in Silver City; the courthouse (now known as the Billy the Kid Gift Shop) in La Mesilla, where Billy was convicted for the murder of Sheriff Brady; and Lincoln, where the Kid was promised a pardon from Governor Lew Wallace (who reneged on the deal). The Billy the Kid National Scenic Byway was designated by the Federal Highway Commission in 1998. Museums in Lincoln, Santa Fe, Silver City, La Mesilla and Las Cruces also display artefacts related to the Kid, such as his knife, the hearse of Pat Garrett and his jail cell.

There are also events linked to Billy the Kid such as the Billy the Kid Pageant, which has been staged since 1940 (see www.billythekidpageant.org). It depicts the escape of the Kid from the Lincoln County courthouse (Gomber 2003). The New Mexico Tourism Department also promotes a trail ride of 125 miles, tracing the route of "Billy the Kid's Last Ride" from the Lincoln County jail to Fort Sumner (NMTD 2007), which one of the trail committee members describes as resulting in people "coming from all over the US and bringing tourism dollars to rural new Mexico" (O'Hara 2005).

Ned Kelly

The notorious bushranger Ned Kelly (1855–1880), it is argued, is Australia's greatest cultural icon and the closest thing to a national hero (Seal 1996: 145). In 1878 his mother was imprisoned on trumped-up charges and Kelly went into hiding. In a gun battle at Stringybark Creek with a police party sent to catch him, he killed three policemen. Outlawed and with a bounty placed on each of their heads, Kelly and his gang engaged in daring bank robberies and, with help from a strong network of supporters, eluded the colonial police for two years. The final violent and bloody confrontation with the authorities took place in June 1880 at Glenrowan. This is where Kelly wore his iconic metal armour and helmet, as he attempted to derail a police train. But his plan went wrong, and the gang was besieged in a local pub. Kelly himself was wounded and captured and the rest of his gang killed. He was subsequently tried, found guilty of murder and executed.

The history of Ned Kelly and the siege is strongly contested (Frost 2006; Frost *et al.* 2008; Jones 1995; Seal 1996), and there is a wide range of sites connected with him and artefacts of varying importance and provenance held in both public and private hands (Sinclair Knight Merz 2003). However, a number of small country towns have built their tourism image around their association with Kelly (Beeton 2004; Frost 2006; Pearce *et al.* 2003). There are tourism trails such as "The Ned Kelly Touring Route" and "The Ned Kelly Trail"; private attractions such as an animatronic theatre and a giant statue in Glenrowan; notable sites such as Stringybark Creek and Glenrowan; historic buildings (including court houses and jails); museums; and a wide variety of wineries, accommodation, cafes, souvenir shops and other retail outlets utilising Kelly as part of their appeal.

While Glenrowan is closely connected with Kelly, tourism development has been problematic on account of a lack of tangible heritage remains, conflict between stakeholders, and a lack of resources and support. Glenrowan itself has the sense of a forgotten moribund backwater, not necessarily what one would expect of a place of such heralded national historical significance. Its collection of souvenir shops and private museums often attracts negative comment, perhaps most famously through the well-known travel writer Bill Bryson, who wrote that the animatronic theatre was "so bad it was worth more than we paid" (2000: 173). A range of plans for an interpretive centre (see, for example, Sinclair Knight Merz 2003) have come to nothing, and the siege site was severely damaged by ill-conceived "beautification" by the local council. A recent archaeological dig there was featured in the documentary *Ned Kelly Uncovered* (2009) by Tony Robinson and provided further impetus for a future heritage centre to house interpretive artefacts. Furthermore, as in the case of Billy the Kid, a long-running dispute over Kelly's actual gravesite is tied to the spectre of potential tourism.

Kelly has increasingly become the subject of commemorative events – for example, the annual "Ned Kelly Festival Weekend" in Beechworth, which since 2005 has marked the capture, imprisonment and committal of Ned Kelly in the town, and the memorialisation of the siege held intermittently in Glenrowan. These commemorations illustrate how events have meanings which are of fundamental importance to a diverse range of stakeholders, particularly local community members and groups, but which are not necessarily captured within tourism development and marketing (Frost *et al.* 2008).

The Ned Kelly Touring Route is an example of a successful development which appears to have overcome some of the obstacles discussed above in terms of providing a coherent visitor experience focused around the Kelly story. It is a joint initiative between seven rural municipalities, linking a number of towns, and was initially created to tie in with the film *Ned Kelly* (2003), which Tourism Victoria thought might be as beneficial to local tourism as *Lord of the Rings* was to New Zealand (Tourism Victoria 2003). Indeed, the brochure featured photos of actor Heath Ledger as Ned Kelly.

James MacKenzie

The wild, remote, romantic beauty of the landscape immediately strikes any visitor to the region branded as MacKenzie Country in the South Island of New Zealand. Equally engrossing for many tourists is the myth and legend surrounding James MacKenzie, the illiterate drover who lent his name to the region of

2 million acres between the foothills and the Southern Alps. The popular historical narrative of his life is drawn largely from James McNeish's novel *MacKenzie*
(1970) and Beattie's history (1940), which recounts the various illegal activities
of MacKenzie in 1855. When settlers arrived in South Canterbury the following
year, they named the region after the Scots-born outlaw.

MacKenzie endured a long period in the wilderness while on the run from the
authorities for stealing 1,000 sheep (Beattie 1940). An abiding element of the
MacKenzie myth is that his sheepdog Friday was crucial to his survival during
his ordeal in rugged country. In this reading he emerges as a free spirit in the
manner of the now discredited atomised man theory of New Zealand male identity (see Fairburn 1982) – the sort of person who could fix anything with a piece
of number 8 fencing-wire. Arguably this cultural stereotype has best (or effectively) been promulgated in the recent Speight's Brewery advertisements depicting the phlegmatic "Southern Man", almost as a homage to MacKenzie and the
populist and largely fictitious New Zealand "man alone" identity (King 2003).
Today the MacKenzie myth is largely a tourism strategy, intended to package the
spectacular landscapes and experiences that drive so much visitation to the South
Island of New Zealand (AMCMD 2009; Te Ara 2009). In Tekapo there is a
monument erected to MacKenzie and his dog, and tourists still receive a spiel that
frames him as a latter-day antipodean Robin Hood and a victim of the injustices
of the Scottish Highland clearances. In truth, MacKenzie was not an outlaw in the
manner of Ned Kelly (and others in this chapter) and so standing alongside Robin
Hood as a popular heroic rebel, but is better understood as a marketable New
Zealand high plains drifter. As the historian Michael King observed: "New
Zealand had no Ned Kelly, and the smaller number of Irish and convict settlers in
the nineteenth century ensured a narrower band of larrikinism in the population
at large than that enjoyed by Australia" (King 2003: 512).

The present-day interpretation of MacKenzie is very much designed to promote
South Canterbury on the commercially important South Island tourist trail. The
MacKenzie brand fits neatly under the umbrella brand of "100 per cent pure NZ",
promoting an image of a rugged and untamed land populated by attractive independent historical characters. The historical figure of MacKenzie (stripped of his minor
criminal activities) is thus remembered for his penetration of the frontier as opposed
to his sheep rustling – a sanitised version that is a very appealing and that sits com-
fortably with depictions of the region as naturalistic and layered with fascinating
history (AMCMD 2009). It is certainly effective as a promotional device, as the
route to Aoraki Mount Cook or Central Otago is one of the most popular tourist
routes in New Zealand (Te Ara 2009). For many, this trip includes an obligatory
stop at Tekapo to look at the "Sheepdog Monument" or a visit to another statue of
the outlaw at MacKenzie Pass near where he was finally apprehended.

Joaquin Murieta

During the Californian Gold Rushes, a group of Hispanic outlaws known as the
"Five Joaquins" committed a series of robberies and murders. In 1853, two members

of the band were shot by pursuing California state rangers. The head of one (known simply as Joaquin) was preserved in a jar of brandy and displayed in San Francisco and Stockton. This incident became the basis for John Rollin Ridge's highly successful novel *The Life and Adventures of Joaquin Murieta* (1854). In Ridge's fictionalised romance, Murieta is given a classic outlaw backstory, turning to crime only after Anglo miners jumped his claim and raped his wife. The novel is conflicted, with the half-Cherokee Ridge sympathetically portraying the racist elements, but it also takes pains to present a Victorian melodrama where wrongdoing (even if in a good cause) must be penalised (Johnson 2000; Kowalewski 2000). In 1919, the tale of Murieta was recycled, providing part of the basis for the Zorro stories by Johnston McCulley. In the latest cinematic version of Zorro – *The Mask of Zorro* (1998) – Antonio Banderas played Murieta's brother seeking revenge.

Despite his impressive outlaw credentials, Murieta has not spawned much tourist interest or development. His story is sometimes marginally referenced in California, but it is essentially absent from museums, tours, visitor centres, attractions and destination marketing. The landscape in which he operated is blandly promoted as Southern Mines, with no attempt being made to create a "Murieta Country". A Hispanic hero, he is missing from the tourism landscape, with few tourists or operators seeming interested in his story. This does raise the interesting possibility that, as the Hispanic proportion of the US population continues to rise, Murieta may possibly be rediscovered as a tourism icon.

Discussion

Despite their violence and crimes, outlaws are popular tourist attractions. One might ask why normally law-abiding people identify with outlaws and are so interested in travelling to places connected with them. In considering this, we must first recognise that what visitors know about such individuals is a "social product" – that is, a series of stories "constructed by the media and the popular imagination" (Kooistra 1989: 36). These stories are embellished, modified, retold, romanticised, fictionalised, even played with – and tourists are very aware of this. Jesse James, Billy the Kid and Ned Kelly have each been the subject of at least a dozen movies – films that both reflect and magnify their appeal. Ned Kelly has featured in plays and paintings, was the only real historical character portrayed in the 2000 Sydney Olympic Games opening ceremony, and lends his name to the annual prize for Australian crime fiction writing (Holland and Williamson 2003). Jesse James provides the inspiration for the sexy villains in *Pokemon* (1998–) and is used to frame moral lessons for an episode of the television series *The Brady Bunch* (1973), while Billy the Kid parties with the eponymous time travellers in *Bill and Ted's Excellent Adventure* (1989) (note that in all three cases the outlaws interact with the young heroes of these popular productions). These outlaws have become popular culture icons, both real and hyper-real.

The concept of a "frontier myth" is highly attractive to tourists (Belk and Costa 1998; Butler 1996; Frost 2008; Laing and Crouch 2009; Penaloza 2001). The frontier is "the meeting point between savagery and civilization", which others have conceptualised as a "dividing line between worlds" (Zurick 1995) or the boundary "between wilderness and civilized nature" (Hall 2002). The frontier myth continually evolves, with Hains (2002: 5) noting that it is a place "of possibility, an open future, and uncertain outcomes . . . frontiers are stories being written". The frontier is a testing place for virtues such as self-reliance, initiative and ruggedness (Terrie 1990; Belk and Costa 1998), a place to develop or "elevate" moral character (Hains 2002: 83). It is the stage for the outlaw or "social bandit" who takes refuge in, and advantage of, its freedom, anarchy and unsettled nature (White 1981). A zone of uncertain behaviour, uneven government and newly available resources, the frontier attracts conflict. Accordingly, the frontier and the outlaw are intertwined, and both represent an attractive, though contradictory, national identity.

It is widely argued that outlaws conform to a common model (Hobsbawm 1959, 1969; Kooistra 1989; Meyer 1980; Seal 1996; Tranter and Donoghue 2008). They are consistently and distinctively portrayed as Robin Hood figures, protecting the weak and fighting injustice. They "never harm the common folk and, in a sense, don't really steal because these Robin Hoods are only taking property from the corrupt and redistributing it to the poor to whom it rightfully belongs" (Kooistra 1989: 36). The catalyst for the outlaw taking on this role is that some injustice has been vindictively visited upon them or their close family (for Kelly and James it was their mother; for Murietta, his wife). In taking revenge, the outlaw avenges all who have been oppressed. The outlaw is attractively portrayed:

> as a common man who was victimized by injustices perpetuated by those who were corrupting the law. They can be fashioned into a symbol of social and political discontent, and this is what separates them from common robbers and murderers.
>
> (Ibid.: 37–8)

It is paradoxical that being declared an outlaw – intended as a severe legal sanction removing one's rights as a citizen – provides a person with the freedom to right injustice. The outlaw is now unrestrained. However, he is committing crimes not to overthrow law and order but to expose the unjust and corrupt, and to return balance and decency to society. But the outlaw is a tragic outsider. As often portrayed in Hollywood movies or tourist interpretation, he uses his violent and destructive skills to save a society but is doomed, for, with these attributes, he cannot return to a normal life (Kitses 2004; Loy 2004). Though a hero, he has forfeited "social identity after renouncing [his] membership in a 'civilized' community" and is thus "doomed by [his] inner savagery" (Stevens 2001: 603). The outlaw is often struck down in the prime of life and while on the run, and can never grow old gracefully among family and home comforts. Kelly, Billy the Kid and Murieta died violently before the age of twenty-five, while MacKenzie disappeared; James made it to the age of thirty, but was ironically killed by his erstwhile friends while doing housework.

Conclusion

These outlaw stories resonate in the modern world, become integral parts of national identities and accordingly generate tourism interest. The lone individual standing up to injustice is a universal story which crosses boundaries of geography and time. The outlaw is a second cousin to the masked superhero of cartoons. Such stories continue to be told, for they appeal to a broad audience who like to imagine that somewhere out there is someone who will put things right. The idea that outlaws represent the underdog in taking on banks, bad government and big business is just as appealing today as it was in the nineteenth century.

However, not everyone is enamoured of the outlaw myth. Rather, it provides an instructive example of what Tunbridge and Ashworth termed "heritage dissonance", which describes situations where cultural heritage provokes a "discordance or a lack of agreement and consistency" among the community (1996: 20). Many tourists see outlaws as simply lawbreakers deserving no attention or sympathy and are turned off by their glorification. Opinions on individual outlaws vary. For example, our consensus is that James is unattractive, yet there are a feast of events and attractions celebrating him.

This poses difficult questions for destination marketing organisations as to whether or not they should utilise such an image. Outlaws may provoke discord from local businesses and government authorities which would prefer a different identity. Indeed, the celebration of outlaws seems greatest at the local level, with generally less enthusiasm and support from national agencies. Ethnicity may also influence support: it is striking that, of the cases considered here, those that are essentially Anglo-Saxon have the most appeal, whereas those representing ethnic minorities, such as Murieta, are downplayed (Johnson 2000). Furthermore, indigenous resistance fighters, such as Jandamarra (Australia) and Geronimo (USA), while technically outlaws, are regarded quite separately. Again this raises interesting questions as to whose national identities are being portrayed and promoted via tourism.

A final paradox is the longevity of these outlaw myths. Critics of the outlaws often argue that their appeal should logically diminish over time and that they have little relevance in our modern societies (Seal 1996). However, if anything, interest is increasing. Why is this the case? From a tourism perspective, it may be that there is too much money invested in them and there are economic imperatives to keeping their stories alive. From a human perspective, it would appear that these stories are universal and are reinterpreted by successive generations, based on our need for heroes and the romance of the frontier.

References

AMCMD (Aoraki Mount Cook MacKenzie District) (2009) "The history of the Aoraki Mount Cook MacKenzie region", www.mtcooknz.com/mackenzie/history (accessed 16 December 2009).

Anderson, B. ([1983] 2006) *Imagined Communities: Reflections on the Origin and Spread of Nationalism.* Rev edn, London and New York: Verso.

Beattie, H. (1940) *MacKenzie of the MacKenzie Country: Pioneer – Explorer – Sheeplifter: Story of a Remarkable Man*. Dunedin: Otago Daily Times.

Beeton, S. (2004) "Rural tourism in Australia – has the gaze altered? Tracking rural images through film and tourism promotion", *International Journal of Tourism Research*, 6: 125–35.

Belk, R. W., and Costa, J. A. (1998) "The mountain man myth: a contemporary consuming fantasy", *Journal of Consumer Research*, 25 (June): 218–40.

Boyle, A. (2004) "Billy the Kid's lawyers want their client dug up", 3 March, www.msnbc. msn.com/id/4441143 (accessed 3 November 2009).

Butler, R. W. (1996) "The development of tourism in frontier regions: issues and approaches," in Y. Gradus and H. Lithwick (eds) *Frontiers in Regional Development*. Lanham, MD: Rowman & Littlefield.

Bryson, B. (2000) *Down Under*. Sydney: Doubleday.

Caton, K., and Almeida Santos, C. (2007) "Heritage tourism on Route 66: deconstructing nostalgia", *Journal of Travel Research*, 45(4): 371–86.

Chronis, A. (2005) "Coconstructing heritage at the Gettysburg Storyscape", *Annals of Tourism Research*, 32(2): 386–406.

Fairburn, M. (1982) "Local community or atomized society", *New Zealand Journal of History*, 16: 146–67.

Frost, W. (2006) "*Braveheart*-ed *Ned Kelly*: historic films, heritage tourism and destination image", *Tourism Management*, 27(2): 247–54.

Frost, W. (2008) "Projecting an image: film-induced festivals in the American West", *Event Management*, 12(2): 95–103.

Frost, W., Wheeler, F., and Harvey, M. (2008) "Commemorative events: sacrifice, identity and dissonance", in J. Ali-Knight, M. Robertson, A. Fyall and A. Larkins (eds) *International Perspectives on Festivals and Events: Paradigms of Analysis* (pp. 161–72). Amsterdam: Elsevier.

Globe and Mail (2003) "Hunt for Billy the Kid continues", *Globe and Mail*, 10 June; www.evalu8.org/staticpage?page=review&siteid=2459 (accessed 5 December 2009).

Gomber, D. (2003) "The last escape of Billy the Kid – America's longest running folk pageant", www.southernnewmexico.com/Articles/Southeast/Lincoln/Lincoln/TheLastEscapeof BillytheKi.html (accessed 3 November 2009).

Hains, B. (2002) *The Ice and the Island: Mawson, Flynn and the Myth of the Frontier*. Melbourne: Melbourne University Press.

Hall, C. M. (2002) "The changing cultural geography of the frontier: national parks and wilderness as frontier remnant", in S. Krakover and Y. Gradus (eds) *Tourism in Frontier Areas*. Lanham, MD: Lexington Books.

Hobsbawm, E. J. (1959) *Social Bandits and Primitive Rebels: Studies in Archaic Forms of Social Movement in the 19th and 20th Centuries*. Glencoe, IL: Free Press.

Hobsbawm, E. J. (1969) *Bandits*. London: Weidenfeld & Nicolson.

Holland, A., and Williamson, C. (2003) *Kelly Culture: Reconstructing Ned Kelly*. Melbourne: State Library of Victoria.

Johnson, S. (2000) *Roaring Camp: The Social World of the California Gold Rush*. London and New York: Norton.

Jones, I. (1995) *Ned Kelly: A Short Life*. Melbourne: Lothian.

King, M. (2003) *The Penguin History of New Zealand*. Auckland: Penguin.

Kitses, J. (2004) *Horizons West: Directing the Western from John Ford to Clint Eastwood*. London: BFI.

Kooistra, P. (1989) *Criminals as Heroes: Structure, Power & Identity*. Bowling Green, OH: Bowling Green State University Press.

Kowalewski, M. (2000) "Romancing the Gold Rush: the literature of the California frontier", *California History*, 79(2): 204–25.

Laing, J., and Crouch, G. (2009) "Exploring the role of media in shaping motivations behind frontier travel experiences", *Tourism Analysis*, 14(2): 187–98.

Loy, R. P. (2004) *Westerns in a Changing America, 1955–2000*. Jefferson, NC: McFarland.

McNeish, J. (1970) *MacKenzie: A Novel*. London: Hodder & Stoughton.

Maier, T. W. (2003) "Digging up the dead: collecting DNA samples from the grave can help to solve historical mysteries, but critics are calling it ghoulish and disrespectful", *Insight on the News*, 27 October, http://findarticles.com/p/articles/mi_m1571/is_2003_Oct_27/ai_109128669 (accessed 3 November 2009).

Meyer, R. E. (1980) "The outlaw: a distinctive American folktype", *Journal of the Folklore Institute*, 17(2/3): 94–124.

Mullin, R. N., and Welch, C. E. (1973) "Billy the Kid: the making of a hero", *Western Folklore*, 32(2): 104–11.

NMTD (New Mexico Tourism Department) (2007) "Billy the Kid Trail Ride retraces historic escape, April 21–28", www.discovernewmexico.com/articles/dated/apr07/billy_the_kid_trail_ride/index.htm (accessed 3 November 2009).

NMTD (New Mexico Tourism Department) (2009) "Billy the Kid Territory", www.new-mexico.org/billythekid (accessed 3 November 2009).

O'Hara, S. (2005) "State tourism saddles up with Billy the Kid's last ride", *New Mexico Business Weekly*, 22 April, http://albuquerque.bizjournals.com/albuquerque/stories/2005/04/25/story8.html (accessed 3 November 2009).

Pearce, P. L, Morrison, A. M., and G. M. Moscardo (2003) "Individuals as tourist icons: a developmental and marketing analysis", *Journal of Hospitality and Leisure Marketing*, 10(1/2): 63–85.

Penaloza, L. (2001) "Consuming the American West: animating cultural meaning and memory at a stock show and rodeo", *Journal of Consumer Research*, 28 (December): 369–98.

Pitchford, S. (2008) *Identity Tourism: Imaging and Imagining the Nation*. Bingley: Emerald.

Roadside America (2009) "Jesse James Museum", www.roadsideamerica.com/story/2141 (accessed 1 December 2009).

Rothman, H. K. (1998) *The Devil's Bargains: Tourism in the Twentieth-Century American West*. Lawrence: University Press of Kansas.

Seal, G. (1996) *The Outlaw Legend: A Cultural Tradition in Britain, America and Australia*. Cambridge: Cambridge University Press.

Seal, G. (2009) "The Robin Hood principle: folklore, history and the social bandit", *Journal of Folklore Research*, 46(1): 67–89.

Shackley, M. (2001) "The legend of Robin Hood: myth, inauthenticity, and tourism development in Nottingham, England", in V. L. Smith and M. Brent (eds) *Hosts and Guests Revisited: Tourism Issues of the 21st Century* (pp. 315–22). New York: Cognizant.

Sinclair Knight Merz (2003) *Glenrowan Heritage Precinct: Feasibility Study Final Report*. Sydney: Sinclair Knight Merz.

Stevens, J. W. (2001) "Bear, outlaw, and storyteller: American frontier mythology and the ethnic subjectivity of N. Scott Momaday", *American Literature*, 73(3): 599–631.

Stiles, T. J. (2002) *Jesse James: Last Rebel of the Civil War*. London: Pimlico Press.

SJCVB (St Joseph Convention and Visitors Bureau) (2009) "Jesse James driving tour", www.stjomo.com/uploadedFiles/Content/Things_To_Do/Public_Tours/JesseJames_DrivingTour.pdf (accessed 1 December 2009).

Te Ara (2009) "MacKenzie Country", www.teara.govt.nz/en/south-canterbury-places/2 (accessed 16 December 2009).

Terrie, P. G. (1990) "Wilderness: ambiguous symbol of the American past," in R. B. Browne (ed.) *Dominant Symbols in Popular Culture*. Bowling Green, OH: Bowling Green State University Popular Press.

Tourism Victoria (2003) "Ned Kelly tourism boom", *Tourism Victoria Newsletter*, 42: 4.

Tranter, B., and Donoghue, J. (2008) "Bushrangers: Ned Kelly and Australian identity", *Journal of Sociology*, 44(4): 373–90.

Tunbridge, J. E., and Ashworth, G. J. (1996) *Dissonant Heritage: The Management of the Past as a Resource in Conflict*. Chichester: Wiley.

Tuska, J. (1994) *Billy the Kid: His Life and Legend*. Westport, CT: Greenwood Press.

Wallis, M. (2007) *Billy the Kid: The Endless Ride*. New York and London: Norton.

White, R. (1981) "Outlaw gangs of the middle border: American social bandits", *Western Historical Quarterly*, 12(4): 387–408.

Wrobel, D. M., and Long, P. T. (2001) *Seeing and Being Seen: Tourism in the American West*. Lawrence: University Press of Kansas.

Zurick, D. (1995) *Errant Journeys*. Austin: University of Texas Press.

13 Heritage and aspects of nation

Vietnam's Ho Chi Minh Museum

*Huong Thanh Bui, Lee Jolliffe and
Anh Minh Nguyen*

Introduction

The role of heritage tourism in constructing a national identity has been addressed by a number of academics (Ashworth 1991; Palmer 1999). According to Lowenthal (1998), heritage is the focal point of nationalism, while McLean (1998) says it offers representations of a nation's past with which the individuals in that nation may identify. The usefulness of heritage sites in constructing national identity within the visitor imagination depends on the degree to which they act as mediums to convey national stories (Pitchford 2008). Pretes (2003) identifies the viewing of such sites by domestic tourists as a key aspect in the formation and maintenance of a national identity, while Lanfant (1995) observes that national heritage is perceived by international visitors as a marker of the nation. The mythical discourses or the signs of nationhood (Palmer 1999) conveyed by heritage sites are thought to be markedly different for domestic and international visitors.

One way national identity is expressed is through national museums, as the museum reinterprets the culture and traditions of the nation (Prosler 1996). National museums are thus seen as agents of identity formation and nationalism. As Ashley (2005: 5) observes, "what is shown and what is not shown can have a major impact on how society sees itself and presents itself to others". Timothy and Boyd (2003) note that it is not uncommon for nations to use heritage to build nationalism. Globalization has also contributed to an increased public interest in museums and changes in practice as their former neutrality has been influenced by both political and corporate agendas (Mathur 2005). As the concept of the museum as an institution, formerly dominated by a Western agenda, reinvents itself, new discourses are emerging. Little attention has been paid to how nationalism is elaborated and communicated to visitors in the context of socialist developing countries such as Vietnam.

The national museum has both a formative and a reflective role in constructing nationhood (MacDonald 1995). Museums developed and operated by the nation-state "assume a quite particular symbolism and meaning for the nation" (Prosler 1996: 35). It has been observed that the establishment of national museums tends to coincide with surges in nationalism and national identity (Gellner 1996;

Kaplan 1994). Anderson (1991) indicates that museums play a part in shaping national identity by educating people in what it means to be a citizen, giving them a history and a sense of common heritage, presenting the defining characteristics of nationhood, and exhibiting tangible evidence of its existence. Museums are thus noted to be one of the more effective ways of conveying messages of national identity (Kirshenblatt-Gimblett 1998).

The creation of national identity can operate through the use of what Shumway (1991: ix) calls "guiding fictions", which are commonly held beliefs that shape people's attachment to the nation. These beliefs are disseminated through school curricula, textbooks, public statements, monuments, festivals and official documents. Heritage sites, including museums, support a national ideological movement reflecting the narratives of their creators (Pretes 2003). As such, the presentation of national heritage is an ideological process. Allcock (1995) notes: "to speak of heritage is to speak of politics". The political role of museums is thus to represent and reinforce national ideologies and hierarchies of power (Robinson and Smith 2006) as, in particular at the national level, they are regulated and managed through state cultural policy (Butcher 2006).

This chapter examines the case of the Ho Chi Minh Museum, discussing the role it plays in conveying nationalism. The museum is located in the national capital precinct of Hanoi in the monument and museum complex dedicated to the former Vietnamese president Ho Chi Minh (Logan 2000). The focus here is on visitor perceptions of the museum. The role of heritage sites and museums in Vietnam in addressing the domestic and international audience has previously been examined (Henderson 2000; Sutherland 2006). Furthering this theme, the chapter examines how the Ho Chi Minh Museum presents aspects of a reinvented Vietnamese national heritage, helping to shape a common national identity, or "imagined community" (Anderson 1991), among a diverse population of hosts and guests and elaborating linkages between nationalism and the museum in a Vietnamese context.

The Ho Chi Minh Museum in context

There is no single national museum of Vietnam. However, seven national museums, managed by the National Cultural Heritage Department of the Ministry of Culture, Sport and Tourism, display particular aspects of the nation. These are the Vietnam History Museum, the Vietnam Revolutionary Museum, the Ho Chi Minh Museum, the Vietnam Fine Arts Museum, the Vietnam Ethnic Cultural Museum, the Army Museum and the Vietnam Museum of Ethnology (Ministry of Culture, Sport and Tourism 2009). Logan (2006: 563) notes that some of these are located in former French colonial buildings given "new capital-city but socialist and /or nationalist functions". For example, the old customs house became the Vietnam Revolutionary Museum, the colonial army barracks is now the Army Museum, and the Far East Research Institute is now the Vietnam History Museum. In contrast, the four-storey Ho Chi Minh Museum was purpose built. It is the most popular in

Table 13.1 Visitor numbers at the Vietnam Revolutionary Museum, the Ho Chi Minh Museum and the Vietnam Fine Art Museum, 1998–2001

Year	Revolutionary Museum		Ho Chi Minh Museum		Fine Art Museum	
	Domestic	International	Domestic	International	Domestic	International
1998	173,000	2,097	942,983	49,397	22,000	17,751
1999	172,927	3,221	1,331,957	132,446	27,700	21,004
2000	182,232	3,747	1,520,747	89,113	29,031	23,228
2001	155,425	4,936	1,465,280	90,101	30,200	21,004

terms of visitor numbers, with domestic visitors accounting for between 90 and 95 per cent of the total – which is ten times that of the Revolutionary Museum and thirty times that of the Fine Art Museum (Table 13.1).

The Ho Chi Minh Museum presents the personal life of Ho Chi Minh as a symbol of Vietnamese independence from the French and Americans in the twentieth century, giving birth to the current Socialist Republic of Vietnam. It thus has the political function of educating domestic visitors about nationalism. The contemporary design of the museum, built with technical assistance from a group of artists of the Moscow Association of Art and Decoration, is what Edensor (2002) refers to as an edifice reflecting the modernity of the nation and is a symbol of its progress (Figure 13.1). The Ho Chi Minh Museum reflects the role of the museum as part of heritage tourism to formulate and reinforce the sense of nationalism among its visitors.

The museum opened on 19 May 1990 in celebration of what would have been Ho Chi Minh's 100th birthday. It is located adjacent to the historical Ba Dinh Square, a sacred space for many national events and military marches, and the surrounding area, which has symbolic significance to the Vietnamese government and people, includes what Logan (2006) refers to as a full package of national symbols – Ho Chi Minh's mausoleum, the former presidential palace, the parade ground, the small house on stilts used by Ho Chi Minh, the State Assembly, the Communist Party headquarters, the Ministry of Foreign Affairs, and the historic Mot Cot Pagoda.

A visit to the Ho Chi Minh Museum, the centrepiece of this capital precinct, can be described as a pilgrimage and a patriotic duty, and it is an ultimate tourism goal for many rural Vietnamese (Jolliffe and Bui 2009), as reflected by the high numbers of domestic visitors. Between its opening in 1990 and the end of 2008, the museum welcomed nearly 20 million people. Numbers reached a peak of 1.6 million in 2000 (Figure 13.2), a year in which there were some significant anniversaries – for example, 990 years since the foundation of Thang Long–Hanoi, the 110th anniversary of Ho Chi Minh's birth, the forty-fifth anniversary of independence (ending nearly a hundred years of French colonization) and the twenty-fifth anniversary of reunification after the Vietnam War. Another peak is expected in 2010, when the capital city of Hanoi celebrates 1,000 years of history.

Figure 13.1 The entrance of the Ho Chi Minh Museum (photograph: Anh Minh Nguyen).

At the museum, Ho Chi Minh himself is situated at the centre of the Vietnamese revolutionary process in three exhibition sections divided into eight different themes. The museum brochure profiles three of these sections: "Ho Chi Minh's life and revolutionary cause", "The Vietnamese land and the struggle and the victories of the Vietnamese people in the Ho Chi Minh era" and "World historical events that exerted an impact on Ho Chi Minh's revolutionary cause and the victories of the Vietnamese people". Thus, the story told is that of modern Vietnam rather than the personal life history of an individual. The attempt to balance these two themes in the museum may have created different perceptions among domestic and international visitors, an issue that we explore in this chapter through a post-visit survey.

Visitor perceptions of the Ho Chi Minh Museum

Domestic and international visitors to the Ho Chi Minh Museum were interviewed by a bilingual researcher in late September and early October of 2009. They were asked about their reasons for visiting the museum and about their perceptions of the displays and were encouraged to talk about this within the wider context of visiting Vietnam. The sample for this exploratory research consisted of ten domestic tourists and seventeen international tourists, and the researchers used thematic analysis to encode the qualitative information gathered.

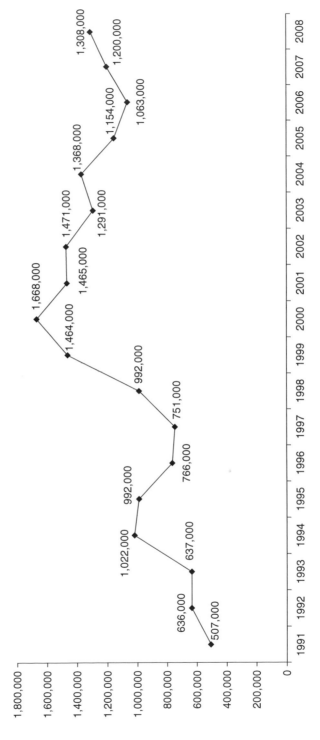

Figure 13.2 Number of visitors to the Ho Chi Minh Museum between 1991 and 2008.

Source: Ho Chi Minh Museum, personal information.

Patterns in the data were noted and labelled to allow distinctions to be drawn. As the coding progressed, categories were refined by restructuring and linking codes.

Impressions of the museum

The majority of international visitors interviewed told us that the museum was different to those they had visited in Vietnam or elsewhere. First, they identified the imposing architecture of the building, which is on a large physical scale. A centrepiece is the 4 metre bronze statue of President Ho Chi Minh, which impressed many visitors. Second, they noted that there are few museums dedicated to one person and one era, observing that in few other countries in the world would authorities build a museum dedicated to one individual on such a massive scale. A British tourist named Brown (58-year-old male) indicated there are many other museums "about culture, about history, science and art, but not [dedicated] to one person".

Respondents commented on the concise temporal dimension of the exhibits. In comparison to many Western art, history and science museums, often portraying hundreds of years of history, the Ho Chi Minh Museum covers a period of about a hundred years. Some individuals noted that exhibits reflected the role of Ho Chi Minh in war and military history: "I know that he was a big part of the Vietnamese War" (Mette, 24-year-old female, Danish).

As Ho Chi Minh played an essential role in leading the Vietnamese to independence, claiming victory first over the French and later over the Americans, his life story represents a critical time in the transformation of Vietnam from a feudal, colonial state to the Democratic Republic of Vietnam (later the Socialist Republic of Vietnam). Thus the exhibits dealing with significant events remind the visitors of turbulent times in Vietnamese history. As one respondent suggested: "It is where Vietnamese young people come and learn more about Vietnamese history" (Doan, 19-year-old male, Vietnamese).

Motivations for visiting the museum

A prime motivation among visitors to the museum is to learn more about Ho Chi Minh himself. There is an assumption that people know something about his life before their visit. However, fourteen of the seventeen international respondents interviewed revealed they had known more about Vietnam than about Ho Chi Minh. This reflects a particular relationship between Vietnam and Ho Chi Minh, with the museum serving the function of a contemporary history museum, educating international visitors about the country.

Other respondents mentioned that they knew the story of Ho Chi Minh from school, via textbooks and documentaries. While they were at the museum they gained further insight as to why his name is linked so closely with the country: "Because Ho Chi Minh is a very important person . . . I know the role he played for the independence of your country" (Clement, 29-year-old female, Austrian).

On the one hand, the museum recalls images of Vietnam fighting for independence: "I think it is very good to have this museum. I understand more about the long time of revolution of Vietnam. I think it is a part of Vietnamese history" (Maya, 32-year-old female, Finnish). On the other hand, the museum continues to present a contemporary vision of the country. Informants indicated they learned about Vietnam when visiting this museum: "We now know more . . . of how Vietnam is changing" (Beth, 22-year-old female, Australian).

Despite any overall impressions, Ho Chi Minh is a central symbol of the story about Vietnam, as demonstrated by another respondent who recognized his contribution: "He spent his life and effort for Vietnam" (Fabiel, 26-year-old male, French).

Messages conveyed by the museum

By restructuring the past image of Vietnam and linking it into present, the museum has created a strong connection between Ho Chi Minh's personal life and his influence over the development of an independent country. Interpreting the revolutionary process that led to the creation of the current Socialist Republic, the museum presents Ho Chi Minh's personal life story in the context of a larger picture of Vietnam. Here it is delivering a message from the nation-state, and a few respondents expressed their disappointment at there not being enough information about the personal life of Ho Chi Minh, which they expected to be the main message conveyed: "Because mostly it talks about the war, about the history and other people, [there is] not much information about Ho Chi Minh himself" (Clement, 29-year-old female, Austrian).

Some respondents reported being confused as to whether the museum was dedicated to the life of Ho Chi Minh and his ideology or to the promotion of Vietnam.

Clement and her friend Lucy (29-year-old female, Austrian) speculated on why there is no such personal information: "I think it depends on the country and the people doing the museum, depends on what they want to convey." The displays thus seem to be selected to communicate communism: "Yes, it's like the communist museum" (Fabiel, 26-year-old male, French).

From the impression and atmosphere created by the museum, interviewees expressed a positive impression of Ho Chi Minh:

It's a very great museum, very well organized, very nice . . . it's easy to follow the way. And it also follows the history of Ho Chi Minh, when was he born, his life and so on. I like the end of the visit with a peaceful text. Because, at the first part, we see many things about the war, but at the end it's a peaceful aspect.

(Arnaud, 23-year-old male, French)

A key theme presented in the museum is that of love and respect – a message that could convey a new perspective for international visitors: "You can count how much Vietnamese people love him and how much he helped Vietnam in the past.

I didn't know that before I came here. But now I know how much your Vietnamese people love Ho Chi Minh" (Beth, 22-year-old female, Australian).

For Vietnamese visitors a trip to the museum is a part of their formal school education. Some domestic respondents therefore mentioned that they had been numerous times. Despite this, nationalism is reinforced, as one respondent noted: "Also I admire Uncle Ho very much and I want to study about his life, his contribution to the revolution in Vietnam" (Yen, 19-year-old female). Another domestic visitor noted how the visit contributed to and reinforced her impressions of Ho Chi Minh:

> I know Ho Chi Minh is our greatest president. I have read many stories about him since I was a child and I admire him. After visiting the Ho Chi Minh Museum I know more about him, about places where he lived and worked during the war time. Then I admire him more and I want to try my best to imitate him.
>
> (Tam, 22-year-old female)

Visitor experience

It is common in some museums for displays relating to a person to be static, captured in a particular period of time. However, displays in the Ho Chi Minh Museum are constantly changing, with exhibits concerning contemporary Vietnam. What visitors see, therefore, is not simply a chronicle of the life of Ho Chi Minh but also an image of a modern, dynamic and changing Vietnam. This was noted by some international visitors: "We know more about the background of Vietnam, of how Vietnam is changing until now . . . through the museum" (Beth, 22-year-old female, Australian).

For some of our respondents the journey to visit the museum was described as part of a spiritual transformation. Some interviewees had read of Ho Chi Minh at school and had known that he was popular. One visitor commented: "I think it is really spiritual and emotional for me. It is about the nation" (George, 27-year-old male, Irish). The sense of Ho Chi Minh as a hero of his country was reflected by another respondent, who compared him to Ghandi: "I have heard a lot of good things about him. He seems to be like Ghandi" (Brown, 58-year-old male, British).

While international visitors noted it was unusual that a museum on such a large scale should be dedicated to one person, the Vietnamese do not mention this. To them, it is taken for granted that Ho Chi Minh should be recognized, and they were impressed more by the modern facilities, the architecture and the atmosphere created by the museum. For them, there is no confusion as to whether the theme of Ho Chi Minh or Vietnam dominates, as they see the man as an absolute symbol of the country.

Influence of travel media

This qualitative investigation would be incomplete if there were no mention of the fact that the Ho Chi Minh Museum achieves a good level of coverage in political education, both in the country's schools and in major travel guidebooks. Guidebooks and travel media do not play much of a role in motivating domestic visitors. However, themes relating to Ho Chi Minh are covered by national television channels, school textbooks and communist posters. Some Vietnamese informants noted the importance of a visit to the museum: "I think young people should visit such a historical museum like this to know more about the history of the country and to be more proud of our country" (Tam, 22-year-old female).

Ten of the seventeen international visitors interviewed mentioned that they came to the museum as the result of reading a guidebook. Six other respondents visited the museum as part of a tour or because it happens to be located in one of the most popular areas of the capital. Both its strategic location and official coverage in travel media have thus encouraged the museum's popularity among international visitors.

Discussion

The Ho Chi Minh Museum, in the view of the respondents, demonstrates Urry's (1996) concept of travelling culture. First, such travel occurs at the culture's sacred sites – here a key cultural site in Hanoi. Second, it is travel to the location of central written or visual texts, and the museum's location within a historic quarter symbolizes over a thousand years of Vietnam's history of feudalism, colonialism and socialism. Third, the travel is to view particular noteworthy individuals or their documentary record: within the museum, Ho Chi Minh is portrayed as the national hero of Vietnam. Fourth, the travel is to view other cultures so to reinforce one's own cultural attachments, and exhibits in the museum tell the story of Ho Chi Minh's journey to find a model of socialism for an independent Vietnam, reinforcing the national identity of the country.

Smith (1991: 71) argues that "nationalism . . . may be regarded as a form of culture as much as a species of political ideology and social movement". The Ho Chi Minh Museum can be viewed as a form of culture delivering messages that reinforce nationalism. From another perspective, as Smith ascertains, there are political and social movements to form nationalism. Heritage is employed for ideological reasons, often connected to national buildings and the conceptualization and construction of official preferred national identities (Palmer 1999). As observed by the respondents, the Ho Chi Minh Museum is an effective vehicle for communicating Vietnam's nation-state narrative.

In communist countries such as Vietnam, China and the former Soviet Union, leaders such as Ho Chi Minh, Mao Tse Tung and Lenin have often been likened in the hearts and minds of citizens to gods. Thus, mythical discourses about these leaders operate largely for political movements. Ho Chi Minh's life story has been constructed as a role model for many generations of Vietnamese, with courses such as "Study Ho Chi Minh ideology" introduced into public schools, universities, government offices and state-owned enterprises. While the Ho Chi Minh Museum is the centrepiece and main attraction of Hanoi's national capital precinct, other heritage sites in the city and elsewhere in Vietnam carry a similar message reinforcing the nationalist discourse. These attractions include Ho Chi Minh's home in Nghe An, his father's tomb in Dong Thap, and the house in Hanoi where he wrote the Declaration of Independence.

Smith (1991) argues that the metaphor of family is indispensable to nationalism. In this theory, the nation is depicted as one great family, and the members are brothers and sisters of the motherland or fatherland. In this way the family of the nation can override and replace the individual's family and evoke similarly strong loyalties. Since he remained single, Ho Chi Minh's individual family life was overridden by a greater national family. In this sense, he is commonly called "Uncle Ho" or the "Father of the Nation".

As indicated by the respondents, the Ho Chi Minh Museum can be seen as symbolic of the determination of the Vietnamese people to construct a new nation during one of the most turbulent periods in their history. Interviewees recognize both the historic and contemporary versions of Vietnam portrayed in the museum as reflecting the political movement to strengthen the country's communist identity.

The Ho Chi Minh Museum is arguably an effective medium for developing nationalism. As the interviewees noted, visiting the museum is a kind of pilgrimage for the Vietnamese. As Smith (1991) observes, nationalism can be used to achieve political goals and to realize the national will. The goal of the nation presented in this museum is that of independence and communism. The theme of war and peace is among the most obvious themes and is well received by visitors. The national will for communism is strengthened with an emphasis on the glories of the social group which constitutes the nation, according to the socialist theory of the workers and farmers. As museums are both the products and the agents of political and social change (Sandell 1998), the Ho Chi Minh Museum serves as a platform to reinforce national ideologies and hierarchies of power in contemporary Vietnam.

The story of Ho Chi Minh's life did not end when he passed away in 1969, but the images and myths associated with his life have continually been disseminated in the public media. In the context of tourism, the references to the Ho Chi Minh Museum in travel media reflect this tendency and influence visitors.

Conclusion

This chapter has focused on examining the role of the museum in nurturing national identities and analysed how the Ho Chi Minh Museum portrays national identity and nationalism to visitors. It reflects the fact that this type of museum is an effective medium to convey national narratives. In this case, the strategy to promote nationalism is reflected in the way an individual person is portrayed as a national hero, disseminating the ideologies of communist Vietnam.

Heritage is thus successfully employed by the Vietnamese national museum authorities to convey a national story and to evoke feelings of nationalism and impressions of nationhood among both domestic and international visitors. In this way the museum is socially inclusive. Here, aspects of the story of an individual central to the creation of the current nation are woven together to create a narrative that, while carrying a different message for domestic and international visitors, is equally powerful in its impact and impression upon the visitors.

While this exploratory research has focused on the impressions of visitors at one of the central national museums of Vietnam, there is potential for a more extensive survey of perceptions of the Ho Chi Minh Museum with a larger sample of interviewees. The research could also be expanded on a comparative basis to other sites in Vietnam. Such research could determine if the other national museums in Hanoi are as effective as the Ho Chi Minh Museum in conveying nationalism and contributing to the portrayal of the ideology of the country.

Overall, this chapter has furthered earlier work that examined the qualities of Hanoi as a capital city tourist destination (Jolliffe and Bui 2009). It has turned from the general to the specific, making a beginning towards understanding how the narrative of the nation-state is communicated through the museum to diverse domestic and international audiences.

References

Allcock, J. B. (1995) "International tourism and the appropriate of history in the Balkans", in M. F Lafant, J. B. Allcock and E. M. Bruner (eds) *International Tourism: Identity and Change*. London: Sage.

Anderson, B. (1991) *Imagined Communities: Reflections on the Origin and Spread of Nationalism*. Rev edn, London: Verso.

Ashley, S. (2005) "State authority and the public sphere: ideas on the changing role of the museum as a Canadian social institution", *Museum and Society*, 3: 5–17.

Ashworth, G. J. (1991) "From history to heritage: from heritage to identity: in search of concepts and models", in G. J. Ashworth and P. J. Larkham (eds) *Building a New Heritage: Tourism, Culture, and Identity in the New Europe*. London: Routledge.

Butcher, J. (2006) "Cultural politics, cultural policy and cultural tourism", in M. Smith and M. Robinson (eds) *Cultural Tourism in a Changing World: Politics, Participation and (Re)presentation*. Clevedon: Channel View.

Edensor, T. (2002) *National Identity, Popular Culture and Everyday Life*. Oxford: Berg.

Gellner, E. (1996) "The coming of nationalism and its interpretation: the myths of nation and class", in G. Balakrishnan (ed.) *Mapping the Nation*. London: Verso.

Henderson, J. C. (2000) "War as a tourist attraction: the case of Vietnam", *International Journal of Tourism Research*, 2: 269–80.

Jolliffe, L., and Bui, H. T. (2009) "Reinvented national capital city: the case of Hanoi, Vietnam", in R. Maitland and B. W. Ritchie (eds) *City Tourism: National Capital Perspectives*. Wallingford: CABI.

Kaplan, F. (1994) *Museums and the Making of "Ourselves": The Role of Objects in National Identity*. Leicester: Leicester University Press.

Kirshenblatt-Gimblett, B. (1998) *Destination Culture*. Los Angeles: University of California Press.

Lanfant, M. F. (1995) "Introduction", in M. F Lafant, J. B. Allcock and E. M. Bruner (eds) *International Tourism: Identity and Change*. London: Sage.

Logan, W. (2000) *Hanoi: Biography of a City*. Seattle: University of Washington Press.

Logan, W. (2006) "The cultural role of capital cities: Hanoi and Hue, Vietnam", *Pacific Affairs*, 78: 559–75.

Lowenthal, D. (1998) *The Heritage Crusade and the Spoils of History*. Cambridge: Cambridge University Press.

MacDonald, S. (1995) "Theorizing museums: an introduction", in S. MacDonald and G. Fyfe (eds) *Theorizing Museums*. Oxford: Blackwell.

McLean, F. (1998) "Museums and the construction of national identity: a review", *International Journal of Heritage Studies*, 3: 244–52.

Mathur, S. (2005) "Social thought and commentary: museums globalization", *Anthropological Quarterly*, 78: 697–708

Ministry of Culture, Sport and Tourism (2009) "Vietnam cultural profile", www.cultural-profiles.net/viet_nam/units/1035.html (accessed 19 November 2009).

Palmer, C. (1999) "Tourism and the symbols of identity", *Tourism Management*, 20: 313–21.

Pitchford, S. (2008) *Identity Tourism: Imaging and Imagining the Nation*. Bingley: Emerald.

Pretes, M. (2003) "Tourism and nationalism", *Annals of Tourism Research*, 30: 125–42.

Prosler, M. (1996) "Museums and globalization", in S. MacDonald and G. Fyfe (eds) *Theorizing Museums*. Oxford: Blackwell.

Robinson, M., and Smith, M. (2006) "Politics, power and play: the shifting contexts of cultural tourism", in M. Smith and M. Robinson (eds) *Cultural Tourism in a Changing World: Politics, Participation and (Re)presentation*. Clevedon: Channel View.

Sandell, R. (1998) "Museums as agents of social inclusion", *Museum Management and Curatorship*, 17: 401–18.

Shumway, N. (1991) *The Invention of Argentina*. Berkeley: University of California Press.

Smith, A. D. (1991) *National Identity*. London: Penguin.

Sutherland, C. (2006) "Repression and resistance: French colonialism as seen through Vietnamese museums", *Museum and Society*, 3: 153–6.

Timothy, D. J., and Boyd, S. W. (2003) *Heritage Tourism*. Harlow: Pearson.

Urry, J. (1996) "How societies remember the past", in S. MacDonald and G. Fyfe (eds) *Theorizing Museums*. Oxford: Blackwell.

14 Battlefield tourism and Australian national identity

Gallipoli and the Western front

Caroline Winter

Introduction

In 1914, a little over a decade after federation in 1901, Australia followed the British Empire into the Great War of 1914–18. Many Australians saw the war as an opportunity for the fledgling nation and her citizens to prove their collective and individual worth on the global stage. Enlistment was voluntary throughout the war, and about half of the eligible population, a total of 416,809, signed up to the AIF (Australian Imperial Force). The proportion of casualties to embarkations was over 65 per cent (compared with approximately 52 per cent for Britain): 153,509 people returned wounded or gassed and 61,829 were killed (AWM 2010; Inglis 2005; Rickard 1996). These statistics, if applied to Australia's population in 2009, of 21,874,900 (five times higher than the pre-war level), would see the dead number around 300,000 and the wounded 750,000 – a total of 1,050,000 (ABS 2009). Given the scale of the sacrifice, it is perhaps not surprising that the men of the AIF, the Anzacs (Australian and New Zealand Army Corps), became the basis for the development of a national character and that their exploits were used to validate the historic and geographic claims of the new Australian nation.

As the noted Australian historian Ken Inglis (2005) observed, even though three-quarters of the Australians were killed on the Western Front, the relatively small and disastrous campaign on the Gallipoli peninsula has now become foremost in popular remembrance of the war and, as such, central to our images of identity. Carlyon (2001: 533) wrote that "Gallipoli has become Australia's Homeric tale". A recent survey at the Shrine of Remembrance in Melbourne, for example, found that 84 per cent of the sample had heard of Anzac, yet fewer than 30 per cent had heard of major battles on the Western Front such as Villers-Bretonneux, Pozières and Bullecourt (Winter 2009).

The Great War resulted in the production of many myths and memories, of which national identity is but one. This chapter does not claim, nor does it wish to deny, the nationalist myths of the Anzacs that were developed with respect to Gallipoli: there are numerous reasons why Gallipoli has to date more easily accommodated the claims for such myths. It does, however, wish to point out that it is time that we recognize the thousands of men and women who gave so much in the campaigns on the Western Front. In practical terms, those who returned suffering the psychological and physical wounds of war, and the additional grief caused by the loss of the dead, have played a significant role in forming a national psyche for Australia.

Tourism provides one way in which a developing interest in, and Australia's attitudes towards, the Great War can be analysed. As Urry (2002a: 2) claimed, the way in which tourists gaze upon attractions and destinations can reflect their own society and that, "rather than being a trivial subject, tourism is significant in its ability to reveal aspects of normal practices which might otherwise remain opaque". A number of changes are now being observed with respect to people visiting battlefields, and tourism will play an important role in operationalizing the experiences, knowledge and understanding of Australians to these places, not only on the Gallipoli peninsula, but at the Western Front and in the Middle East.

Defining the new nation

A great deal is made of Australia's role in the Great War in defining the national character and distinguishing the country as a nation in its own right, but Inglis (2005: 191) observes that, in 1914, "country" could mean the British Empire or Australia and, in the years just after the war, "The imagined community invoked on memorials was still, as after the war in South Africa, both empire and nation". It has been noted that loyalty to the Empire can be attributed partly to the fact that, in Commonwealth countries such as Australia, a reasonable proportion of the population had been born in Britain (Inglis 2005; Vance 1997; Winter 2006). In 1911, the population of Australia was around 4,455,000 and, of those, 591,000 (13 per cent) had been born in the United Kingdom (Stonham 1921). Yet, as Winter observed:

> They died in an imperial effort; but they contributed not only to the survival of the Empire, but also to its supersession. The day Australians landed at Gallipoli is the day they mark the emergence of their separate and distinctive national identity.
>
> (Winter 2006: 158)

Creating a nation's "qualifications"

For new nations, particularly settler societies such as Australia, New Zealand and Canada – whose societies had been suddenly transplanted into new lands – the development of nationhood was not straightforward. Before the war Australia was a predominantly British and imperial society, a result of the international and national contexts of social ideology, institutional rituals and anti-nationalist propaganda (Alomes 1993). Links with the land extended for just over a century, and grand nation-defining events were limited to a short battle at the Eureka Stockade in 1854 and a war between the white settlers and indigenous Australians that has never been fully appreciated in the nationalist ideology. Furthermore, the land of Australia was deemed to be "*terra nullius*", not belonging to any people, and this imagined status meant that ownership could be justified without reference to nation-defining battles.

National myths and memories are created for particular purposes within an overall context of social continuity and meaning for the citizens (Anderson 1991; Kapferer 1988). The first memories created in the aftermath of the Great War were to allay grief and to provide some sense or purpose for the mass death and destruction that had occurred (Inglis 2005; Lloyd 1998; Mosse 1990; Winter 2006). In most cases, memorials were built not as victorious monuments to nations but in order to remember the war, the dead and those who had served (Inglis 2005; Winter 2006). As Mosse (1990: 6) stated, social memories were created where "The aim was to make an inherently unpalatable past acceptable, important not just for the purpose of consolation but above all for the justification of the nation in whose name the war had been fought". It is notable that in the 1930s, when some of Australia's large memorials were built, the names of many battles were inscribed upon them – places were as important as the names of the dead and the survivors. From these numerous sites, sixteen were selected for memorialization at the Shrine of Remembrance in Melbourne (Box 14.1). The Australian National Memorial just outside Villers-Bretonneux in France lists the names of twenty-seven conflicts on the Western Front in which the AIF served, as well as those of nearly 11,000 of the Australians reported missing (Box 14.2).

Box 14.1 Australian First World War battle honours listed at the Shrine of Remembrance, Melbourne

Landing at Anzac	Villers-Bretonneux
Sari-Bair	Amiens
Rumani	Mont St Quentin
Gaza-Beersheba	Hindenburg Line
North Sea	Ypres
Cocos Islands	Messines
Megiddo	Pozières
Damascus	Bullecourt

Box 14.2 Conflicts on the Western Front in which Australians were involved

Albert 1918	Bullecourt	Mont St Quentin
Albert 1918 (Chuignes)	Epehy	Passchendaele
Amiens	Hamel	Poelcapelle
Ancre 1918	Hazebrouck	Polygon Wood
Arras 1917	Hindenburg Line	Pozières
Aure	Lys	Somme 1916–18
Bapaume 1917	Marne 1918	St Quentin Canal
Beaurevoir	Menin Road	Villers-Bretonneux
Broodseinde	Messines 1917	Ypres 1917

It was only in later years, particularly after the Second World War, that the tradition based on the Anzacs at Gallipoli was so extensively used in Australia as to form the basis of a national identity (Carlyon 2001, 2006). Today a further change is occurring with the interest of a new generation of Australians in the war, and tourism is helping to validate these claims once more through travel to battlefields.

An Australian character?

Kapferer (1988: 200) has argued that Australian national identity is unique in that there exists "a strong sense that society – and by extension the state – does not create the person". He also argues that, in this respect, the legend of Anzac is important: "The Anzac legend declares the nation to be whole and unified, outside the mechanism of the state, and this autonomous integrity is reproduced in its parts, in individual Australian citizens" (ibid.: 23). In other words, he suggests that "the individual is the fundamental unit of value. The individual is ideologically conceived of as preceding society and as the building block upon which society is constituted" (ibid.: 14). This further reinforces "the egalitarian individualistic logic of Australian nationalism" demonstrated by the tradition of Anzac (ibid.: 197). The notion of egalitarianism was a key attribute of the Anzacs, which was emphasized as a point to distinguish Australia from Britain and her class system. The humorous stories of Anzacs refusing to salute British officers is one example which illustrates this point (Carlyon 2006).

The official war historian C. E. W. Bean is often cited as being the creator of the Anzac myth. His histories of the war describe the qualities of the Anzacs as being derived from the bush – in spite of the realities of urbanization (Rickard 1996). Although the men of the AIF were pictured as "country lads", the reality was that, of the 416,809 enlistments, only 57,430 (14 per cent) were from country callings (Carlyon 2001). Similar claims were made with respect to the Canadians, even though under 10 per cent were from farming backgrounds (Vance 1997). Even as late as the 1980s, the archetypal Australian has been characterized as male, white and a country dweller. This myth has been criticized because it excluded a large proportion of the population, such as indigenous people, women, migrants and urbanites (Alomes and Jones 1991; Inglis 1997; Ward 1966).

Ironically, many Anzacs were also excluded from the national myth (Inglis 2005; Rickard 1996). Larsson (2009: 272) states that "The selective nature of Australia's national memory of war means that the sacrifices of disabled soldiers and their kin have largely been suppressed within the public domain". She argues that these men were Australia's "shattered Anzacs", whose realities were excluded from the images created about the war. Despite the importance of family relationships to returned servicemen and women during and after the war, Larsson maintains that they were passed over in favour of mateship. The families of the returned servicemen often had difficulty in obtaining adequate compensation from the government for their plight and their efforts at caring for the wounded were largely unacknowledged. Australia was not unique in this respect, and Vance (1997: 53) found that, in Canada too, "the ruined veteran had little place in the myth of the war". Not only have individual Anzacs been forgotten, but most of the battles in which they served have been overshadowed by Gallipoli (Carlyon 2006; Charlton 1986).

Gallipoli's claim

There are many reasons why Gallipoli has formed the basis of the nation's identity and history. The battles on the peninsula comprised the first major campaign of the Great War in which Australians were involved, and commemorations of the landing, on 25 April 1915, were held as early as 1916. The nature of the conflict also meant that claims for the attributes of bushmanship, egalitarianism, mateship and the heroic struggle of individuals could be more easily supported in the battles at Gallipoli than in those on the Western Front involving the spectre of industrial slaughter. One of the very important reasons that Gallipoli has become such an iconic feature of nationhood is that it satisfies one of the critical requirements for a nation, that of geographic definition and sovereignty. As Gammage reminded us recently:

> In July 1923 the Treaty of Lausanne granted the Commission the Helles and Suvla cemeteries plus "the whole of Anzac" as one cemetery and this was confirmed by the 1936 Montreux convention . . . Since 1918 the Commission has let Australians care for Anzac. Practically, as well as emotionally, Anzac is part of Australia and New Zealand.
>
> (Gammage 2007: 129)

A series of connections can be made between the Outback and Gallipoli which satisfy the theoretical demands for a nation with respect to an ancient history and a defined geographic homeland. McGrath (1991: 122) argues that the myth of Outback satisfies our need for a "distant past" and that "The Outback is conveniently remote and ancient and so are its original people . . . It is intrinsic to our colonial identity, symbolising our history, our soul, our acquisition". It has also been argued that, through the use of Outback mythology and the selective appropriation of Aboriginal culture, white settler society has been able to create its own links with the land (Lattas 1990; McGrath 1991). Hoffenberg (2001) argued that the struggles of the AIF in the Gallipoli landscape echoed the myths of Outback and thus helped to extend the links between Australia and the nation-defining events of the Great War.

Travel, tourism and the nation

Until recent years, by virtue of their distance from the battlefields and cemeteries of the Great War, Australians and New Zealanders were forced to develop ways of dealing with their grief often in the absence of a body or grave (Ziino 2007). Research by Scates (2006) has found that, even today, decades after the war's end, Australians are still making journeys to the battlefields to express grief. Such journeys reflect Urry's argument that physical travel is not substitutable and that we need corporeally to experience other people, places and events (Urry 2002b: 255). He describes this as "facing the place" where "there is a further sense of co-presence, physically walking or seeing or touching or hearing or smelling a place" (ibid.: 261). Tourism can be important to a people's sense of national identity because it serves to operationalize the stories, the history and the linkages with the land. Slade (2003: 792) found for Australians and New Zealanders that, at Gallipoli, "Generally, they come to see the place where their great nation building stories happened".

Tourism can have a strong influence on the development of a battlefield by sacralizing and "marking" a site to provide interest and attraction for tourists (Seaton 1999; Henderson 2006). From a pragmatic perspective, travel and tourism is a necessary component of Australian war commemoration because these sites of conflict lie outside the nation's political boundaries.

As Hodge and Turner (1987: 121) stated, "Touring 'our country' is both a symbolic assertion of our 'ownership' of it and an affirmation of our identity as 'Australians' that such an ownership entails". In Australia, the myth of "Outback", located somewhere in the vast deserts of the country's centre, has been pictured as the ancient heart of the nation. McGrath (1991: 114–15) argues that travel can authenticate this myth of "Outback" and its associated notions of national identity, and that the act of travelling "out there" seems to prove that the myth exists. For example, travellers can see, touch, hear and smell the "Outback" and, through the experience of physical emersion in the landscape, extend their sense of reality to the nation.

In comparison with the area known as Anzac on the Gallipoli peninsula, the Western Front creates a number of significant problems for constructing the abstract components of an Australian nation. First, most of the land in France and Belgium was and remains good farmland, and this meant that, immediately after the war, the bodies, barbed wire and munitions were cleared. By 1931 farming had resumed and people had moved back to their homes and villages (Carlyon 2006; Gammage 2007; Osborne 2001). In other words, there was very little evidence by which visitors could attempt to imagine how the war actually was, or to provide "markers" by which to interpret the landscape and to understand the events (Carlyon 2006; MacCannell 1999; Scates 2006; Seaton 2000). Figure 14.1 depicts a scene on the Somme today, illustrating the close proximity of the war cemetery to farmland. In most cases, and with only a few exceptions (for example, VC Corner is the only all-Australian cemetery in France), the Australian dead share cemeteries with the dead of other nations – Britain, Canada, New Zealand, South Africa, India and, sometimes, Germany and France. Clearly, Australia cannot claim a national homeland on the Western Front as it can at Gallipoli.

Recognition of changes on the Western Front

Since the 1960s the increase in the provision of cheap airfares has allowed more Australians to travel to Europe and to visit the graves and memorials to the Great War (Davidson and Spearritt 2000). In recent years, the numbers of Australian

Figure 14.1 The Somme today: a communal cemetery in the midst of a dairy farm (photograph: C. Winter).

visitors to Gallipoli have increased, from 5,000 in 1995 to 20,000 in 2005, and the number of people attending the Dawn Service has also grown, from 300 in 1984 to 15,000 in 2000 (Carlyon 2001; Department of Veterans' Affairs 2007). Gammage (2007) expressed his concern that the events have become so large that they threaten Anzac itself.

The Somme Tourist Board (Comité du Tourisme de la Somme 2006b: 7) noted changes in the nature of those visiting battlefields, from the initial perspective of remembrance and honouring the dead to the historical and educational aspects of today. It predicts that the future will involve a move towards acceptance and a greater ethical understanding of the Great War. This recognizes the different needs, experiences and knowledge of subsequent generations as their distance from the war lengthens. The Australian government, for example, is actively developing sites on the Western Front to help those wishing to visit and seek information. In 2007 the National Australian Archives completed a $5 million project to digitize the records of over 370,000 soldiers from the Great War (Burke 2007). This source allows people, for the first time, to trace their relatives' journey to the Great War battlefields. The Department of Veterans' Affairs also launched a new website for travellers providing easily accessible information about all of Australia's overseas war memorials. The minister for veterans' affairs, Alan Griffin, stated: "I encourage all Australians to consider visiting an overseas memorial as part of future travel plans, or a part of research into our wartime history" (Griffin 2009a). He also announced that $10 million will be set aside to develop an "Anzac Trail" on the Western Front which "will foster a deeper appreciation of what Australians achieved and endured in the main theatre of conflict of the First World War". Australian memorials and museums at seven sites – Villers-Bretonneux, Pozières, Bullecourt, Fromelles, Mont St Quentin, Ypres and Tyne Cot – will be developed (Griffin 2009b).

After the war, local memorials and cemeteries were the focus for remembrance and grief, and the construction of national memorials was relatively rare (Inglis 2005; Laqueur 1994). A review of some of the tourist brochures for the Somme in 2008 revealed that, in spite of their relatively low numbers, national memorials have become a feature of the battlefields. The memorials of a number of the victorious nations have been represented, including Australia, France, Canada, South Africa, Ireland, Britain and the United States. Importantly, relatively few cemeteries and divisional memorials are mentioned in the brochures (although these are available through information sites maintained by the Commonwealth War Graves Commission). There are, perhaps, some pragmatic reasons for the focus on national memorials. Many of the divisional or regimental memorials offer little explicit information as to their significance and meaning. The national memorials, however, are large and distinctive structures, and some have recently built large visitor centers on site with the express purpose of providing educational displays to accommodate large numbers of people.

Figure 14.2 shows the Australian National Memorial, situated near the village of Villers-Bretonneux in France. The village is also important to Australians because it is the location of the Adelaide Cemetery, from which an unknown Australian soldier was taken in 1993 and reburied at the Australian War Memorial in Canberra. Visitor numbers to the Franco-Australian museum in the village have risen from 45 in 1992 to 3,300 in 2005. In 2008 a dawn service was introduced at the Australian National Memorial which was attended by 5,000 people. The event is now being described as "Australia's second Anzac Day", acknowledging the famous capture of the village on 25 April 1918 by the AIF (Button 2006; Carlyon 2001; Department of Veterans' Affairs 2007).

Australians are likely to combine a visit to the battlefields with a broader overseas trip in order to help justify the travel distance and expense. Visitors do not always have the time or knowledge to visit the hundreds of sites and memorials (the Western Front trench line extended 760 km, from the English Channel to the Swiss border). The average length of stay in the Ypres area, for example, is only 2.6 days (Vandaele and Monballyu 2008). A number of organizations, including the Australian Department of Veterans' Affairs and the Somme and Flanders tourist boards, have extensive websites which provide travellers with information about the Great War and the memorials, as well as such advice as routes and

Figure 14.2 The Australian National Memorial, Villers-Bretonneux, France (photograph:
C. Winter).

accommodation. In the area known as "Poppy Country", around the town of Albert, there is a "Poppy Trail" to assist visitors to find the most memorable sites.

The major guide, *The Visitors' Guide to the Battlefields*, provides information about more than ninety memorials and places of interest relating to the Great War (Comité du Tourisme de la Somme 2006a). It incorporates a four-tiered rating system to indicate the relative importance of the various sites using the poppy: x indicates "a site of secondary interest", one poppy indicates "an interesting site", two poppies mark "a very interesting site" and three poppies signify "an exceptional site". Table 14.1 demonstrates that memorials to battles, including cemeteries, divisional or regimental memorials and actual battlefields, comprise more than half of the sites. However, none are rated above "1" (an interesting site). Of the fifteen sites given two- or three-poppy ratings, six are museums and five are national memorials. The most highly ranked sites in the guide (three poppies) are La Boiselle crater, the Historial de la Grande Guerre (a museum) at Péronne, Thiepval, the Newfoundland Caribou, the Albert Trench Museum, the Albert Basilica, the Australian National Memorial and the South African Memorial. This focus upon large, distinctive and national monuments suggests that, overall, fewer visitors need to express grief and more have an educational and national interest in the war. Within this contemporary scenario, the Pozières sites have been given a low ranking because of their lack of visually distinctive attractions. However, the battles at Pozières in 1916 resulted in some of the greatest numbers

Table 14.1 Poppy rating by memorial type

Memorial type	x	1	2	3	Total sites
Cemetery	12	2	–	–	14
Museum/visitor centre	–	–	2	4	6
National	–	1	1	4	7
Divisional	21	5	–	–	26
General memorial (detail not stated)	2	1	–	–	3
Personal	1	2	–	–	3
Church	4	1	2	–	7
Statue	5	2	–	–	7
Battle site	7	4	–	1	12
Other	4	3	1		9
Total	56	21	6	9	92

Source: Comité du Tourisme de la Somme (2006a).

Notes: X = A site of secondary interest
   1 = An interesting site
   2 = A very interesting site
   3 = An exceptional site

3 ratings: *Historial de la Grande Guerre* museum; South African National Memorial and Museum; Franco-British Memorial, Thiepval; Visitor Centre, Thiepval; Newfoundland Memorial Park; Lochnagar Crater; Albert Museum; Australian National Memorial.

2 ratings: Chapel of Souvenir Francais; Ulster Tower; Albert Basilica; Museum and railway, Froissy; Hall of Sole Command; Villers-Bretonneux Museum/School.

of casualties of Australians in the entire war, and were the cause of widespread sadness and grief for people at home.

As Table 14.2 indicates, the Australian memorials that were built in the period up to the late 1930s were dedicated to military units, and they were simple structures offering very little explicit information. Figure 14.3 shows the Australian First Division Memorial, which was built at Pozières and opened some time between 1919 and 1925. Interpretive panels have now been placed near the site to help visitors understand its significance. Many memorials built in the past twenty years, particularly the memorial parks at Le Hamel, Fromelles and Bullecourt, now have such interpretive panels. Plaques have been laid at sites where "markers" have been absent, such as at the Windmill in Pozières and Mouquet Farm. Johnson (1995: 54) wrote that "These new sites of memory are not simply arbitrary assignations of historical referents in space but are consciously situated to connect or compete with existing nodes of collective remembering". These sites will cater to a new generation of visitors who may have no first-hand knowledge of the war or of those who either fought at these places or experienced the war directly.

Conclusion

In the early years following the Great War the underlying motivation for visiting a battlefield was to express grief for loved ones who were killed or lost. The way

Table 14.2 Australian war memorials on the Western Front

Memorial name	Country	Year opened
5th Division Memorial, Polygon Wood, Zonnebeke	Belgium	1919
1st Australian Tunnelling Company, Hill 60, Ypres	Belgium	1923
1st Division Memorial, Pozières	France	1919–25
2nd Division Memorial, Mont St Quentin	France	1925/1971[a]
3rd Division Memorial, Sailly le Sec	France	1919–25
4th Division Memorial, Bellenglise	France	1919–25
CWGC Memorial to the Missing, Villers-Bretonneux Military Cemetery – Australian National Memorial	France	1938
Australian Slouch Hat Memorial	France	1981
Cross Memorial, Bullecourt	France	1982
Australian Memorial Park, Bullecourt	France	1992
Windmill site, Pozières (plaque)	France	1993
Mouquet Farm Battle Exploit Plaque	France	1997
Australian Corps Memorial Park, Le Hamel	France	1998
Australian Memorial Park, Fromelles	France	1998

Sources: Department of Veterans' Affairs website (http://memorials.dva.gov.au/Default.aspx); Inglis (2005).

Note: [a]The original statue of a Digger bayoneting an eagle was completed in 1925, but was removed by

Figure 14.3 The Australian First Division Memorial, Pozières, with the Franco-British memorial on the horizon (photograph: C.Winter).

in which Australians remembered the war and those who fought in it was similar to that of other young nations, such as New Zealand and Canada, who sent an entire generation of their youth to fight thousands of kilometres from their homelands. Later again, at least in Australia, the relatively small and disastrous campaign on the Gallipoli peninsula gained status as one of the nation-building events of the war, overshadowing the far greater battles in which the AIF had engaged on the Western Front.

The centenary commemoration of the Great War will begin in Belgium and France in 2014, and this will provide an opportunity for Australians to acknowledge the part played by their own nation in this world-changing event. While Gallipoli will probably remain Australia's primary site for defining the nation in wartime, there are some indications that the battles on the Western Front and those who were involved in them may be given the acknowledgment they deserve by future generations of Australians. This will not be easily achieved, however, given the profile lent to the Gallipoli campaign in recent years. Tourism has the capacity to operationalize our understanding of these significant events in which great numbers of Australians were killed or wounded, because it provides people with direct experience of the landscapes and battlefields. In these places, many organizations are actively encouraging educational experiences for contemporary visitors in order for them to understand the magnitude and impacts of the war across the globe.

The men and women of the first AIF contributed to our identity as Australians, not through mythic exploits, but through their physical and emotional experiences on the battlefields and in their lives after the war as husbands, wives, friends, parents, grandparents and great-grandparents. Perhaps, too, we can appreciate not just the Anzacs of the Great War, but those from all of the conflicts and peace-keeping missions in which Australians have served.

References

ABS (Australian Bureau of Statistics) (2009) *Australian Demographic Statistics, June 2009*, Cat. 3101.0. Canberra: ABS.

Alomes, S. (1993) "Australian nationalism in the eras of imperialism and internationalism", in J. Arnold, P. Spearritt and D. Walker (eds) *Out of Empire: the British Dominion of Australia*. Port Melbourne: Mandarin.

Alomes, S., and Jones, C. (1991) *Australian Nationalism: A Documentary History*. North Ryde, NSW: Angus & Robertson.

Anderson, B. (1991) *Imagined Communities: Reflections on the Origin and Spread of Nationalism*. Rev edn, New York: Verso.

AWM (Australian War Memorial) (2010) "Australian fatalities at Gallipoli", www.awm. gov.au/encyclopedia/gallipoli/fataities.asp (accessed 21 January 2010).

Burke, N. (2007) "Aussie WW1 records online", *Daily Telegraph*, News Ltd. Online. Available: http://0-global.factiva.com.alpha2.latrobe.edu.au/ha/default.aspx (accessed 12 April 2007).

Button, J. (2006) "No hitches, just pilgrims showing the right spirit", *Sydney Morning Herald*, 21 April.

Carlyon, L. (2001) *Gallipoli*. Sydney: Macmillan.

Carlyon, L. (2006) *The Great War*. Sydney: Macmillan.

Charlton, P. (1986) *Pozières, 1916*. North Ryde, NSW: Methuen Haynes.

Comité du Tourisme de la Somme (2006a) *The Visitors' Guide to the Battlefields*. Amiens: Comité du Tourisme de la Somme.

Comité du Tourisme de la Somme (2006b) *Commemorations: 90th Anniversary of the Battle of the Somme: Programme of Events*. Amiens: Comité du Tourisme de la Somme.

Davidson, J., and Spearritt, P. (2000) *Holiday Business: Tourism in Australia since 1870*. Carlton South, Vic.: Miegunyah Press.

Department of Veterans' Affairs (2007) "Proposed Anzac commemorative site, Gallipoli, June 1999", www.anzacsite.gov.au/3building/concept.html (accessed 16 January 2007).

Gammage, B. (2007) "The Anzac cemetery", *Australian Historical Studies*, 38(129): 124–40.

Griffin, A. (2009a) "Search online for overseas Australian memorials", Media Release VA098, 24 April, Department of Veterans' Affairs.

Griffin, A. (2009b) "$10 million for Anzac trail on Western Front", Media Release VA028, 24 April, Department of Veterans' Affairs.

Henderson, J. (2006) "War as a tourist attraction: the case of Vietnam", *International Journal of Tourism Research*, 2: 269–80.

Hodge, B., and Turner, G. (1987) *Myths of Oz*. Sydney: Allen & Unwin.

Hoffenberg, P. L. (2001) "Landscape, memory and the Australian war experience, 1915–18", *Journal of Contemporary History*, 36(1): 111–31.

Inglis, K. (1997) "Men, women, and war memorials: Anzac Australia", in R. White and P. Russell (eds) *Memories and Dreams: Reflections on Twentieth-Century Australia*. St Leonards, NSW: Allen & Unwin.

Inglis, K. (2005) *Sacred Places: War Memorials in the Australian Landscape*. Carlton, Vic.: Melbourne University Press.

Johnson, N. (1995) "Cast in stone: monuments, geography, and nationalism", *Environment and Planning D: Society and Space*, 13: 54–65.

Kapferer, B. (1988) *Legends of People, Myths of State: Violence, Intolerance, and Political Culture in Sri Lanka and Australia*. Washington, DC: Smithsonian Institution Press.

Laqueur, T. (1994) "Memory and naming in the Great War", in J. Gillis (ed.) *Commemorations: The Politics of National Identity*. Princeton, NJ: Princeton University Press.

Larsson, M. (2009) *Shattered Anzacs: Living with the Scars of War*. Sydney: Univeristy of New South Wales Press.

Lattas, A. (1990) "Aborigines and contemporary nationalism: primordiality and the cultural politics of Otherness", in J. Marcus (ed.) *Writing Australian Culture*. Adelaide: University of Adelaide Press.

Lloyd, D. (1998) *Battlefield Tourism: Pilgrimage and the Commemoration of the Great War in Britain, Australia and Canada*. Oxford: Berg.

MacCannell, D. (1999) *The Tourist: A New Theory of the Leisure Class*. Berkeley: University of California Press.

McGrath, A. (1991) "Travels to a distant past: the mythology of the Outback", *Australian Cultural History*, 10: 113–24.

Mosse, G. L. (1990) *Fallen Soldiers: Reshaping the Memory of the World Wars*. New York: Oxford University Press.

Osborne, B. S. (2001) "In the shadows of monuments: the British League for the reconstruction of the devastated areas of France", *International Journal of Heritage Studies*, 7(1): 59–82.

Rickard, J. (1996) *Australia: A Cultural History*. 2nd edn, London: Longman.

Scates, B. (2006) *Return to Gallipoli: Walking the Battlefields of the Great War*. Cambridge: Cambridge University Press.

Seaton, A. V. (1999) "War and thanatourism: Waterloo 1815–1914", *Annals of Tourism Research*, 26: 130–58.

Seaton, A. V. (2000) "Another weekend away looking for dead bodies . . . battlefield tourism on the Somme and in Flanders", *Tourism Recreation Research*, 25: 63–77.

Slade, P. (2003) "Gallipoli thanatourism: the meaning of ANZAC", *Annals of Tourism Research*, 30: 779–94.

Stonham, J. (1921) *Official Year Book of the Commonwealth of Australia 1901–1920*. Melbourne: Commonwealth of Australia.

Urry, J. (2002a) *The Tourist Gaze*. 2nd edn, London: Sage.

Urry, J. (2002b) "Mobility and proximity", *Sociology*, 36(2): 255–74.

Vance, J. (1997) *Death So Noble: Memory, Meaning and the First World War*. Vancouver: University of British Columbia Press.

Vandaele, D., and Monballyu, M. (2008) "Understanding battlefield tourism in the Westhoek", in K. Lindroth and M. Voutilainen (eds) *Proceedings of the Travel and Tourism Research Association Europe 2008 Annual Conference*, Helsinki, pp. 539–46; www.ttra-europeconference.com/images/downloads/Proceedings_2008.pdf (accessed 3 November 2010).

Ward, R. (1966) *The Australian Legend*. 2nd edn, Oxford: Oxford University Press.

Winter, C. (2009) "The Shrine of Remembrance, Melbourne: a short study of visitors' experiences", *International Journal of Tourism Research*, 11: 553–65.

Winter, J. (2006) *Remembering War: The Great War between Memory and History in the Twentieth Century*. New Haven, CT: Yale University Press.

Ziino, B. (2007) *A Distant Grief: Australians, War Graves and the Great War*. Crawley: University of Western Australia Press.

15 Travelling to the past

Narratives of place and national identity on the Chatham Islands

Adriana Campelo and Robert Aitken

Introduction

The purpose of this chapter is to demonstrate how narratives of history and community experience have formed the basis for place identity on some remote islands in the Pacific Ocean. The idea of national and identity boundaries has particular relevance for small islands such as the Chathams off the east coast of New Zealand. For islands especially, the physical boundaries are clear and incontestable. On the Chathams, the physical boundaries that reinforce separation from mainland New Zealand are complemented by the importance of ownership, the strength of local culture, and the influence of genealogy and history. Together these create a powerful sense of place identity and nation.

This chapter discusses ideas of cultural and heritage tourism, place identity and habitus to provide a theoretical framework for the narratives and stories that contribute to create the identity and ethos of the Chatham Islands. The researchers collected the narratives using multi-sited ethnography through historiography and participant observation during three field trips, for periods of one, three and two weeks, in November 2007, January 2008 and February 2009, respectively. Very little is published about the Chatham Islands; therefore all the information about the lifestyle, habitus, beliefs and values of the people were gathered through our ethnographic experience on site.

The attractiveness and appeal of the Chathams embrace their natural, cultural and historical heritage. The narratives that keep alive the islanders' cultural and historical heritage are not only a starting point for the incipient tourism industry but also serve to strengthen the islands' identity. For visitors and tourists, heritage reconnects people with their past and with their present, reinforcing their self-identity. For places, heritage tourism protects, preserves and reaffirms their ethos. Heritage and history are the cornerstones for place, people and community identities.

Cultural and heritage tourism

Heritage tourism embraces a wide spectrum of tourism possibilities that relate to different human experiences and various accounts of life. According to Hollinshead (1988), among these are history, social customs and cultural traditions, communication and expression (arts and crafts) and ethnicity. Heritage tourism goes beyond the consumption of cultural products from the past (Smith 2003) and creates opportunities to represent the past in the present (Nuryanti 1996). This provides the possibility of witnessing and experiencing the "way of life" of a people and a place connected to a specific time.

The demand of tourists to experience and understand different ways of life by rediscovering the past developed as a niche tourism market in the late 1990s (Poria, Butler and Airey 2001, 2004; Bonn *et al.* 2007). Focusing on the history, culture and natural appeal of places, heritage tourism encompasses a wide variety of connections that link landscape to the cultural and natural heritage of people. The fascination of discovering something that happened in the past can appeal in different ways. For instance, historical attractions may appeal to tourists who are interested in visiting built heritage (museums and historical buildings) and archaeological and natural heritage (Bonn *et al.* 2007). However, these are always heavily influenced by the history and experience of the different people whose culture shaped the past.

Heritage tourism involves everything inherited from the past – arts, history, wildlife and landscape (Sharpley 1993; Christou 2006; Yale 1991). Heritage is defined by Graham *et al.* (2000) as "a view from the present, either backward to a past or forward to a future" (cited in Smith 2003: 2), which is created via interpretation. Unlike other forms of tourism, such as adventure tourism, it joins the past to the present by connecting the outside world of tourists to the inside world of locals (even locals from the past).

The engagement with the past is largely dependent on a number of precise features, such as a specific location or site, a specific moment in time, a specific event, and/or a specific history of a group of people. The distinctiveness of the experience is of central importance to the heritage tourist. These features stand very much for a pre-modern kind of experience that privileges authenticity, slow pace and, in some cases, nostalgia. It is opposed to a postmodern experience that is characterized by an emphasis on the here and now (Dann 2006). The engagement is therefore about specific connections with particular locations in a certain fragment of time, through scenic landscapes, landmarks, archeological remains and/or cultural manifestations (Caton and Santos 2007). Frequently, this engagement occurs through the combination of all these specificities plus the narratives of the local people, which create a sense of proximity with the past and endorse perceptions of authenticity.

Heritage tourism involves emotions and motivations that include nostalgic romanticism, curiosity and the desire to taste diverse "cultural scapes" (Ashworth and Goodall 1990, cited in Christou 2006). The experience is nurtured by reviving a sense of time and space that, perhaps, no longer exists. Heritage tourism is the "contemporary use of the past" (Smith 2003: 82) through its interpretation and its representation. The feeling of nostalgia surrounding the experience of travel across time is part of the distinctiveness. It cannot be repeated or replicated authentically in other places because it happened in only one place and in only one socio-cultural context, and this makes it a unique experience. The importance of this cannot be underestimated, both for the reinforcement it provides for its protagonists and for the vicarious experience it offers to its recipients. For tourists and visitors, heritage tourism promotes self-improvement by refining educational and cultural sensibilities. For local people, it is part of the continuous process of identification and personal and collective ownership. It also engenders a sense of responsibility towards protecting the social capital that makes each community unique (Prohaska 1995).

Criticisms and concerns regarding heritage tourism (Walsh 1992) are linked to the risks of commodifying the past, distorting and fossilizing history for commercial purposes, leading eventually to a loss of authenticity. On the one hand, it brings to the present pieces of history and of the past and contributes towards keeping them alive. On the other hand, the constant "recycling" of those pieces can render them banal and empty of their intrinsic meanings. Approaches that avoid such threats must include the central role of the community in managing and ensuring an accurate interpretation of meaning and an authentic representation of their identity.

More recently, a branch of heritage tourism has emerged that emphasizes visiting "spaces considered by the visitors as relevant to their own heritage" (Poria, Biran and Reichel 2009: 92). This form of heritage tourism is of interest to those who are either searching to understand their own sense of identity (Prentice and Andersen 2007) or looking to create their own interpretation of the past. In the latter case, visitors might make use of personal knowledge and combine it with the site experience to gain insights about their individual heritage (Poria, Biran and Reichel 2009). Accordingly, heritage tourism has developed a sub-segment that relates more to personal identity. This is called genealogical tourism (Santos and Yan 2009). Genealogy provides a sense of belonging to a broader family or ethnic group, and the distinctiveness of this belonging allows individuals to reconstruct and reaffirm their identities. Genealogical tourism, or legacy tourism, as it is called by McCain and Ray, provides an opportunity to attract tourists who find personal meaning in the sites they visit and who "recognize personal legacy motives" (McCain and Ray 2003: 716).

Place identity

Place identity encompasses a set of features and a variety of dynamic interactions and influences (Massey 1995; Lewicka 2008; Kneafsey 2000; Carter, Dyer and Sharma 2007) that create a distinctive character of a place (Stedman 2003). Fluidity and dynamism, for example, are recognized by many authors (Kneafsey 2000; Carter, Dyer and Sharma 2007; Massey 1995) as part of the concept of place identity on account of a variety of interactions. The ways in which these interactions are established and experienced create the peculiar ontology or ethos of each place. According to Borgerson and Schroeder (2005: 19), "ontology centers on notions of being or identity – including human identity". The ontology and genuine aspects of a place refer to its specific attributes (Gilmore 2002; Lewicka

2008; Kotler and Gertner 2002). A communal culture, its beliefs and habitus are part of the shared identity of a certain people living in a certain place at a certain time. This communal state of being might be understood as the ethos of place – an original essence that shapes (Reynolds 1993), characterizes and creates its distinctiveness (Kotler and Gertner 2002). The ethos, or the ontology, of a place is based largely on the meanings of people's social interactions, constructions and understanding of the past and of their relevance to the present experience. The ways in which relationships are established shape the place identity and a collective sense of being and belonging (Dixon and Durrheim 2000).

Communal and shared narratives are created by "the selective recollection of past events which are thought to be important for the members of a specific community" (Halbwach 1985, cited in De Cillia *et al.* 1999: 155). These contribute to the development of a collective memory that is foundational to the construction of nation or place identity, and they disseminate and underpin the values and beliefs that characterize a community each time they are retold. The reproduction and repetition of such stories reinforce the meanings of what has been learnt and understood from the past and inform future actions and behaviour. In this way, the narratives carry the sense of identity of the people and of the place.

Habitus

The concept of habitus can be traced back to Aristotle's writings, and was refined and elaborated upon by Bourdieu, who defines it as "the product of history, which produces individual and collective practices, and hence history, in accordance with the schemas engendered by history" (1977: 82). Later, Bourdieu revisited the concept to explain: "The habitus – embodied history, internalised as a second nature and so forgotten as history – is the active presence of the whole past of which it is the product" (1990: 56).

Habitus has roots in the embeddedness of social exchanges. It is "a set of acquired characteristics which are the product of social conditions" existing among a group or community (Bourdieu 2002: 29). The flip side of these exchanges contributes to ascribe meanings (Carter, Donald and Squires 1993) to places. This definition reinforces the idea of interrelations between the concept of habitus, modus operandi and lifestyle directly and specifically related to a social group. To De Cillia, Reisigl and Wodak (1999), the habitus is part of a national identity. A shared place or national identity embraces a system of common perceptions and concepts "of related emotional attitudes intersubjectively shared within a specific group of persons" and "of similar behavioural dispositions" (De Cillia *et al.* 1999: 153).

In fact, Bourdieu links habitus and lifestyle, saying that the latter is "the best example of the unity of human behaviour" (2002: 29) as an individual or as a group, and it reveals and expresses manners and ways of doing things in terms of practicalities of life, in terms of affective engagements, and in terms of expression and communication.

Narratives of a shared identity: the case of the Chatham Islands

The interactions and narratives about a place confirm symbolic meanings and validate the discourses of people (Ryden 1993), update memories and rituals, and reinforce myths, fables, traditions and icons (Stokowski 2002). Stories and narratives are of central importance in the formation of a place identity. Narratives maintain the connections between place, people, time and physical settings (Stokowski 2002); through them, people share stories of the past, engage with experiences of the present, and make predictions for the future that perpetuate meanings through developing and reinforcing habitus (Kyle and Chick 2007). To Hillier and Rooksby (2002; 5), "habitus is thus a sense of one's (and others') place and role in the world of one's lived environment".

The following sections present the narratives that create a shared sense of nation identity on the Chatham Islands. The narratives emerged through participant observation on site and were informed and confirmed by historiography.

The Chatham Islands

The Chatham Islands are an archipelago of ten islands that cover an area of 966 sq km, located 800 km east of Christchurch, New Zealand. The two main islands, Chatham and Pitt, are the only inhabited ones, the others being conservation reserves. The population in 2006 numbered 609 people, of whom 369 were identified as being of Maori and Moriori descent. Maori are the native people of New Zealand, and Moriori are the native people of the Chatham Islands. It is believed that both groups share the same ancestors from East Polynesia (King 2000). Maori was spoken by 13.7 per cent of the population – a high percentage considering the rate for New Zealand was 4.1 per cent (Census 2006).

The economy of the Islands is based on pastoral farming, fishing and an incipient tourism industry. The median annual income in 2006 was $24,200, just a little lower than the New Zealand median, which was $24,400. However, just over 40 per cent received an annual income of $20,000 or less, which was below the New Zealand average rate of 43.2 per cent; 16.7 per cent earned more than $50,000, while the rate for New Zealand was 18.0 per cent (Census 2006). These figures indicate a socio-economic environment more homogeneous than that of mainland New Zealand.

The biggest island in the group is named Chatham, after the first European ship which arrived there in 1791, the brig *HMS Chatham*. The Maori and Moriori names are Wharekauri and Rekohu, both of which describe the misty sunlight that surrounds the islands. A significant landmark is Te Whanga lagoon, covering approximately 20,000 hectares/180 sq km, or one-fifth of the island's area. The second inhabited island, Pitt (called Rangiauria in Moriori), lies to the south of Chatham, covers an area of 62 sq km and has approximately fifty inhabitants (Census 2006).

Ethnic history

The Moriori were the first indigenous people to live on the islands. They were organized into nine tribes – Hamata, Wheteina, Eitara, Etiao, Harua, Makao, Matanga, Poutama and Rauru – and lived in kin-based groups of between thirty and a hundred people. Moriori society seemed to be more egalitarian and democratic than that of their traditional Polynesian ancestors, with their leaders elected as much for their fishing and hunting prowess as for their hereditary rights. The population was without outside human contact for over 400 years (King 2000; Davis and Solomon 2005).

The group of islands was discovered by Europeans in 1791, with the advent of *HMS Chatham* commanded by Lieutenant William Robert Broughton. Although the Chatham Islands were officially on the British Royal Navy map of the known world by 1793, they remained unvisited until 1804, when the first sealers started to arrive. From 1810 the visits of Europeans vessels (from England, Portugal, France and Ireland) looking for seals and whales became more frequent. These visits not only reduced the population of seals, which were killed indiscriminately to be sold in China, Russia and England, but also severely affected the Moriori population, who were not equipped to deal with the inevitable ravages of European diseases. The islands were declared part of New Zealand in 1842 and became a target for British colonisation. By 1843 five German missionaries had arrived and had introduced literacy and farming (King 2000).

In 1835, Maori tribes, escaping from the intertribal wars on the North Island of New Zealand, invaded the Chathams. Their settlements were characterized by a violence and brutality that led, ultimately, to the decimation and enslaving of the Moriori people. It is estimated that the Moriori population at this time numbered around 2,000 but by 1862, as a result of this destructive experience and the deadly diseases introduced by Europeans, it had plunged to just over a hundred. The last full-blooded Moriori died in 1933 (Davis and Solomon 2005).

Narratives that create the Chathams' experience

Organized tourism on the Chathams is currently limited to week-long tours offered by the islands' main operators. Because of the absence of public transportation and the very few place and road signs indicating areas of interest, tourists rely heavily on their hosts to determine itineraries, plan activities, receive directions and obtain access. The Chathams' experience requires a much closer working relationship with local inhabitants than is usual and inevitably enhances the visitors' sense of adventure and immersion into the place's history and culture. The majority of tourist activities, always related to ecotourism and/or heritage tourism (including both natural and historical heritage), are weather dependent, and thus a closer affinity with the natural environment is developed.

Narrative 1

Ecotourism celebrates the islands' natural history. The Chathams emerged in the last 4 million years, creating a complex archipelago comprised of ancient volcanic and schist rock and more recent sediments, including limestone, basalt and dune sand. The land has been uplifted, eroded and drowned several times. This has resulted in a variety of landscapes whose mosaic of habitats support a considerable richness and diversity of flora and fauna (Department of Conservation 2009). The islands form a natural repository of fossilized bones of birds and maritime species, accessible to visitors on the beaches and shores of the Te Whanga lagoon. The lagoon, in addition to being a remarkable landmark on account of its size, has special meanings for local inhabitants relating to its importance as an abundant source of food. It is also an important place for recreation where, for generations, families have traditionally camped during Christmas. Further, it is a place where heritage (historical and natural) can be experienced through such activities as visiting Nunuku's cave, where Moriori carvings can be seen, or hunting for fossilized shark teeth along the shores of Te Whanga. Other activities involve a combined interest in the islands' history and heritage, such as visiting the J. M. Baker (Hapupu in Moriori) National Historic Reserve, a kopi forest where ancient Moriori tree carvings are located (King and Morrison 1990), or the two main scenic reserves of Ocean Mail and Henga, both important sites of early Moriori occupancy.

Narrative 2

One aspect of Moriori culture highlighted by King is how the tribes abolished all internecine mortal combat, and how they developed a method to solve disputes which did not "threaten annihilation" (2000: 26). This peaceful characteristic is represented by Nunuku's law. Nunuku-whenua was an ancestral tribal leader who ordered peace between the Rauru and Wheteina tribes, who were more commonly accustomed to bloodshed and cannibalism. The Nunuku tradition was adopted and honoured by all the Chatham Island Moriori and would seem to explain their peaceful overtures to the traditionally warlike Maoris when they arrived later in the nineteenth century. The ensuing conflict between the expansive Maori and the entrenched Moriori contributed significantly to a discontinuity in Moriori history, language and culture (King 2000).

The Treaty of Waitangi (the treaty between the British and Maori chiefs establishing rights of ownership to the new "colony" of New Zealand) was signed in 1840, but only in 1863 were Moriori finally recognized under the jurisdiction. In more recent years Moriori have started to re-establish their identity and are now experiencing a renaissance of language and culture. In 2005, the first Moriori *marae* (sacred place) was built, in the shape of an albatross, a bird which has great symbolic resonance for Moriori (Davis and Solomon 2005); it is now a communal space for meetings, gatherings and celebrations. It is also a place for quiet reflection and for Moriori to walk through and among the stories of their ancestors.

Visiting the *marae* is an immersion in Moriori history and culture, which, unlike that of the Maori, remains unknown to the majority of New Zealanders. This indigenous heritage is thus of noteworthy importance as a tourist attraction on the islands, principally because the indigenous people remained isolated from the rest of the world for 400 years, and their story of violent combat, brutal oppression and defiant survival is a poignant reminder both of the frailties of human endeavour and of the resilience of the human spirit. The present effort of Moriori to reconstruct their identity, re-establish their culture and reconnect with their neighbours is a dynamic experience that is continuing to unfold. Further, their stories remain barely written and published, which make them little known in New Zealand and other countries.

Narrative 3

The European heritage of the Chathams is equally celebrated through the stories of the settlers, sealers and whalers. The most prominent of these recount the story of Frederick Hunt, an Englishman who was the first European settler. He arrived with his family in 1842 on Chatham, then moved to Pitt and took ownership of land, trading half of the island for a red jacket from Apitea, a Maori chief. Hunt introduced farming on Pitt, and his descendants still own land and farm there. Among many stories about Hunt, one is relevant to understand the importance of genealogy to Pitt islanders in the sense that ownership is related not only to possession of the land, but also to family history. Frederick Hunt had two daughters, and, in order to protect his name and preserve it for future generations, his sons-in-law were obliged on marriage to take his surname to be part of his family estate. The name has been continued through succeeding generations, and members of the current generation tell this story with the clear intention of honouring the obligation and establishing their part in its history.

Narrative 4

The lines of descent and paths of genealogy are clear and vital for the people of the Chathams. In casual conversation, locals proudly trace back six generations of their family history on the islands. Indeed, the majority of the population today is related to particular immigration phases – Moriori, Irish, Portuguese, English and French whalers, British colonisation, Maori, and German missionaries. Not surprisingly, these ethnicities have become interwoven over time, and the stories and memories of how and when this patchwork originated are well preserved and perpetuated among the community. Knowledge about genealogy, or *whakapapa* (Maori for genealogy), is considered of high importance in the community in order to determine the sense of self- and family identity. In particular, knowledge extends to the land on the islands where their ancestors used to live, which, in most cases, is still under the same family ownership. Genealogy is experienced through this attachment to the family land and to its place in the islands' communal history, which is transmitted through a strong oral tradition (there is no written equivalent).

Narrative 5

Even though it is part of New Zealand, and separated by only a two-hour flight, the community shares a strong feeling that New Zealand is a different country. In reality, a number of factors contribute to creating a symbolic and literal distance between the Chathams and the mainland. For example, the flight between the two is often delayed or cancelled when weather conditions deteriorate. The weekly supply ship is also vulnerable, and essential deliveries of food, stock and fuel can be delayed for days. Indeed, the barriers to a physical approach to the islands reinforce their isolation, impacting not only the perception of separateness and differentiation from the mainland but also the notion of time, which on the islands is clearly determined more by the weather than by the clock. This creates a particular rhythm of life on the Chathams.

Besides the strong connection with an ancient past, a visit to the Chathams provides a glimpse of a lifestyle that has disappeared from the New Zealand mainland, and indeed from most developed countries, but which remains here as genuine and authentic. The slow pace of life combined with the small size of the community provides a taste of what rural New Zealand was like twenty or thirty years ago. Doors unlocked and cars parked with keys inside are a reminder not only of a different time but also of a different set of values.

Conclusion

Fundamental to the relationship between nation and identity on the Chatham Islands is how people perceive themselves. Place identity takes shape when similar perceptions are shared across a community. These perceptions influence attitudes and perspectives on life, defining which values matter and the degree of their importance in the community's life. Great importance is given on the Chatham Islands to the maintenance of family ties, not only those in the present but especially those with the past. People are proudly aware of their ancestors and the stories that link them together. Indeed, the importance of carrying a family name from generation to generation plays a significant part in the culture and the continuation of the bonds with the past. This is further reinforced by the importance of the ownership of land and natural resources, which links identity to ancestors and to place. The strength of this sense of identity and place has considerable appeal for those interested in exploring their own heritage in a living community with explicit and direct links to the past. This has created a niche opportunity to develop heritage tourism on the islands.

The limited number of public meeting places on the Chathams (just one hotel and two cafes) promotes a natural contact between tourists and locals, facilitating access to the community's lifestyle. These contacts create opportunities for locals to tell their stories about the islands – stories that inevitably involve their ancestors – and the locals naturally take the perspective of the narrator. Listening to stories from sixth-generation descendants of the original protagonists rein-forces a sense of authenticity and connectedness that links the past to the present. Each retelling also serves to revive, reaffirm and re-enliven the individual family histories that comprise the islands' collective past. For tourists, "witnessing" the past through its re-presentation is an experience that is at once immediate and unique to the moment and privileged. However, such narrative reinforcement of the islanders' culture is less about creating new perspectives on tourism products and more about confirming and celebrating community history, ways of life, fam-ily duties and, ultimately, place identity.

Self- and communal identity, involving people and place, are based on two strong pillars – family history and attachment to the land – both of which rein-force the importance of ownership and belonging. Ownership from a more indi-vidual perspective is about private possession in terms of land and family names. From a communal perspective, the sense of ownership is about landscape, natu-ral resources, history, ancestry, traditions, community duties, rights and roles. Such ownership nurtures a feeling of belonging and fosters a sense of responsi-bility. As the population is a food-gathering society, there is a strong emphasis on sharing (Bird-David 2005, cited in Belk 2010). Sharing goes beyond eco-nomic and reciprocal forms of exchange objects and possessions, and adopts an alternative model of exchange experiences that widens the perspective to include unwritten knowledge about ways of life and the past. The culture of sharing traditions and day-to-day practices is, in large measure, related to how people survive in their environment, and is responsible for extending individual owner-ship to communal ownership. Therefore, sharing becomes a practice that rein-forces the feeling of unity and a mutual identity (Belk 2010). Ownership embraces family duties and roles and is related to community services. For example, certain families have specific duties on occasions such as funerals, marriages, births, sporting events and social gatherings. These duties are expected to be passed from generation to generation in order to preserve com-munity culture and identity.

This chapter demonstrates the experience of a destination where the identity and ethos of place are of high importance in creating a niche for the development of heritage tourism. The attractiveness and appeal of the Chathams stems from their natural and historical heritage. Both are the essence of the place and are central to people's identity and, at same time, form the main attraction for tour-ists. The development of tourism creates challenges not only for the preservation and conservation of the islands' cultural heritage but also to its identity. The retelling of narratives helps to reinforce the identity and ethos of the place and their sense of nation among the community.

References

Belk, R. W. (2010) "Sharing", *Journal of Consumer Research*, 36: 715–34.
Bonn, M. A., Joseph-Mathews, S. M., Dai, M., Hayes, S., and Cave, J. (2007) "Heritage/cultural attraction atmospherics: creating the right environment for the heritage/cultural visitor", *Journal of Travel Research*, 3: 345–54.

Borgerson, J. L., and Schroeder, J. (2005) "Identity in marketing communications: an ethics of visual representation", in A. J. Kimmel (ed.) *Marketing Communication: New Approaches, Technologies, and Styles.* Oxford: Oxford University Press.

Bourdieu, P. (1977) *Outline of a Theory of Practice.* Cambridge: Cambridge University Press.

Bourdieu, P. (1990) *The Logic of Practice.* Stanford, CA: Stanford University Press.

Bourdieu, P. (2002) "Habitus", in J. Hillier and E. Rooksby (eds) *Habitus: A Sense of Place.* Aldershot: Ashgate.

Carter, E., Donald, J., and Squires, J. (1993) *Space and Place: Theories of Identity and Location.* London: Lawrence & Wishart.

Carter, J., Dyer, P., and Sharma, B. (2007) "Dis-placed voices: sense of place and place-identity on the sunshine coast", *Social and Cultural Geography*, 5: 755–73.

Caton, K., and Santos, C. A. (2007) "Heritage tourism on Route 66: deconstructing nostalgia", *Journal of Travel Research*, 4: 371–86.

Census, Statistics New Zealand (2006) "2006 census of population and dwellings: final report on contents", www.statisticsnz.govt.nz (accessed 15 April 2008).

Christou, E. (2006) "Heritage and cultural tourism: a marketing-focused approach", in M. Sigala and D. Leslie (eds) *International Cultural Tourism: Management, Implications and Cases.* Oxford: Elsevier.

Dann, G. M. S. (2006) "Promotional issues", in G. Baldacchino (ed.) *Extreme Tourism: Lessons from the World's Cold Water Islands.* Oxford: Elsevier.

Davis, D., and Solomon, M. (2005) "Moriori", *Te Ara: The Encyclopedia of New Zealand*; www.teara.govt.nz/en/moriori (accessed 6 January 2008).

De Cillia, R., Reisigl, M., and Wodak, R. (1999) "The discursive construction of national identities", *Discourse and Society*, 10: 149–73.

Department of Conservation (2009) www.doc.govt.nz/by-region/chatham-islands (accessed 11 February 2009).

Dixon, J., and Durrheim, K. (2000) "Displacing place-identity: a discursive approach to locating self and other", *British Journal of Social Psychology*, 39: 27–44.

Gilmore, F. (2002) "A country – can it be repositioned? Spain – the success story of country branding", *Journal of Brand Management*, 9: 281–96.

Hillier, J., and Rooksby, E. (2002) *Habitus: A Sense of Place.* Aldershot: Ashgate.

Hollinshead, K. (1988) "First blush of the longtime: the market development of Australia's living Aboriginal heritage. Tourism research: expanding boundaries", in *Proceedings of the 19th Annual Conference of the Travel and Tourism Research Association* (pp. 183–98). Salt Lake City: University of Utah.

King, M. (2000) *Moriori: A People Rediscovered.* Auckland: Penguin Books.

King, M., and Morrison, R. (1990) *A Land Apart: The Chatham Islands of New Zealand.* Auckland: Random Century.

Kneafsey, M. (2000) "Tourism, place identities and social relations in the European rural periphery", *European Urban and Regional Studies*, 1: 35–50.

Kotler, P., and Gertner, D. (2002) "Country as brand, product, and beyond: a place marketing and brand management perspective", *Journal of Brand Management*, 9: 62–82.

Kyle, G., and Chick, G. (2007) "The social construction of sense of place", *Leisure Sciences*, 29: 209–25.

Lewicka, M. (2008) "Place attachment, place identity, and place memory: restoring the forgotten city past", *Journal of Environmental Psychology*, 3: 209–31.

McCain, G., and Ray, N. (2003) "Legacy tourism: the search for personal meaning in heritage travel", *Tourism Management*, 24: 713–17.

Massey, D. (1995) "Places and their pasts", *History Workshop Journal*, 39: 182–92.

Nuryanti, W. (1996) "Heritage and postmodern tourism", *Annals of Tourism Research*, 2: 249–60.

Poria, Y., Biran, A., and Reichel, A. (2009) "Visitors' preferences for interpretation at heritage sites", *Journal of Travel Research*, 1: 92–105.

Poria, Y., Butler, R., and Airey, D. (2001) "Clarifying heritage tourism", *Annals of Tourism Research*, 4: 1047–9.

Poria, Y., Butler, R., and Airey, D. (2004) "Links between tourists, heritage, and reasons for visiting heritage sites", *Journal of Travel Research*, 1: 19–28.

Prentice, R., and Andersen, V. (2007) "Interpreting heritage essentialisms: familiarity and felt history", *Tourism Management*, 3: 661–76.

Prohaska, S. (1995) "Trends in cultural tourism", in M. Conlin and T. Baum (eds) *Island Tourism: Management Principles and Practice*. London: Wiley.

Reynolds, N. (1993) "Ethos as location: new sites for understanding discursive authority", *Rhetoric Review*, 11: 325–38.

Ryden, K. C. (1993) *Mapping the Invisible Landscape: Folklore, Writing, and the Sense of Place*. Iowa City: University of Iowa Press.

Santos, C. A., and Yan, G. (2009) "Genealogical tourism: a phenomenological examination", *Journal of Travel Research*, 49: 56–67.

Sharpley, R. (1993) *Tourism & Leisure in the Countryside*. Huntington: Elm.

Smith, M. K. (2003) *Issues in Cultural Tourism Studies*. London: Routledge.

Stedman, R. C. (2003) "Is it really just a social construction? The contribution of the physical environment to sense of place", *Society and Natural Resources*, 8: 671–85.

Stokowski, P. (2002) "Languages of place and discourses of power: constructing new senses of place", *Journal of Leisure Research*, 34: 368–83.

Walsh, K. (1992) *The Representation of the Past: Museums and Heritage in the Post-Modern World*. London: Routledge.

Yale, P. (1991) *From Tourist Attractions to Heritage Tourism*. Huntingdon: Elm.

16 Dark tourism and national identity in the Australian history curriculum

Unexamined questions regarding educational visits to sites of human suffering

Jacqueline Z. Wilson

Introduction

In 2008, the newly constituted Australian National Curriculum Board (NCB) identified the study of history in schools at all year-levels as one of the key elements of the development of young Australians into "successful learners" and hence "active and informed citizens" (NCB 2008: 3). "Successful learners", the board stated, are able "to make sense of their world and think about how things became the way they are". The NCB subsequently proposed a national history curriculum that accords fully with its aims, affirming that history "provides the means whereby individual and collective identities are formed and sustained" (NCB 2009: 4).

However, despite its acknowledged value in the growth of intellectual character and civic awareness in young people, history is notorious among educators for presenting difficulties when it comes to student engagement – especially Australian history, and especially at secondary level (Clark 2008: 1–16). It is here, as the NCB acknowledges (2009: 16), that the historical excursion comes into its own. An increasingly popular tourist practice all over the world is that of visiting historical sites that memorialise human suffering, trauma and death. In a growing phenomenon broadly known as "dark tourism", former prisons, battlefields, war memorials, concentration camps and even the remnants of natural disasters receive many thousands of visitors a year (Lennon and Foley 2000). At first sight, the term "dark tourism" may imply little more than a general fascination with the dire and macabre, but there is more to it than that. The sites themselves often embody multiple layers of contested historical and cultural meaning, and the motivation of those visiting tends to be at least as complex (Strange 2000; Loo and Strange 2000; Strange and Kempa 2003; Wilson 2008). A monument to fallen soldiers, for instance, may simultaneously be a venue for straightforward "sightseeing", a destination of reverent pilgrimage and an educational resource. Importantly, it may also stand as a material contribution to the "social memory" of a society, and hence attain the status of a symbol of national identity (Scates 2006: 184–7; Winter 2009: 609).

The creation or preservation of iconic sites of social memory can occur as a consciously directed project. This was the case in many countries, including Australia, after the First World War, with the construction of numerous monuments and memorials honouring the fallen and celebrating those who had returned

(Scates 2006; Winter 2009). It can also be a consequence of a spontaneous general recognition, over time, of a site's significance in the process of society – or nation-building. These sites often pass through phases of contested meaning or significance, being reviled as shameful in one era, only later, as historical sensibilities shift, to be celebrated.

One of the lessons conveyed by international examples is that social memory is often affirmed, and national identity thus served, by those sites that embody the darkest narratives. And these can result both from "official" attempts to direct the public consciousness and "unofficial" impromptu acts of remembrance by ordinary citizens. Davison (2006: 104–5) cites South Africa's Apartheid Museum as a case in point, confirming its ability movingly to evoke the evils of the apartheid era, while contrasting its sophisticated representational structure to the equally evocative "improvised monument to the victims of the [Berlin] Wall, [located] close to the Reichstag". In recounting his South African experience, Davison (2006: 104) also notes in passing "the busloads of schoolchildren" expected on any weekday at the Apartheid Museum. This highlights an aspect that almost all such institutions, the world over, regard as an everyday component of their visitor demographic (and in many cases rely on as a significant source of funds) – namely, the role of educational resources – and the most direct and tangible way in which they fulfil this role is as a destination for school excursions. This is no less true in Australia than anywhere else in the world where such sites operate.

Dark tourism, education and Australian identity

Teachers in all disciplines have long recognised the value of temporarily transforming students' learning environments through abandoning the conventional classroom, either transferring to an alternative locale within the school or visiting sites and facilities outside the school (Zarmati 2009; Lorenza 2009; Whitty 2003; Cullen 2005; Munday 2008; Schiller 2006; Hobart 2005). As Lorenza (2009: 23) suggests, "Excursions offer a sensory learning opportunity whereby students explore the reality of an environment, be it geographical, mathematical, scientific, social or artistic, through a range of sensory experiences".

The key questions, then, from an educational standpoint, are: What is meant by "the reality of an environment"? and What constitutes a "sensory learning opportunity" in that environment when its significance rests centrally on the commemoration of suffering and death? Each year thousands of Australia's primary and secondary schoolchildren visit such environments. The excursions they undertake can range from a short walk to a nearby cemetery or war monument and back, to a full day touring, say, a former prison or convict site, or an extended period visiting interstate memorials or even overseas battlefields. Minor sites, usually local to schools visiting them, are numberless. Some of the major sites of social memory commonly visited by school groups within Australia are the Port Arthur Historic Site; Old Melbourne Gaol; Old Adelaide Gaol; Fremantle Prison; the Shrine of Remembrance at Melbourne; the Holocaust museums in Melbourne, Sydney and Perth; Sovereign Hill's Eureka Stockade "Sound and Light Show" at

Ballarat; the Cyclone Tracy Exhibit at Darwin Museum; and the Australian War Memorial in Canberra. Overseas sites regularly toured by groups from Australian schools include Gallipoli, the Kakoda Track, and European battlefields and war graves of both world wars.

The extensive educational patronage of these sites does not obviate the questions arising from their contested meanings. Interpretation of historical sites of any kind is often cause for debate, and those sites whose cultural or historical significance rests on the highly emotive issue of human suffering tend to excite especially deep and intensely fought divisions among both scholars and stakeholders (Strange 2000; Strange and Kempa 2003; Loo and Strange 2000; Sunter 2003; Williams 2004; Hughes 2008; Wilson 2008). It is therefore problematic to define precisely how, and to what extent, experience of such sites actually influences the teaching and learning of Australian history and to determine the nature of their contribution to students' perception and understanding of national identity.

The issue of Australian identity has been a self-conscious and at times somewhat vexed question for the past four decades or so. The settlement in 1788 that founded the proto-nation-state that is today called Australia (originally the colony of New South Wales) established a near-total British monoculture that endured, at least in its citizens' self-definition and the view of influential observers, for a century and a half (Trollope 1873; Hancock 1930; Pringle 1961; Horne 1964). Not until the mid-twentieth century did it begin to occur to significant segments of the population – and, crucially, their leaders – that "British" Australia was conceptualised at the expense of substantial sections of its society, especially its Aboriginal peoples, non-British migrant groups and women. The result has been a growing attempt to redefine the nation along more inclusive lines, with a fairly effective (albeit still partial) embracement of feminism, a movement towards reconciliation between indigenous and non-indigenous Australians, and immigration and social policies explicitly aimed at creating and promoting a multicultural society (Curthoys 1983; Attwood and Markus 1999; Manne 2001).

Perhaps inevitably, over the past decade there has been a reaction among conservative politicians and scholars, in company with certain prominent media commentators, intent in part on re-creating a simplified national image which, if it does not regress all the way back to the "days of Empire", at least pays due homage to key aspects of Australia's British legacy. This movement has essentially focused on two key issues: consolidating the iconic status of the role in the First World War of the nation's military archetype, the soldiers of the Australian and New Zealand Army Corps (Anzacs); and attempting to rehabilitate Anglo-Australian (white) society in the matter of the dispossession and mistreatment of the Aborigines. The former aim – extolling the Anzacs – has been highly successful, not least because it is very much in accord with existing popular sentiment (Lake and Reynolds 2010). The latter issue, however, in its "playing down" of Aboriginal suffering, proved far more contentious and led to an extraordinarily bitter public debate, dubbed the "History Wars", encompassing legalistic scholarly disputation, political interference and journalistic rancour (Macintyre and Clark 2004).

Even the relatively straightforward mythologising of the Anzacs has its paradoxes and contested aspects. The genesis of the Anzac "legend" lies in Australian troops' participation in one of the Allies' most unfortunate campaigns of the Great War: the landings on the Turkish coast at Gallipoli. Thus for many Australians the focus of national identity is a benighted strip of coastline in a foreign country, too remote for the vast majority to hope ever to visit, and moreover the site of a defeat. They must also, each in their own way, deal with the fact that the traditional image of the "typical" Anzac has in recent years come under the scrutiny of revisionist historians. A freshly critical eye cast on the contemporary accounts of the Gallipoli and Western Front campaigns has questioned the long-established notion of unflinching courage and unfailingly sound character as hallmarks of the Australian soldier (Lake and Reynolds 2010; Kent 1985; Serle 1965).

Australian national identity has become, it seems, irrevocably tangled. A societal skein of disparate political dispositions, ethnicities, socio-economic circumstances, gender perceptions, personal narratives and personal stakes in the historical narratives combine to render consensual answers elusive (yet all the more compelling to pursue). These, then, are some of the imperatives involved below the surface, as it were, in the inclusion of national identity as a goal in the history curriculum.

Two Australian case studies

Most teachers put a great deal of thought into choosing and organising excursions. Some make the decision to take their students to a particular location on the basis of little more than assumed or "obvious" relevance to the subject being taught and/or a pedagogically sound but hazily defined desire to come up with activities that will "engage" them. However, in the case of dark tourism sites, even excursions that are very carefully planned and rationalised are potentially problematic. By way of illustrating this, two exemplary dark tourism sites are discussed. Both have considerable standing as signifiers of Australian identity and are regularly visited by school groups, but upon closer scrutiny they present unexamined facets that prompt questions regarding the exact nature of their educational role.

The Port Arthur Historic Site

One of the most popular dark tourism sites in Australia, and one of the most visited by schoolchildren, is the Port Arthur Historic Site, on the Tasman peninsula in south-east Tasmania. The earliest British settlement of Tasmania (then called Van Diemen's Land, the name given it by the Dutch explorer Abel Tasman) was founded in 1803 and, as in most of the other colonies on the Australian continent, the first settlers on the island were convicts – penal transportees from Britain, sent across the world in their thousands from the late eighteenth to the mid-nineteenth century. Port Arthur was established as a penal settlement in 1830, with the intention of expanding the colony's "secondary punishment" venues and, further, to "exploit the convict labour force" (Robson 1997: 15). It housed prisoners until 1877, twenty-four years after the cessation of convict transportation and twenty-two years after the colony had officially become Tasmania (Weidenhofer 1981: 1). By that time, of the approximately 61,000 convicts who had served their sentences in the island colony, an estimated 12,700 had actually been imprisoned at Port Arthur (ibid.: 2).

In the course of its life as a penal settlement, Port Arthur came to be the site of a township; a military barracks; a complex of industrial and commercial establishments including a shipyard; an asylum for the criminally insane; and three distinct prisons, reflecting developments in the economic significance of the convicts as a labour force, the nature of the site as both a general prison and a place of punishment for multiple-offending or incorrigible transportees from elsewhere, and the correctional philosophies of the day. From the late 1830s, the settlement was self-sustaining in terms of certain food staples (Weidenhofer 1981: 39, 100–3), and for much of its existence it made a sizable contribution to the Tasmanian economy, producing a variety of goods of sufficiently high quality to be exported to Britain and elsewhere (ibid.: 98–100).

Port Arthur was, and remains, notorious for its rigorous and brutal regime of punishments and enforcement of regulations (Convict Department, Tasmania [1868] 1991). Much of its reputation rests on the second prison to be established there, the so-called Separate Prison, in the early 1850s, which was modelled on the "experimental" prison at Pentonville in London, where prisoners were placed in solitary confinement for the purpose of reform through education and the acquisition of trade skills (Brand 1990: 4–8; Johnston 2000). This establishment was, in the words of the colony's comptroller-general of convicts, expressly to confine:

> men who, in consequence of having committed serious crimes, are under orders of removal to Norfolk Island for lengthened periods, as well as those who by their general troublesome refractory conduct interfere with the discipline of the stations in Van Diemen's Land.
>
> (Cited in Brand 1990: 9)

Throughout its existence, Port Arthur was one of the most feared destinations among the Australian penal colonies.

When Port Arthur's prisons closed in 1877, the nearby township promptly renamed itself Carnarvon. The buildings of the penal settlement, which had been in physical decline for years (Weidenhofer 1981: 121), were permitted to deteriorate apace, culminating in a series of fires that destroyed or left a number of major structures gutted (ibid.: 126–8). For a while after the closure, at least some of the townspeople and other residents of the neighbourhood preferred "to deny Port Arthur's existence" (ibid.: 3); but (dark) tourism had started almost as soon as the prisons closed and quickly took over as the area's staple industry, with visitors presumably drawn, in the words of the site's modern promotional literature, "to see first-hand the 'horrors' of a penal station" (Port Arthur Historic Site 2010b).

The Port Arthur Historic Site, which today comprises more than sixty buildings in varying states of disrepair and/or restoration on 100 hectares of land, has received significant government support for several decades and consistently attracts in the order of a quarter of a million visitors a year (Weidenhofer 1981: 3; Port Arthur Historic Site 2010a).

The renaming of the town at the moment the last inmate had departed is significant. For many years after the penal centre's closure, and notwithstanding the area's immense popularity as a tourist attraction, local residents – residents all over the island, in fact – were quite literally ashamed of the site, as they were ashamed of even the possibility that they might be related to or descended from a convict. This sense of stigma came to be known as the "convict stain". Not until the late 1960s were social historians able to suggest that Australia as a society had come to terms with its past, and that the "stain" was fading (Reynolds 1969).

In relation to the connections between dark tourism sites and national identity, Australia's convict origins are apparently more accepted than in the past. Nevertheless the convict stain, in a variety of forms, is still very much a factor, albeit hidden, in the national psyche (Wilson 2008). As evidence of this, the 2000 Sydney Olympics opening ceremony, which provided – for a global television audience of approximately 3.7 billion people (Australian Bureau of Statistics 2007) – an extended and spectacularly staged depiction of the national historical narrative that included every social phase, every major event, every significant character type, omitted only one group – the convicts (Wilson 2008: 204–5). This is despite their central and indispensible role in the founding of the colonies, and despite, too, the fact that approximately one-fifth of modern Australians are their descendants. Not a single Australian media commentator of any prominence thought their omission worth mentioning in their subsequent reviews and analyses of the event (ibid.: 205). Where, then, does a site such as Port Arthur, whose origins are intrinsically bound up with convict society, stand in relation to the modern Australian's personal narrative? Where does it stand in relation to the society's shared sense of nation? That it has iconic status among the nation's landmarks is undeniable, yet it is not actually clear just why. Like so many dark tourism sites, it is deeply ambiguous. This ambiguity leads to the further questions – namely, What do schoolchildren see in the site? What is the appropriate pedagogical process of preparing them for such conflicted meanings? and, In what way does it further their education?

These questions are compounded by the fact that there is more to Port Arthur, as an archetypal dark tourism site, than its convict origins. On the morning of 28 April 1996, a young Tasmanian man with a long history of disturbed personal relations armed himself with three military assault rifles, travelled the short distance from his home to the Port Arthur Historic Site, and began a random murder spree that lasted almost twenty-four hours. He left thirty-five people dead and nineteen wounded. Most of the victims were shot on the grounds of the site.

It is no exaggeration to say that the entire nation was to a degree traumatised by the Port Arthur massacre. The enormity of the crime, its psychopathic pointlessness, the seemingly "fated" choice of the already "dark" location, and the recriminations at Tasmania's notoriously lax firearms laws which had allowed the gunman so easily to acquire his weapons combined to produce a moment of collective grief and dismay that itself almost immediately became iconic, a macabre landmark in the national narrative. The words "Port Arthur" suddenly identified not merely a place, but an event.

But the focus of the experience was, of course, felt most strongly, and most lastingly, at Port Arthur itself. To this day, visitors to the site are expressly discouraged from raising the topic of the massacre. Its promotional website succinctly recounts the massacre's terrible narrative, pointedly omitting the killer's name throughout (he is simply "the gunman"), and speaks of the ongoing emotional vulnerability of the Port Arthur personnel, "many of whom lost close friends, colleagues or family members". Tourists wanting information are invited to "read the plaque at the Memorial Garden" (Port Arthur 2010c).

The teacher organising a historical excursion to Port Arthur can find abundant advice and information available on the same website. On one of the "school visits" pages, concerned specifically with presenting a "Code of Conduct for school visits", a number of points are made about visitors' treatment of the site's scenic, archaeological and social integrity, observance of safety principles, respectful dealings with site personnel, and so on. As a final item the 1996 massacre is briefly noted, and the invitation to visit the Memorial Garden reiterated. The teacher is then urged "to view the details on this topic on our website and discuss with your students before visiting" (Port Arthur 2010d).

The teacher is, in other words, being given a cue to address pre-emptively the issue of students' behavioural response to the massacre – that is, showing appropriate respect both for the dead and for the living who remain affected by the event. Such concerns on the part of site operators and teachers are, of course, both reasonable and realistic – few would doubt the potential for even well-intentioned schoolchildren inadvertently to behave or speak in ways that could upset people, and those people certainly have the right to manage their grief undisturbed. Yet this raises questions about other, unspoken, aspects of the issue: aside from admonishing his/her students to behave appropriately, just how, and on what pedagogical basis, does the teacher prepare them for a visit to the scene of a historically recent mass murder? The implication in Port Arthur's "official" treatment of the massacre is, of course, that, although obviously terrible, the event of 1996 is essentially irrelevant to the overall purpose and meaning of the site – that is, visitors are there to experience a locale of "convict" history, where there just happens to have been a recent catastrophe. This, however, raises the question, noted earlier, of the perennially "multi-layered" nature of dark tourism sites and their intrinsically contested meanings. It may reasonably be assumed that, to some people – presumably a minority, but that does not in itself disqualify it from acknowledgement – the Port Arthur Historic Site is primarily the scene of a historically recent mass murder, and there just happens to have been a convict settlement there, long ago. This highlights the evolving nature of national identity and its innate links with the manifold and often contested strands of the national narrative. No doubt many would think it unlikely, but there is potential for the ambiguity that permeates Port Arthur to expand to encompass fully the massacre as an "iconic" moment of national grief similar to other disasters, defeats, and so on. Given the centrality of national identity in the curriculum, the implications of such ambiguities upon the schoolchild's experience and conceptualisation of the excursion destination deserve some examination.

Fremantle Prison

The issue of recent versus distant past is also played out at Fremantle Prison in Western Australia. Unlike Tasmania and the other eastern colonies, the 1829 British settlement at the mouth of the Swan River, in the south-west corner of what would come to be named Western Australia, began as a "free settlement" – that is, no transportees were involved in its foundation. The colony (named Fremantle after the naval captain who staked Britain's claim to Australia's west coast) initially failed to thrive, however, and for two decades its long-term viability was precarious at best. In the early 1840s it was agreed that it would take on a contingent of juvenile convicts from England's Parkhurst Prison, and in 1850, just at the moment that the eastern colonies were radically scaling back their convict intake, full-scale penal transportation to Fremantle began.

Although the arrival of the convicts solved many of the settlement's difficulties by providing a cheap labour force, it also presented a significant "law and order" problem. Hence plans were almost immediately drawn up for a major prison of a thousand beds, to be built using convict labour. Fremantle Prison was commissioned in 1857. It remained continuously in operation as Western Australia's main maximum-security prison for almost a century and a half, until its decommissioning in 1991.

Shortly after its closure, Fremantle Prison began operating as a prison museum; while not quite as well known or as popular as Port Arthur, it still attracts well over 150,000 visitors a year (Fremantle Prison 2009a). Given the continuity of its life as a prison into the recent past, it is conceptualised by many visitors in terms of its "modern" inmates, with its colonial/convict history a relatively incidental, "long-ago" aspect. The site's representational focus tends to run counter to that perception, however, with tour topics and promotional material by and large heavily emphasising the convict era. A highly popular "Descendants' Day" is run annually for patrons claiming descent from convicts, and the site has links with local genealogists who assist at such events. For some, the site's balance of meanings has very personal ramifications – such that the genealogist who organises Descendants' Day often has to "counsel" people who are terribly distressed at their discovery of convict ancestry (Wilson 2008: 204). In her opinion, the "convict stain" is still a very real factor in Western Australia.

Like the Port Arthur Historic Site, Fremantle Prison regularly hosts school excursions, and the site operators take their educational responsibilities seriously. Curriculum-focused tours are advertised, and the prison's website offers substantial downloadable resources for students and teachers designed to be printed off at school, including worksheets, visual material and themed information packages (Fremantle Prison 2009b). But here the convict emphasis noted above becomes extreme: in all the teacher/student resources provided by the website (which total almost fifty pages), not one word or image mentions or in any way acknowledges the prison's century-long post-convict career as a general prison. From a child's relatively uninformed perspective, the inference is clear: Fremantle Prison is a site where convicts were imprisoned long ago, and just happens to have had "ordinary" prisoners locked up in it recently.

The tours advertised do make some mention of recent inmates, but in terms that seem designed to water down the realities of prison life. The visitor can expect, for instance, to "marvel at original prisoner works of art" and "laugh as our entertaining guides show you the lighter side of prison humour" (Fremantle Prison 2009c). Such an approach is consistent with euphemising tendencies at many Australian dark tourism sites, especially former prisons (Wilson 2008), but whether it is consistent with the pedagogical integrity one would hope for in history education in schools is questionable.

The issue of contested meanings at Fremantle is not confined merely to questions of how long ago people were locked up, or how awful it was, whatever the era. There is a further dimension to children's experience of the prison that highlights the hidden complexities of its narratives. On one of the days the author visited the site, a group of Aboriginal boys, about nine or ten years old, arrived on a bus from an area in the north of the state. It was a weekend, and they were not there as a school group; they were in Perth to see a football match the following day, and all wore identical sweaters sporting a corporate sponsorship logo. One of the adults accompanying them had thought a visit to Fremantle Prison would "keep them occupied", and a tour was duly organised for them.

The boys followed their guide in what appeared more a state of bemusement than interest. An observer had no way of knowing just what they made of their experience. But of one thing it was possible to be certain: they did not see all there was of the site. An aspect of prisons rarely discussed or even revealed in tours, but ubiquitous in operational prisons, is inmate graffiti. Usually drawn or written on cell walls but sometimes on surfaces in communal areas both indoors and outside, graffiti is for many inmates the most natural, accessible and in some degree cathartic mode of self-expression available (Wilson 2008: 67–130). The typical inmate of a prison such as Fremantle would record, in pencil, marker or anything else he could lay hands on, thoughts of sex, revenge, rebellion or self-reflection. On the day before the Aboriginal children toured the prison, in cells sequestered from public view, the author had photographed a number of images on walls depicting the red, yellow and black flag of Aboriginal nationality and various other assertions of indigenous resistance. These images were consistent with similarly styled messages of defiance found in other prisons, including, in some cases, explicit claims to ownership of the land on which the prison stands (ibid.: 124).

While the Aboriginal boys who toured the prison that day were not there as a school group, their tour guide indicated that they were in many ways typical of the school groups that routinely visited. Given the calamitous rates of indigenous incarceration in Australia today and throughout the twentieth century, one cannot help but question the relevance, to children of Aboriginal background, of a prison museum that presents itself primarily as a site of convict imprisonment and virtually ignores the hundred or more years that followed the convict era. This highlights, once again, the manifold and radically contested meanings of such sites. As an iconic architectural entity, Fremantle Prison stands – and is represented – as an archetype of Australia's social, legal and institutional history and hence a monumental signifier of national identity; yet its place in the collective memory remains both ambiguous and potentially confronting.

Conclusion

Dark tourism in Australia takes an unusually narrow form in the global context of the phenomenon. As we have seen, virtually all the battlefields with which Australians identify are overseas, and although sites of Aboriginal suffering abound on Australian soil, very few as yet are widely known; thus former prisons and prison museums are by far the most commonly visited sites falling within the dark tourism spectrum. This trend accords with an abiding fascination with prisons among the tourist public all over the world – a fascination whose reasons are diverse, complex, and relatively little studied. However, it may, in light of the country's origins, be seen as especially apposite in Australia. As the only nation-state to have been founded as a prison, Australia has a unique relationship with its centres of incarceration – colonial or contemporary – that is intrinsically linked (whether the tourist is conscious of it or not) to the national identity. But this connection still falls short of an explanation as such, the issue of identity itself being so multifaceted. (For instance, notwithstanding the sites' status as venues of human suffering, very many Australian tourists cite "architectural" interest as a central motivation for visiting them (Wilson 2008: 42).) It must necessarily be considered along with (if not fully distinguished from) issues of contested personal and social narratives of the kind touched upon in the discussion above.

It is reasonable to assume that most adult visitors may be aware, to some degree, of the ambiguities inherent in a site such as Fremantle or Port Arthur without being unduly troubled or confused by them. But what of the schoolchild? By what pedagogical approach or method does the teacher account for those ambiguities? If the purpose of the historical excursion lies in something we call a "sensory learning opportunity", and if the excursion destination chosen is one that fits very precisely into the category of dark tourism, in what way and to what degree is that "darkness" to be part of the "sensed" educational experience? Such questions remain relatively unexamined in many educational settings. The key points are that schoolchildren regularly visit dark tourism sites, that dark tourism sites are very often characterised by profoundly contested historical and cultural interpretation, and that in many cases there is little or no acknowledgement of this in an educational context. This chapter does not suggest that excursions to such sites should never be made by schools; rather, it submits that the expectations and preparation of educators, both on site and in the classroom, may need some revision before the visit.

References

Attwood, B., and Markus, A. (1999) "The fight for Aboriginal rights", in R. Manne (ed.) *The Australian Century: Political Struggle in the Building of a Nation*. Melbourne: Text.

Australian Bureau of Statistics (2007) "Year Book Australia, 2002: a look back at the Sydney Olympics and Paralympics," www.abs.gov.au/ausstats/abs@.nsf/featurearticlesbytitle/E7E546D49DCA1D97CA257298000CED32?OpenDocument (accessed 9 November 2010).

Brand, I. (1990) *The "Separate" or "Model Prison", Port Arthur*. Launceston, TAS: Regal.

Clark, A. (2008) *History's Children: History Wars in the Classroom*. Sydney: University of New South Wales Press.

Convict Department, Tasmania ([1868] 1991) *Rules and Regulations for the Penal Settlement on Tasman's Peninsula*. Port Arthur, TAS: Port Arthur Historic Site Management Authority.

Cullen, M. (2005) "Enhancing multiple intelligence through museum visits", *SCIOS: Journal of the Association of Science Teachers of Western Australia*, 41(2): 27–9.

Curthoys, A. (1983) "Revisiting Australian history: including Aboriginal resistance", *Arena*, 62.

Davison, G. (2006) "What should a national museum do? Learning from the world", in M. Lake (ed.) *Memories, Monuments and Museums: The Past in the Present* (pp. 91–109). Melbourne: Melbourne University Press.

Fremantle Prison (2009a) "News", 22 November, www.fremantleprison.com/ABOUT_US/NEWS/Pages/default.aspx (accessed 4 November 2010).

Fremantle Prison (2009b) "School tours", www.fremantleprison.com.au/Education/schooltours/Pages/default.aspx (accessed 5 November 2010).

Fremantle Prison (2009c) "Prison tour", www.fremantleprison.com.au/Education/schooltours/prisontour/Pages/default.aspx (accessed 4 November 2010).

Hancock, W. K. (1930) *Australia*. London: Ernest Benn.

Hobart, P. (2005) "Authentic learning beyond the classroom: authentic learning, VELS and PoLTs", *Ethos* 13(1): 12–19.

Horne, D. (1964) *The Lucky Country*. Rev. edn, Harmondsworth: Penguin.

Hughes, R. (2008) "Dutiful tourism: encountering the Cambodian genocide", *Asia Pacific Viewpoint*, 49(3): 318–30.

Johnston, N. (2000) *Forms of Constraint: A History of Prison Architecture*. Urbana: University of Illinois Press.

Kent, D. A. (1985) "The Anzac book and the Anzac legend", *Historical Studies*, 21(84): 376–90.

Lake, M., and Reynolds, H. (2010) *What's Wrong with Anzac: The Militarisation of Australian History*. Sydney: University of New South Wales Press.

Lennon, J., and Foley, M. (2000) *Dark Tourism*. London: Continuum.

Loo, T., and Strange, C. (2000) "'Rock prison of liberation': Alcatraz island and the American imagination", *Radical History Review*, 78: 27–56.

Lorenza, L. (2009) "Beyond four walls: why go beyond the bounds of school?" *Teacher*, January–February: 22–5.

Macintyre, S., and Clark, A. (2004) *The History Wars*. Melbourne: Melbourne University Press.

Manne, R. (2001) *In Denial: The Stolen Generations and the Right*. Melbourne: Schwartz.

Munday, P. (2008) "Teacher perceptions of the role and value of excursions in years 7–10 geography education in Victoria, Australia", *International Research in Geographical and Environmental Education*, 17(2): 146–69.

NCB (National Curriculum Board) (2008) *The Shape of the National Curriculum: A Proposal for Discussion*. Canberra: Australian Government.

NCB (National Curriculum Board) (2009) *Shape of the Australian Curriculum: History*. Canberra: Australian Government.

Port Arthur Historic Site (2010a) "Another record year for Port Arthur – despite the rain!", http://portarthur.org.au/index.aspx?sys=Archived%20News%20Article&intID=1727 (accessed 9 November 2010).

Port Arthur Historic Site (2010b) "Post convict era", http://www.portarthur.org.au/index. aspx?id=6325 (accessed 9 November 2010).

Port Arthur Historic Site (2010c) "Sunday 28 April 1996", http://www.portarthur.org.au/ index.aspx?id=6334 (accessed 9 November 2010).

Port Arthur Historic Site (2010d) "Code of conduct for school visits", http://portarthur.org. au/file.aspx?id= (accessed 9 November 2010).

Pringle, J. (1961) *Australian Accent*. London: Chatto & Windus.

Reynolds, H. (1969) "'That hated stain': the aftermath of transportation in Tasmania", *Historical Studies*, 14(53): 19–31.

Robson, L. (1997) *A Short History of Tasmania*. Melbourne: Oxford University Press.

Scates, B. (2006) *Return to Gallipoli: Walking the Battlefields of the Great War*. Cambridge: Cambridge University Press.

Schiller, W. (2006) "Children's voices", *Teacher*, December: 26–33.

Serle, G. (1965) "The Digger tradition and Australian nationalism", *Meanjin*, June.

Strange, C. (2000) "From 'place of misery' to 'lottery of life': interpreting Port Arthur's past", *Online Museum Journal*, 2; http://hosting.collectionsaustralia.net/omj/ vol2/pdfs/ strange.pdf (accessed 4 November 2010).

Strange, C., and Kempa, M. (2003) "Shades of dark tourism: Alcatraz and Robben Island", *Annals of Tourism Research*, 30(2): 386–405.

Sunter, A. B. (2003) "Contested memories of Eureka: museum interpretations of the Eureka Stockade", *Labour History*, 85: 29–45.

Trollope, A. (1873) *Australia and New Zealand*. Melbourne: George Robertson.

Weidenhofer, M. (1981) *Port Arthur: A Place of Misery*. Melbourne: Oxford University Press.

Whitty, H. (2003) "Visiting museums as a learning experience", *Classroom*, 23(3): 12–13.

Williams, P. (2004) "Witnessing genocide: vigilance and remembrance at Tuol Sleng and Cheung Ek", *Holocaust and Genocide Studies*, 18(2): 234–54.

Wilson, J. (2008) *Prison: Cultural Memory and Dark Tourism*. New York: Peter Lang.

Winter, C. (2009) "Tourism, social memory and the Great War", *Annals of Tourism Research*, 36(4): 607–26.

Zarmati, L. (2009) "Why a national curriculum needs a museum site study", *reCollections: Journal of the National Museum of Australia*, 4(1): 1–12.

17 Research directions for tourism and national identities

Elspeth Frew and Leanne White

Tourism and national identities: a conclusion

This volume considered the ways in which tourism and national identity intersect and the means by which they do so. These themes were addressed from a supply and demand perspective via a variety of case studies from around the world. The various chapters highlighted, in particular, the importance for tourism operators of understanding these connections, since these are the people who have the opportunity to enhance such interest and use it in the marketing of a destination. Because it represents one way in which a country can seek to project a particular self-image to the wider international community, tourism is an important component of the process of identity-building (Light 2001).

Summary of the chapters

In the first part of the book, "Identity and image", each of the five chapters demonstrated how tourism authorities have used aspects of national identity to promote their region. The authors in this section demonstrated that, in each country considered, the authorities have recognised the opportunity to capture the imagination of tourists by referring to various aspects of national identity. The kitsch aspects of Irish culture have been exploited to promote Ireland, while the authorities in Washington, DC, have emphasised the sense of size and importance of the monuments and museums to highlight national identity. In Hungary, the government has tried to distance itself from the country's Soviet past and has sought to create a new image employing more traditional aspects of Hungarian heritage and culture. In the Australian context, the horse has been strongly tied into national identity via movies such as *The Man From Snowy River* and sporting events such as the Melbourne Cup. Similarly, tourism authorities have used the success of the *Lord of the Rings* film trilogy to help in the domestic and international branding of New Zealand.

Tourism has been described as a complex construction "constituting a powerful interface between cultures and societies that is organized within a global framework, but which takes place very much at a local level" (Burns 2005: 402). To this end, the second part of the book, "Culture and community", considered the complex relationships between national identity, the community and tourism. The case study of Canadian National Day demonstrated that national identity is reinforced through various events and activities engaged in by local participants. The impact of the 2008 Olympic Games on Beijing residents was considered, and it was noted that the locals were generally supportive of the event as it provided the opportunity to showcase China to the world. In the Kyrgyz Republic, the authorities identified the importance of developing community-based tourism which reflects aspects of the local culture as an important means of developing a sustainable industry. The example of novelty world championship events was examined in the context of local landscape and culture, revealing that these location-specific events play an important part in the identity of the region. The Pakistani community in the United Kingdom was discussed in relation to an individual's desire to travel to their home-land and their associated identity. All these chapters reflect the notion that the movement and activities of domestic and international tourists are often culturally influenced and for the "purpose of maintaining social threads between communities" (Coles *et al*. 2005: 475). Thus, this section highlighted the strong connection between the community, tourism and national identity.

The final part of the book, "Heritage and history", considered the relationship between heritage, national identity and tourism. Australia's national identity was discussed in relation to the First World War, and the author reflected on the growing importance of the events on the Western Front for future Australian national identity. The traditional heritage of the Chatham Islands was identified as being an attractive draw card for tourists. Similarly, the Ho Chi Minh museum in Vietnam was shown to be important in creating a strong sense of Vietnamese identity among domestic and international tourists. The tourism activities surrounding four outlaws in frontier nations were discussed in relation to national identity, and it was established that many local businesses in the relevant regions have successfully exploited the legacy of three of the four villains as tourism products. In an exploration of dark tourism at two former Australian prisons it was shown that the sites' curators have been selective in the historic aspects they portray to visitors; in particular, schoolchildren possibly receive an ambiguous image of Australian convict history, which may influence their perception of their own national identity. Thus, the final section of the book demonstrated that a country's heritage is of interest to tourists and reflects various aspects of national identity.

Final remarks

The book has demonstrated that national identity and tourism intersect, overlap and traverse. Gaining a better understanding of national identity is itself a worthwhile endeavour, and integrating this with links to tourism adds significantly to the innovative element presented here. The authors have shown that the connection between tourism and national identity is apparent via the promotional activities of tourism authorities in relation to both cultural activities and heritage. The benefit of such an awareness of society and a formal appreciation of the role of national identity and tourism is likely to lead to much better informed policies and practices in the management of such products. The case studies, representing aspects of tourism and national identity from various parts of the world, reinforce the fact that many countries encourage and support forms of tourism that "accord with, and affirm, [the] sense of [their] own cultural and political identity" (Light 2007: 747). From a social, cultural and economic perspective, the book helps to provide a better understanding of the multifaceted and complex connections between people and places, including the need for appropriate development of such national identity-related products. The strategic development of such tourism products may have the potential to enhance a region both economically and socially and to create high levels of post-trip satisfaction among visitors, leading to repeat visits and positive word of mouth recommendation.

In the coming decade, there is likely to be increased competition in the tourism and hospitality industries among destinations worldwide, among domestic destinations, and among firms within a destination. This increased competition has implications for destination management organisations, marketing, policy, planning and development, strategic management and human resource development (Dwyer 2005). Thus, since they reflect the unique and distinctive aspects of an individual country, tourism products related to national identity have the potential to gain ascendancy in such competition.

However, another force which may influence the relationship between tourism and national identity is globalisation. Globalisation can be defined as the increasing integration of economies, societies and civilisations, with aspects of travel and tourism being described as among the many causes and results of such processes (Hjalager 2007). Globalisation because of tourism is particularly obvious in developing countries when Western culture is encountered at hotels, resorts and attractions and the local indigenous culture is superseded or ignored. With the advance of globalisation, nations need to ensure that their cultures are maintained, and one way of guaranteeing this is to develop products that reflect a unique national identity.

This book has centred on creating an awareness of the importance of national identity and tourism in a range of settings and regions in the world. However, the relationship is complex and dynamic. Further research and discussion is required to identify ways in which national identity and tourism can be developed in a mutually beneficial manner. In other words, research should consider the best way of developing interesting and sustainable tourism products and creating related national identities that avoid the worst commodification of culture and preserve the distinctive culture and identity of the country.

References

Burns, P. M. (2005) "Social identities, globalization, and the cultural politics of tourism", in W. F. Theobald (ed.) *Global Tourism*. Burlington, MA: Elsevier Science.

Coles, T., Duval, D. T., and Hall, C. M. (2005) "Tourism, mobility, and global communities: new approaches to theorizing tourism and tourist spaces", in W. F. Theobald (ed.) *Global Tourism*. Burlington, MA: Elsevier Science.

Dwyer, L, (2005) "Trends underpinning global tourism in the coming decade", in W. F. Theobald (ed.) *Global Tourism*. Burlington, MA: Elsevier Science.

Hjalager, A. M. (2007) "Stages in the economic globalization of tourism", *Annals of Tourism Research*, 34(2): 437–57.

Light, D. (2001) "Facing the future: tourism and identity-building in post-socialist Romania", *Political Geography*, 20: 1053–74.

Light, D. (2007) "Dracula tourism in Romania: cultural identity and the state", *Annals of Tourism Research*, 34(3): 746–65.

Index